MW01617854

Globalization and the Digital Divide

Globalization and the Digital Divide

EDITED BY

Kirk St.Amant and Bolanle A. Olaniran

Amherst, New York

Copyright 2011, 2022 Kirk St.Amant and Bolanle A. Olaniran

All rights reserved.
Printed in the United States of America

No part of this publication may be reproduced, stored in or introduced into a retrieval system, or transmitted, in any form, or by any means (electronic, mechanical, photocopying, recording, or otherwise), without the prior permission of the publisher.

Requests for permission should be directed to:
permissions@cambriapress.com, or mailed to:
Cambria Press
100 Corporate Parkway, Suite 128
Amherst, NY 14226

Library of Congress Cataloging-in-Publication Data
on file for hardcover edition.

Hardcover ISBN 978-1-60497-770-7 (2011)
Paperback ISBN 978-1-63857-040-0 (2022)

For my daughters, Lily and Isabelle, who are a source of inspiration in all that I do; for my wife, Dori, whose continued patience and support were essential to this project; to Dr. Mark D. Hawthorne, and to the memory of Dr. Victoria Mikelonis—the individuals who introduced me to the concept of computing in global contexts.

—Kirk St.Amant

First, I would like to give all honor and glory to the Lord. And I am deeply grateful to my wife, Adeline, who allows me to spend the necessary time on my research; her undying love is essential in all that I do and accomplish. My mother, Alice, and my brothers, Dan and Sunday, I thank for their prayers, love, and support. My thanks go also to Gus Friedrich, my mentor and adviser, for believing in me. I am grateful to all who have found my work useful in the areas of globalization, technology, and culture; I am humbled. Finally, I dedicate this work to the memory of my father, who helped instill in me the need to keep reaching for the stars.

—Bolanle A. Olaniran

TABLE OF CONTENTS

List of Illustrations

List of Tables

Globalization and the Digital Divide

Introduction

Globalization and the Digital Divide

Understanding the Connections between Technology and Communication in a Global Context

Kirk St.Amant

Globalization as Communication

In essence, globalization is about integration at an international level. In many cases, this integration is economic and is driven by business practices and trade agreements. In other cases, it is ideological, occurring as different ideas and perspectives move back and forth across nations and regions. In every instance, however, globalization involves one central factor—communication. Effective communication provides individuals with the information they need to participate in today's global society as consumers, workers, and citizens. It is only through the effective sharing of information on a global level that everything from policies on international trade to the diffusion of MP3 files can take on a truly international nature.

Within this communication framework, the concept of *access* is central. That is, only people with access to essential information can participate effectively in today's global marketplace for goods, services, and ideas. Access, in turn, is often dependent on media or on the technologies used to present and exchange ideas. In the case of globalization, the media requisite for access are usually electronic or online in nature. What makes such media critical is the speed and directness with which they allow individuals to locate and exchange information on a global scale. E-mail, for example, allows a person in Boston to exchange information with someone in Beijing almost as quickly and directly as that person could convey the same information to a neighbor across the street.

GLOBALIZATION AND ONLINE ACCESS

As of this writing, almost 2 billion people around the world can connect to the online environment (Adair, 2010; "Internet Usage Statistics: The Internet Big Picture," 2010). Although this number represents roughly one third of the world's population, international online access continues to increase with amazing speed. The number of Internet users in Australia, for example, grew by almost 400,000 between June and August 2004 ("Active Internet Users," 2004), and today Australians spend more time interacting via Web 2.0 media than any other culture (Marshall, 2010). In Japan almost 80% of the population has online access ("Internet Usage in Asia," 2010), and in South Korea 39 million of the nation's 48 million citizens can connect to the Internet. In addition, broadband access in South Korea has continued to grow rapidly—by almost 1 million individuals between 2008 and 2009 alone

("Internet Usage in Asia," 2010; Whitney, 2009). This degree of online access has placed the connected, or the "wired," nations of the world at the forefront of globalization as it relates to both international trade and the sharing of ideas, entertainment, and policies on a global scale.

The most astounding growth in online access is taking place in developing nations. The number of Internet connections in India, for example, was expected to grow by over 40% in 2009, and this number includes some 51 million active Internet users—almost double the number of Internet users in the ultrawired Scandinavian countries ("Internet Usage in Europe," 2010; Lau, 2010). Online access in China grew exponentially—by almost 2000%—during the last decade: Individuals with online access increased from 22.5 million to almost 420 million individuals in that time ("Internet Usage in Asia," 2010). Furthermore, China's mobile-phone markets—another source of potential online access—are expected to include some 1.3 billion subscribers by the middle of the next decade (Lau, 2010). Similarly, the number of individuals going online in Eastern Europe has grown markedly since the turn of the millennium. For example, Lithuania, Latvia, Poland, and Russia have all experienced increases in online access of over 500% during in the last decade ("Internet Usage in Europe," 2010), and broadband use is rapidly increasing; Ukraine, for one, experienced more than 15% growth in broadband access in 2009 (Whitney, 2009).

Though this growth in online access seems remarkable, the ratio of such growth in comparison to the population of developing world paints a very different picture. In truth, the world's emerging economies appear to be at a distinct disadvantage when it comes to participating in the global information economy. For example, whereas Asia is home to just over half of the world's population, as of this writing only 22% of those living there have Internet access (Adair, 2010; "Internet Usage Statistics: The Internet Big Picture," 2010). Likewise, only about 10% of the population of Africa—a continent with a population of just over 1 billion—has online access (Adair, 2010; "Internet Usage Statistics for Africa," 2010). A similar situation obtains in many other less economically developed regions of the world, including South and Central America and parts of the former Communist Bloc.

Yet this situation is far from hopeless. Over the last decade, various projects have been undertaken with the goal of increasing online access in the world's developing nations. In Africa, a mix of public- and private-sector ventures focuses on increasing online access across the continent ("High Speed Internet Access," 2010; Kalia, 2001; Lister, Dovey, Giddings, Grant, & Kelly, 2003). In Latin America, similar public and private ventures have been proposed, and although less than half of South America's population is currently online, impressive gains have been made in the nations of Brazil, Argentina, and Chile (Ballve, 2008; "Internet Usage And Populations in South America," 2010; "Tying Latin America Together," 2001). These developments, combined with some of the world's lowest Wi-Fi costs and Latin America's fast-growing markets for mobile phones, might assist with the spread of online access there (Ballve, 2008; Burger, 2004; "11 Trends," 2004).

At the same time, a number of organizations have started developing online communication technologies that could provide individuals in developing nations with more affordable online access (Ballve, 2008; "Beyond the Digital Divide," 2004; Kalia, 2001; "Vision," n.d.). Some of these organizations have also begun developing inexpensive hubs for online access in nations such as India, Ghana, Brazil, and South Africa ("Beyond the Digital Divide," 2004; Warschauer, 2003). In addition, the international diffusion of open-source software has allowed a wider range of individuals around the world to use software and interact in cyberspace ("Open Source's Local Heroes," 2003; van Reijswoud & Mulo, 2007). Thus the potential exists for even more cultures and regions to participate in the globalization process as related to communication and online media. For such solutions to be realized, however, organizations and individuals must first understand the factors that affect Internet access and use across a range of cultures, regions, and nations. Until this happens, the effective and even global diffusion of online access will remain an elusive goal.

Globalization and the New World Paradigm

The interrelation of globalization, communication, and media has prompted many to view the world in terms of a new dichotomy: the global "wired" (nations with widespread online access) and the global "tired" (nations with very limited online access). These differing levels of online access have created an international rift—a global digital divide. The nature of this rift, its current status, and future projections about it have important implications for all of the world's citizens. As Gili S. Drori and Yong Suk Jang (2003) noted,

> To keep up with the rest of the world, a country is required not only to be "Internet ready" but mainly to be "Internet sophisticated." In other words, the world of IT is no longer about making the initial connection; rather, it is currently all about intensity of e-use and sophistication of e-use. (p. 156)

These problems, however, are not intractable. Rather, with time, attention, and the correct level of understanding, public policies and private-sector practices can be developed or revised to close this divide and bring more of the world's citizens to the global stage. Consider, for example, how the global war on HIV/AIDS has progressed as more organizations and nations have aligned their practices in order to treat a common problem for the good of all (Thomas & Weber, 2004). If an analogous degree of international cooperation and coordination—in combination with an understanding of the unique, local needs of different areas—can be achieved in relation to global Internet access, perhaps the digital divide might begin to disappear.

The first step in addressing such problems is understanding. That is, organizations and individuals must understand which factors contribute to this global digital divide in order to address such factors effectively. From this foundational understanding, organizations and individuals can take the focused, coordinated actions needed to successfully rectify international disparities in online access. In order to develop such an understanding, interested parties need to review the perspectives and practices of organizations and individuals located on both sides of the divide. Only through such a comprehensive examination can approaches be developed that address the specific needs and requisite conditions for establishing online access in different regions of the world.

A good deal has been written on globalization (e.g., Bhagwati's *In Defense of Globalization* and Cohen's *Globalization and Its Enemies*) and on the global digital divide (e.g., Warschauer's *Technology and Social Inclusion: Rethinking the Digital Divide* and Norris's *Digital Divide: Civic Engagement, Information Poverty, and the Internet Worldwide*), but these texts tend to represent the perspectives of the wired nations of the world. In order to gain the understanding needed to address the complex factors contributing to the global digital divide, one must also hear and consider perspectives from the other side.

Overview of this Collection

This collection represents an initial step toward examining the global digital divide from the perspective of developing nations. The contributors examine the challenges faced by the citizens of these nations and their prospects for truly collaborative programs. Several contributions in this volume present insights into the digital divide as it is seen and understood within developing nations—many of which have been overlooked in previous discussions of this topic. Other contributions examine forces or programs that might affect online access and the uses of online media in these countries.

The collection begins with Tuğba Kalafatoğlu's overview of culture and communication factors that can affect interactions—and participation—in international cyberspace. In her chapter, Kalafatoğlu discusses certain communication approaches individuals can apply so as to avoid problem areas commonly associated with interacting in global contexts. She also explains why individuals and organizations need to distinguish the economic, political, and social aspects of globalization in order to recognize the cultural factors that affect international interactions. Kalafatoğlu's chapter thus provides a foundation for understanding how cultural preferences and expectations can affect international online exchanges and can contribute to the existence of the global digital divide.

In the book's second chapter, Kehbuma Langmia examines globalization, information sharing, and communication from an African perspective. Langmia uses theoretical concepts of Africana critical theory and Afrocentricity to review the globalization experience through Internet-based communication technologies in Africa. He also focuses on the importance of bringing an appreciation of African cultures to communication technology design and whether that design should reflect the cultures that created the technologies or those that use them. Langmia then explains how design based on the culture of the designer can actually impede the use of such technologies and thus deepen the global digital divide.

In chapter 3, Victor van Reijswoud and Arjan de Jager review programs designed to close the information and knowledge gaps between developing and developed nations. The two note how the appropriate technology (AT) approach can facilitate the effective adoption of information communication technologies (ICTs) in emerging economies. Van Reijswoud and de Jager also propose a preliminary theory in which AT guides system development in order to create ICT scenarios that best address local needs. Through example cases, the authors illustrate how this AT approach can lead to improved online access and ICT use in developing nations.

The fourth chapter, by Anas Tawileh, explores the potential low-cost wireless networks have to bridge the global digital divide. Tawileh reviews two projects from different parts of Africa. The first is a community center in Tanzania that used wireless communication technologies to provide information services to a large, dispersed group of individuals; the second is an initiative involving wireless networking and open-source software that allowed a group of schools in South Africa to develop a network for e-learning. Tawileh identifies factors that contributed to success in both cases and suggests directions for future research.

Francesca da Rimini's chapter provides a focused examination of community uses of technology. Da Rimini presents a conceptual framework for considering new forms of socially engaged, creative projects based on community participation through technology. To illustrate this approach, she focuses on the Container Project, an innovative computing and creative arts initiative in an impoverished Jamaican township. By examining the ways this project allows local communities to engage a wider, global context, da Rimini reveals the role meaningful collaborative mechanisms can play in bridging the global digital divide.

In many ways, the global digital divide is about presence—specifically, the extent of a nation's or a culture's presence in international cyberspace. In the book's sixth chapter, Alireza Noruzi uses Google-related counts of Web pages from European and Middle Eastern countries to investigate the Web presence of countries in these regions. Noruzi focuses on how specific features (e.g., Internet access, language, and ICT literacy) influence a particular nation's Web presence in global cyberspace, revealing that the global digital divide is not simply a matter of equal access to the Internet—rather, it also involves a nation's and a culture's ability to maintain significant online presence in order to share its national or cultural perspectives equally in global cyberspace.

The importance of equal access to information is a central issue for Yun Xia, who uses a study of socioeconomic and cultural factors to examine the nature of the digital divide in one particular nation: China. Xia explains that a range of factors—including age, gender, income, education, and employment—can affect digital divides *within* a nation as much as they can *between* nations. Such internal digital divides can affect a nation's effective participation in international cyberspace. Xia also explains ways that understanding the internal digital divide in China could help researchers and policy makers better address issues that determine a nation's position on either side of the global digital divide.

Yasmin Ibrahim's "Globalization, Epidemics and Politics: Communicating Risk in the Digital Age" examines the idea of the Internet as a mechanism for collaboration and information sharing. In contrast to Xia's chapter, Ibrahim's piece reviews ways different national governments create policies that limit the flow of information across their borders—in both directions—selectively imposing information-based digital divides upon their citizens. Specifically, Ibrahim examines how online media have been used to address recent global crises in public health. She reveals that ICTs can effectively address such situations or further complicate them.

The collection concludes with Tatjana Takševa's examination of how the commercialization of higher education can widen the global digital divide. Takševa examines global trends in higher education and examines the implications these trends have for developing nations—places where higher education is an important instrument for national development. She also reviews ways in which many current approaches to globalizing education actually contribute to the global digital divide and do not attempt to address it. Takševa concludes with strategies for creating more equitable approaches to the globalization of higher education—approaches that could address many of the factors currently contributing to the global digital divide.

Conclusion

By addressing this range of topics and cultures, and by doing so from a variety of perspectives, the authors who have contributed to this collection provide important insights into a particular cross section of the global digital divide. The chapters they have written can serve as a foundation for further research into a particular theory, approach, or region—whether that research is of an academic, public policy, or business-focused nature. In each of these cases, an enhanced understanding of the factors contributing to the global digital divide can help individuals make more informed decisions about media, communication, and globalization.

REFERENCES

11 trends to watch in 2004. (2004). *eMarketer*. Retrieved May 15, 2004, from http://www.emarketer.com/news/article.php?1002633&format=printer_friendly.

Active Internet users by country, July 2004. (2004, August 25). *ClickZ*. Retrieved October 6, 2004, from http://www.clickz.com/stats/sectors/geographics/article.php/3397231.

Adair, D. (2010, October 19). Internet users to surpass 2 billion. *Indie Pro Pub*. Retrieved October 19, 2010, from http://indiepropub.com/internet-users-to-surpass-2-billion/311248/.

Ballve, M. (2008, April 3). In Brazil, Internet access grows rapidly, even among poor. *World Politics Review*. Retrieved October 1, 2010, from http://www.worldpoliticsreview.com/articles/1891/in-brazil-internet-access-grows-rapidly-even-among-poor.

Beyond the digital divide. (2004, March 13). *The Economist: Technology Quarterly Supplement*, 8.

Bhagwati, J. N. (2004). *In defense of globalization*. New York, NY: Oxford University Press.

Burger, A. (2004, June 16). Broadband WiFi spreads in Latin America. *E-Commerce Times*. Retrieved October 1, 2010, from http://www.ecommercetimes.com/story/34517.html.

Cohen, D. (2006). *Globalization and its enemies*. Cambridge, MA: MIT Press.

Drori, G. S., & Jang, Y. S. (2003). The global digital divide: A sociological assessment of trends and causes. *Social Science Computer Review, 21*, 144–161.

High speed Internet access in Africa takes off. (2010, June 21). *Stratsis incite: Current security, economic, and energy trends on the African continent* (Weblog). Retrieved October 1, 2010, from http://stratsisincite.

wordpress.com/2010/06/21/high-speed-internet-access-in-africa-takes-off/.

Internet usage and populations in South America. (2010). Internet world stats. Retrieved October 1, 2010, from http://www.internetworldstats.com/stats15.htm.

Internet usage in Asia. (2010). Internet world stats. Retrieved October 1, 2010, from http://www.internetworldstats.com/stats3.htm.

Internet usage in Europe. (2010). Internet world stats. Retrieved October 1, 2010, from http://www.internetworldstats.com/stats4.htm.

Internet usage statistics for Africa. (2010). Internet world stats. Retrieved October 1, 2010, from http://www.internetworldstats.com/stats1.htm.

Internet usage statistics: The Internet big picture. (2010). Internet World Stats. Retrieved October 1, 2010, from http://www.internetworldstats.com/stats.htm.

Kalia, K. (2001, July/August). Bridging global digital divides. *Silicon Alley Reporter*, 52–54.

Lau, A. (2010, June 28). Why Asia should matter to marketers. *ClickZ*. Retrieved September 10, 2010, from http://www.clickz.com/clickz/column/1721892/why-asia-should-matter-marketers.

Lister, M., Dovey, J., Giddings, S., Grant, I., & Kelly, K. (2003). *New media: A critical introduction*. New York, NY: Routledge.

Marshall, J. (2010, January 29). Australians spend most time on social networks and blogs. *ClickZ*. Retrieved September 8, 2010, from http://www.clickz.com/clickz/stats/1705913/australians-spend-most-time-social-networks-blogs.

Norris, P. (2001). *Digital divide: Civic engagement, information poverty, and the Internet worldwide*. Cambridge, UK: Cambridge University Press.

Open source's local heroes. (2003, December 6). *The Economist: Technology Quarterly Supplement*, 3–5.

Thomas, C., & Weber, M. (2004). The politics of global health governance: Whatever happened to "health for all by the year 2000"? *Global Governance, 10*(2), 187–205.

Tying Latin American together. (2001, Summer). *NYSE Magazine*, 9.

van Reijswoud, V. E., & Mulo, E. (2007). Evaluating the potential of free and open source software in the developing world. In K. St. Amant & B. Still (Eds.), *Handbook of research on open source software: Technological, economic and social perspectives* (pp. 79–92). Hershey, PA: IDEA Group Inc.

Vision. (n.d.). *One laptop per child.* Retrieved October 1, 2010, from http://laptop.org/en/vision/index.shtml.

Warschauer, M. (2003). *Technology and social inclusion: Rethinking the digital divide.* Cambridge, MA: MIT Press.

Whitney, L. (2009, June 16). Global broadband access on the rise. Cnetnews. Retrieved September 8, 2010, from http://news.cnet.com/8301–1035_3–10265421–94.html.

CHAPTER 1

THE SPREAD OF CULTURE UNDER THE UMBRELLA OF GLOBALIZATION

Tuğba Kalafatoğlu

New forms of technology are one of the hallmarks of contemporary globalization, and technological progress like that of the last three decades is a good indicator of profound social transformations. Within this framework, culture can be a key factor to understanding processes related to, affecting, and emerging from globalization. For these reasons, an understanding of cross-cultural communication is essential to an effective examination of globalization and its components. This chapter aims to avoid the problem of overgeneralization and to make the analytical and practical distinctions between aspects of economic, political, and social life easier to identify and comprehend. In essence, understanding culture is necessary to success in the modern environment of globalization; therefore this chapter examines whether globalization makes people around the world more similar or more different and examines the role globalization plays in the daily lives of individuals around the globe.

INTRODUCTION

Globalization is economically transforming the world as national borders become increasingly irrelevant to the global flow of money and goods. But globalization also has a great effect on cultures around the world in terms of products. Global brands—including Coca-Cola, Apple, Starbucks, and McDonald's—and an increasing number of services are uniting nations in a global marketplace that makes each culture more interdependent with the others. Although many individuals point to globalization's positive effects, others continue to debate the merits of globalization as both a process and an ideology. The spread of democratic governments, the liberalization of trade, the spread of new liberal economic reforms, the rise of technology, and the emergence of a truly global market for goods and services have resulted in a decline in the significance of national and other barriers to globalization. In fact, globalization has come to represent a growing interdependence among nations.

At the same time, tourism has become a leading global industry, and immigration is taking place on a massive scale. Radio and television have linked the world through a common grid of knowledge. Under the umbrella of globalization, the Internet, in particular, has neutralized distance as a major barrier to communication between people from different societies. All of these developments fundamentally transform the meanings of culture as people increasingly consider themselves members of a global "cultural supermarket" from which they can select their identities.

For the economist, *globalization* is essentially the emergence of a global market. For the historian, the term refers to an era dominated by global capitalism. For the sociologist, it is a process of interaction and integration among people. For the political scientist, it affects the political systems of developing countries around the world. But across all these fields and beyond, there can be no doubt that humanity today is living in an ever more interconnected global economy, a fact with vast social and political implications. Most important, globalization has a cultural dimension resulting from immense worldwide communication. Thus if economic globalization takes place, so too does cultural globalization.

The process of globalization has many undesirable effects on the well-being of people, cultures, and political systems in developing countries around the world. During the last decade, *globalization* became an internationally well-known word, and it that word represents one of the most highly charged issues of the day. It is ubiquitous in public discourse—found in TV sound bites and slogans on place cards, on Websites and in learned journals, in parliaments, in corporate boardrooms, and in labor meeting halls. For this reason, the better one understands globalization, the more effectively one can interact in the various arenas it encompasses.

Perspectives on Globalization

All over the world, different people hold different views of globalization. The following definitions represent some currently influential views on the topic:

> [Globalization is] the inexorable integration of markets, nation-states, and technologies to a degree never witnessed before—in a way that is enabling individuals, corporations, and nation-states to reach around the world farther, faster, deeper, and cheaper than ever before … [it is] the spread of free-market capitalism to virtually every country in the world. (Friedman, 1999, pp. 7–8)

> As experienced from below, the dominant form of globalization means a historical transformation: in the economy, of livelihoods and modes of existence; in politics, a loss in the degree of control exercised locally … and in culture, a devaluation of a collectivity's achievements.… Globalization is emerging as a political response to the expansion of market power.… It is a domain of knowledge. (Mittelman, 2000, p. 6)

> The historical transformation constituted by the sum of particular forms and instances of … making or being made global (i) by the active dissemination of practices, values, technology, and other human products throughout the globe (ii) when global practices and so on exercise an increasing influence over people's lives (iii) when the globe serves as a focus for, or a premise in shaping, human activities. (Albrow, 1996, p. 88)
>
> [Globalization represents] a social process in which the constraints of geography on social and cultural arrangements recede and in which people become increasingly aware that they are receding. (Waters, 1995, p. 3)

Amazingly, despite the term's wide use, it does not appear to have any precise, widely agreed-upon definition. Indeed, the breadth of meanings attached to globalization seems to be increasing rather than narrowing over time. Moreover, with each passing year, the term takes on new cultural, political, and other connotations in addition to the economic ones previously associated with globalization.

IS GLOBALIZATION NEW?

Globalization is not new. Globalization has existed for thousands of years, for people (and later, corporations) have been buying from and selling to each other internationally for centuries—as attested by the famed Silk Road connecting China and Europe during the Middle Ages. In its most current economic incarnation, globalization is an ongoing process that dates back to at least the 1700s. Thus, globalization represents change, but change has always been an integral feature of life.

What is the change today? Technology. New forms of technology are one of the hallmarks of contemporary globalization. Indeed, technological progress of the magnitude seen in the last three decades indicates profound social and cultural transformations. Today, technology breaks new ground in all corners of the globe. Whether in North America, the Asia Pacific region, Europe and Russia, or India and China, investment in technology research and technology development is paying dividends. The globalization of technology means that 20th-century economic advantages and powerbase structures are being rapidly removed. The Internet and the World Wide Web are great international knowledge levelers. Businesses large or small, long established or newly minted, are all equal in the cyber world of RSS feeds, electronic mail, e-commerce, Web portals, and Google hits.

Technology and globalization go hand in hand. Globalization unleashes technology, and technology drives firms to plan production and sales on a global basis. In nearly every case, technology also changes the work people do. The jobs created by globalization, for example, demand more education and training. Globalization also changes the way businesses operate by transforming relationships between suppliers, producers, retailers, and customers. Because of these interrelations, one cannot isolate technology from the world of business and commerce, law and contracts, culture and religion, language and literacy, or well-being and wealth.

The world thrives on change, and change usually reflects progress, perceived or otherwise. Technological advances now underpin change, regardless of the purpose of the endeavor. Today, the globalization of technology is a given. Moreover, technology's evolution creates new facets of globalization with the potential to change the future's course and open new possibilities.

The globalization of technology creates new opportunities as reactions to emerging demands arise from new possibilities. People around the world can now connect easily, quickly, and at a lower cost than ever before: In effect, online communication technologies have eliminated borders. The globalization of technology has already demonstrated that cross-border and intercontinental outsourcing, crossing several time zones, is a viable business model. Such practices are made possible by the leveling nature of common language skills, literacy, and intellectual abilities, which outweigh considerations of workers' citizenship or location. Through the range of possibilities associated with the globalization of technology, people are now increasingly interconnected. Most important, in this new online global context, cultural unawareness or language difficulties accentuated by local dialects and accents can be overcome through innovative uses of technology.

Institutions, practices, and behaviors are, in turn, being changed by the technologies of the digital age. Taking the form of 3G phones, video reporting, and advanced techno gadgets, technology is part of daily life, and people have become part of an e-society. This e-society uses digital media in most relationships, including peer to peer (e.g., personal communications, business-to-business purchases), government to citizen (e.g., online mechanisms citizens use to interact with government), or individual to other (e.g., business to consumer).

THE EFFECTS OF GLOBALIZATION

Not only does globalization help provide for a technological transfer that boosts countries on an economic scale, but it also promotes cultural transfer around the world.

Cultural Integration

One positive effect of globalization is the cultural exchange that it promotes around the world. The spread of culture is evident in several aspects of life in many countries. Globalization now allows (for example) Americans to eat Italian food, rural Vietnamese farmers to watch the daily news on television, the French to eat fast food, Germans to watch American movies, and the Japanese to listen to Scottish music. Today's world is marked by globalization; almost no place or no one is so far away that connecting is entirely impossible. As a result, international interactions in today's world contrast sharply with those presented in Jules Verne's 1873 fantasy-adventure story *Around the World in Eighty Days*. In fact, it is now possible to circle the globe in less than a day and to note changes in the various cultures along the way.

Culture is a society's conglomeration of its language, spiritual practices, social mores, and values that are transmitted from one generation to another. Global culturalization is a diffusion of cultural values and ideas across national borders. A specific example of such cultural integration is the way restaurants not only affect eating habits but also influence the traditions and values in countries where they are located. To illustrate these concepts, I consider the examples of Starbucks and McDonald's, two brands recognized worldwide.

The Starbucks Corporation

Starbucks was founded in 1971 as a local roaster and retailer of whole-bean and ground coffee, tea, and spices; it was a single store in Pike Place Market, Seattle, in the state of Washington. Named after a character in the novel *Moby Dick*, Starbucks is now the largest coffeehouse company in the world, boasting some 16,000 outlets in over 40 countries (Starbucks Corporation, 2011).

The Starbucks phenomenon, however, causes cultural concerns in Italy. Whereas Americans commonly buy takeaway coffee and drink it in the street or at the office, Italians associate coffee with leisurely sidewalk cafés. Coffee in Italy is more than a drink; it is a lifestyle ("Why Starbucks is not present," 2006). The fast-food culture born in the United States does not match Italian culture. Rather, in Italy eating is a part of life to be enjoyed with friends and family. Likewise, Italians drink coffee to relax and chat, not on the go as Americans often do. In this cultural context, Italian coffee shops offer a personal, friendly atmosphere many Italians believe a large chain could not provide. For them, Starbucks cannot supply the unique atmosphere of closeness and companionship that other coffee shops can.

The McDonald's Corporation

Another telling example of globalization is the proliferation of McDonald's restaurants around the world. McDonald's has become emblematic of globalization, such that globalization is sometimes referred to as the "McDonaldization of society" (Ritzer, 1983). McDonald's is the world's largest chain of fast-food restaurants, primarily selling hamburgers, chicken, French fries, breakfasts, milkshakes, and soft drinks. The business began in 1940, with a restaurant opened by siblings Dick and Mac McDonald in San Bernardino, California ("Travel through Time," 2011).

Since then, McDonald's has expanded and now boasts over 32,000 restaurants that serve some 60 million people in 117 different nations each day (McDonald's Corporation, 2011). According to the company's Website, "More than 75% of McDonald's restaurants worldwide are owned and operated by independent local men and women" (McDonald's Corporation, 2011, para. 1).

Consider McDonald's effects on Chinese culture, for instance. In the past, festivities marking a child's birth date were not celebrated in China. McDonald's established a new tradition by successfully promoting American-style birthday parties as part of its marketing strategy ("The influence of U.S. corporations," n.d.). This example might appear trivial, but it shows that the spread of U.S. companies in foreign countries can have unexpected consequences. And such influences are not limited to American companies; rather, in many sectors, globalization represents the important role companies from a variety of nations play in the daily lives of people around the world.

Some individuals might call the spread of culture via globalization "Americanization." They might argue that culture—their native culture—is being lost to the American standard of life, and that globalization is thus detrimental to the preservation of those cultures. However, this argument simply does not explain the whole story. For example, because the Hindu religion proscribes the consumption of red meat, McDonald's restaurants in India serve a certain kind of lamb patty (called a maharaja burger) instead of the original beef patties (Cooper, 1996). This menu item, unique to India, illustrates the multinational organization's adaptation to a particular local culture. Although Indians might eat at McDonald's, they need not compromise any of their traditional or religious values to do so. This is a prime case of globalization's creating new mixtures of cultures as various cultural influences spread to all corners of the globe.

Understanding Other Cultures

Companies are expanding operations to other nations and are following the new trend of outsourcing to do so. "However, expanding operations to other nations means that organizations have to concurrently expand their communication capabilities so that they can interact efficiently with their foreign offices and markets" ("The importance of language," 2010, para. 2). Moreover, "mobility, economic and political interdependence, and communication technology are three reasons to explain why intercultural communication has become an imperative in contemporary society" ("The importance of language," 2010, para. 2). Because communication is so crucial, then, a key initial step to engaging effectively in cross-cultural communication is understanding and accepting the differences of other cultural groups.

Such acceptance, however, does not mean that individuals need to agree with the perspectives and practices of another culture. Rather, it means that people should try understand how they are viewed by the "other" culture in order to devise ways to best collaborate cross-culturally—particularly within the context of online exchanges (Varner & Beamer, 2006). Thus, effective interaction in the age of globalization, particularly via online media, requires individuals to understand the "other" culture. For this reason, individuals can benefit from a system or a framework that helps them identify and understand different cultural aspects that can affect communication practices in global contexts.

Communication across Cultures: What? Who? How?

In the past, many people assumed that cultural differences were barriers that impeded communication and interaction. Today effective global leaders believe that cultural differences, if well managed, are resources, not handicaps. Culture is an intrinsic part of the global marketing environment—particularly the global online marketing environment. Cultural diversity in such international contexts brings with it an immense richness that, if correctly addressed, can lead to high rates of international success. New cultures, for example, might offer a breeding ground for new product ideas; cultural exchanges might lead to new market opportunities in other nations. Thus, cultural differences can be an important resource for companies if the rights steps are taken to understand and address them.

If, in one's homeland, both managers and workers can be taught to communicate more effectively with colleagues and customers—particularly in exchanges involving online media—global organizational successes can follow. Training, briefing, and adequate preparation for both online and on-site interactions with individuals in others cultures can make these exchanges positive and enlightening. However, someone who communicates effectively with American nationals in the United Sate might not necessarily be as effective when communicating with Japanese or Saudi Arabians in the United States, Japan, or Saudi Arabia. To better understand the global leader's role as a communicator, it is vital that one comprehend what the complex process of communication involves: Communication is a dynamic exchange of energy, ideas, and information between and among people. It is verbal and nonverbal and occurs at different levels—informal and formal, intellectual and emotional. Most communication is manifest through symbols that globally differ in their meanings according to time, place, culture, and person. Human interaction, moreover, is characterized by a continual updating of these symbols' meanings. The next section explores the nature of such interactions and symbols.

The Communication Process: One Planet, One Future?

Every individual communicates a unique perspective that reflects his or her own world and reality. Every culture, in turn, reflects its group's worldview. Modern telecommunications, including television and the Internet, have forever changed human beings and their views. These technologies have created a new level of awareness about individuals' actions and forced a review of notions about transparency and accountability. These same technologies confront humanity with the fundamental contradiction between unlimited economic growth and the resources required to maintain that growth. More than at any other time in history, in the 21st century, humankind faces rival and increasingly incompatible viewpoints and realities—delivered almost instantly and directly via online media—and the role of corporations is central to this conflict, representing globalization in a myriad of these situations.

Although the reality that "business as usual" cannot continue is broadly recognized, one can say that international business is different from national business because countries and societies are different. Societies vary because their cultures vary, exhibiting profound differences in social structure, religion, language, education, economic philosophy, and political philosophy. But by any definition, communication is a process of circular interaction that involves a sender, a receiver, and a message. In human interaction, the sender or receiver might be a person or a group of people. The message conveys meaning through the medium or symbol used to send it (the *how*) as well as in its content (the *what*).

Both sender and receiver occupy a unique field of experience. Essentially, this is a private world of perception through which all experience is filtered, organized, and translated. Each person experiences life in a unique way and psychologically structures his or her own distinctive perceptual field. Among the factors that comprise one's field of experience are one's family and one's educational, cultural, religious, and social background. An individual's perceptual field affects the way he or she receives and dispenses all new information. An individual's self-image, needs, values, expectations, goals, standards, cultural norms, and perception have an effect on the way input is received and interpreted. All of these factors also affect how the members of a given culture perceive technology in terms of its uses and its implications. A sense of the similarities and dissimilarities between the sender and the receiver facilitates a successful communication—particularly in the age of the global Internet.

Global Communication

Klopf (1991) defined *communication* as a process individuals use to exchange ideas, information, and opinions through verbal and nonverbal channels. People working and communicating in a multicultural environment must "remember that the message that ultimately counts is the one that the other person gets or creates in their mind, not the one we send" (Simons, Vazquez, & Harris, 1993, pp. 45–50). Key to understanding this is that each person has been socialized in a unique environment, and such socialization creates a wide range of differences. These differences increase across cultures, and therefore the number of misunderstandings or miscommunications increases, as well.

Every person is simultaneously part of many different identity groups through which he or she learns and becomes part of his or her culture. For example, I am Turkish; I was born in Turkey and grew up there, but I have studied and worked in the United States. Thus the two cultures I know are combined in my personal and professional life. In the same way, each individual is culturally unique because each one adopts or adapts differently the attitudes, values, and beliefs of the groups to which one belongs. All communication becomes intercultural because of variations in the group identities of those communicating. What follows is a discussion of different items individuals should consider when addressing cultural differences in the various international contexts that arise through globalization.

High and Low Context

In the anthropological sense, *culture* refers to the cumulative deposit of knowledge, beliefs, values, religion, customs, and mores acquired by a group of people and that is then passed on from generation to generation. In examining the differences that arise between cultures, the anthropologist Edward T. Hall made a vital distinction between high- and low-context cultures (Hall, 1976; see table 1.1). He described the ways this matter of context influences communications—namely, information is either in the physical context or it is internalized in the person and little is communicated in the explicit words or message.

According to Hall, high-context communicators expect others to be able to interpret what they mean based on a knowledge of the cultural values that lie behind the words, what they are actually talking about at the time, the speaker's tone of voice, and of course, eye and body language. People from Japan, Saudi Arabia, Spain, and China engage

Table 1.1. High-context and low-context cultures around the world.

Low-Context Cultures	High-Context Cultures
Nordic and Germanic	The Arab World
Europe	Most of Africa
North America	Latin America
Australia and New Zealand	Asia

Source. Adapted from Hall (1976) and from Hall and Hall (1987).

in high-context communications. For example, compare what the word *difficult* means for Japanese people and what it means to French people. In the Japanese cultural context, the word *difficult* means "absolutely out of the question, impossible." But when the French say *difficult*, they mean "not easy, but not impossible either." Another example is the different levels of directness used by Japanese and Americans. Japanese communicate by stating things indirectly, whereas Americans usually "spell it all out" (Herberger, 1980).

In contrast, in a low-context culture, most information is contained in explicit codes, such as words. Canada and the United States, as well as many European cultures, engage in low-context communication (Hall & Hall, 1987). In other words, low-context communicators tend to express themselves in explicit, concrete, and unequivocal terms. Little cultural baggage comes with it, and listeners can usually take what speakers say at face value. Such differences can affect how messages are presented and received when interlocutors use online media to interact across cultures.

When individuals are communicating, they are attempting to determine how much the listener knows about whatever is being discussed. In low-context communication, the listener knows very little and must be told practically everything. In high-context cultures, however, the listener is already familiar with the context and does not need much background information. Because of this key difference, communication between high-context people and low-context people is often fraught

TABLE 1.2. Communication in high-context and low-context cultures.

High-Context Culture	Low-Context Culture
Context	
Meaning lies in the environment, relationship, status, and protocol	Meaning is explicit and often written
"Yes" may be ambiguous	No ambiguity
Space	
Group space	Individual space
Smaller physical distance	Larger physical distance
Time	
Polychronic[a]	Monochronic[b]
Interlocutors multitask	Interlocutors concentrate on single task
Easily interrupted, allows distractions	Takes deadlines and schedules seriously
Verbal/Nonverbal	
Greater use of nonverbal cues	Mostly verbal communication
Gestures and facial expressions convey meaning	Gestures support speech
Silence accepted as communication	Low tolerance for silence
Agreements	
Emphasis on verbal contract	Emphasis on written contract
Indirectness is considerate and honest	Directness is honest
Laws are flexible and situational	Laws are rigid and universal
Contracts are symbolic of a relationship	Contracts are binding

Notes. [a] Followers of polychronic **time are not comfortable** performing **repetitive tasks that are easy to define within boundaries.** [b] **Followers of** monochronic time excel at repetitive tasks that are easy to define within boundaries.
Source. Adapted from Hall and Hall (1987).

with impatience and irritation because low-context communicators might provide more information than is necessary, whereas high-context communicators may not provide enough information (Hall, 1976). Such irritation might become even more acute when members of these two cultural groups interact through online media—because these media often remove

TABLE 1.3. Tips for overcoming the differences between high- and low-context cultures.

• Keep an open mind	• Answer calmly and reasonably
• Put yourself in other person's position	• Be genuine
• Listen before speaking	• Be yourself
• Ask open-ended questions (who, what, why, where, how)	

the nonverbal cues (e.g., physical appearance, accent, and intonation) that can remind an interlocutor that he or she is interacting with someone from another culture. The characteristics of low- and high-context cultures as they affect communication are contrasted in table 1.2.

Unless global leaders are aware of subtle differences, communication misunderstandings between low- and high-context interlocutors can result, particularly when these individuals are communicating through Web-based media. Global leaders should prioritize intercultural communication and an understanding of the fundamental differences between high- and low-context cultures, for such differences will likely affect their business success throughout the global marketplace or their political success when dealing with others in the world. Table 1.3 provides an overview of different approaches individuals can take to interact more effectively in order to address differing communication expectations associated with high-context and low-context cultures.

NEGOTIATING ACROSS CULTURES IN A GLOBAL WORLD

One of the most difficult and important tasks associated with globalization is international negotiation. Negotiation is a process in which two or more entities come together to discuss common and conflicting interests in order to reach an agreement of mutual benefit. International negotiation is extremely complex and difficult, for it involves laws, regulations, standards, and business practices that differ from one society to the next. Most of the difficulties in international negotiations, however, arise because of cultural differences. Differences in the negotiation process from culture to culture include language, cultural conditioning, negotiating styles, approaches to problem solving, assumptions, gestures and facial expressions, and the role of ceremony and formality.

According to Lewis, there are over 200 national cultures in the world, and many other cultural layers, such as region, generation, gender, class, education, and profession (2006, p. 28). In a theoretical approach to analyzing the broad cultural differences, Lewis divided cultures into three main categories: linear-active, multi-active, and reactive (see table 1.4).

Missing Points: Did You Say That? Did You Mean That? What Do You Mean?

When people communicate, each makes certain assumptions about the perception, judgment, thinking, and reasoning patterns of the other; people make these assumptions without realizing they are doing so. Correct assumptions facilitate communication, but incorrect assumptions lead to misunderstanding and confusion. Awareness of cultural influences is thus essential for transferring concepts, technology, or ideas in international

TABLE 1.4. Lewis's categories of culture.

Linear-Active (e.g., U.S., U.K., Germany)	**Multi-Active** (e.g., Italy, Spain, Brazil)	**Reactive** (e.g., China, Korea)
Talks half the time	Talks most of the time	Listens most of the time
Does one thing at a time	Does several things at once	Reacts to partner's action
Plans ahead step by step	Plans grand outline only	Looks at general principle
Partly conceals feelings	Displays feelings	Conceals feelings
Rarely interrupts	Often interrupts	Never interrupts
Is job oriented	Is people oriented	Is very people oriented
Uses mainly facts	Prioritizes feelings before facts	Considers statements to be promises
Separates the social and professional	Interweaves the social and professional	Connects the social and professional

Source. Adapted from Lewis (2006, p. 127).

exchanges. Depending on the cultures involved, an overlap of values may occur in a specific area; in these cases, the problems related to transferring ideas will be minimal.

According to Graham (1996), there are four problematic areas in international negotiations: language, nonverbal behavior, values, and thinking and decision making. Many promising international deals fall through when problems arise between negotiators from informal cultures and their counterparts from more formal cultures. Armed with knowledge about various cultural perspectives on negotiation, however, international negotiators could take the following steps to reduce difficulties and increase the chance of success in cross-cultural negotiations.

First, negotiators must recognize that counterparts from other cultures differ in their perceptions, motivations, beliefs, and values. Those communicating need to identify, understand, and respect the other side's culture before the negotiation opens. Each side should be prepared to communicate and operate on two discrete cultural wavelengths whether the exchange takes place in cyberspace or in physical space.

International negotiators should avoid assuming that behaviors acceptable in their own culture are also acceptable in all other cultures. This is particularly relevant in relation to cyberspace interactions; one might easily suppose, for example, that the more direct approach to online exchanges common in one's own low-context culture is universal. (Such an assumption might conflict with the expectations of individuals from high-context cultures, in which a more indirect approach would be preferred.) Those involved in intercultural negotiations should adjust the pace of proceedings to that of the people with whom they are trying to do business. In online exchanges, such adjustments might require waiting what seems (to one partner) like an excessive amount of time for a response via a medium designed for speed (e.g., expecting a quick response to e-mails or a quick responding post in an online chat).

In any negotiations with anybody anywhere, any party involved has the option of declining a deal.

Everyone involved in an online or an on-site exchange should be treated with the greatest personal respect. Productive and enduring personal relations between negotiators lead to long-term relationships between their companies; this is a source of mutual prosperity. Adopting a respectful perspective can entail forcing oneself to think carefully about how to structure an online response to an overseas counterpart; often this is a more productive tactic than rapidly posting a quick and direct reply. Related to respect is the idea that negotiators must be culturally neutral; difference does not indicate either superiority or inferiority. Neither party should cast judgment on the other party's cultural mores. The danger of such assumptions can be particularly acute in online exchanges, in which delays between the time a message is sent and the time a response is received could be mistakenly viewed as a negative reflection of the other party's abilities (e.g., intellect) or character (e.g., honesty).

Those involved in international communications need to be sensitive to cultural norms and taboos. They must try to understand what these cultural particularities are and how their behavior relates to them even if abiding by these norms causes discomfort or emotional stress to the interlocutor. Such sensitivities might require a special degree of attention in online exchanges, in which the text-based nature of most media prevents one from viewing nonverbal reactions and responses—important feedback—to messages. Likewise, negotiators should demonstrate interest in, knowledge of, respect for, and appreciation of the other side's culture. Failure to do so can easily be interpreted as reflective of cultural superiority and arrogance. Questions about culture, for example, carefully framed without criticism show that one finds the other side's culture interesting, important, and worth learning about. Such sensitivity, again, can be challenging in cyberspace, where one's impulse is often to provide quick and direct responses to questions or comments.

Finally, in order to reach to their audiences, negotiators should create a central message; even if one is dealing with other cultures, people around the world like to know what the presentation is about and what they will gain from listening to it (though different cultures might expect this factor to be addressed in different ways).

In applying the strategies listed here, individuals engaged in cross-cultural communication first need to determine whether the audience values abundant facts and background information or if such details are considered extraneous. For example, Turks are not inclined to value an amassment of facts; they consider the broader context rather than the minute details. Americans, in contrast, are extremely fact oriented. Evaluating one's audience allows one to select only points that support the central message and that are relevant to the audience, thus increasing the effectiveness of the presentation. If, for example, one's audience comprises Germans, Scandinavians, or Japanese, one should support what one says with plenty of relevant facts and statistics. But if the audience is British, one can present a broad topical overview that includes only the essential details.

Formal cultures tend to be organized in steep hierarchies that reflect major differences in status and power. In contrast, informal cultures value more egalitarian organizations with smaller differences in status and power. These contrasting values can cause conflict in a range of online and on-site negotiations. On the one hand, members of formal and hierarchical cultures might at times be offended by the breezy familiarity used by counterparts accustomed to informal and egalitarian societies. On the other hand, those from informal cultures might perceive their formal counterparts as stuffy or arrogant. Such misunderstandings can be avoided if both sides are aware that different behaviors reflect differing cultural values rather than individual idiosyncrasies. For example, Americans tend to have a short term, distributive view of negotiation. Because Americans are concerned with their own interests and view negotiations competitively, they often arrive at distributive outcomes. In contrast, most Asians view negotiation as a long-term relationship and cooperative task.

Given the variant perspectives on negotiation held by Americans and by those of other nationalities, it is not surprising that international negotiations, both online and on-site, are marred by many difficulties, misunderstandings, and mistakes. Learning about the cultural perspectives of negotiation can reduce some of these problems. The first step toward improving intercultural negotiations is understanding the influence of cultural differences on negotiation styles. In any negotiation situation—be it online or on-site—it does not matter which side one is on; each party is there to win. Therefore the international negotiator should try to learn as much as possible about the other side's culture. Negotiators should be tolerant and respectful of cultural differences. Once differences are understood, negotiators should seek ways of accommodating them.

CONCLUSION

The world has embarked on the most ambitious collective experiment in history: globalization, the long-term effort to integrate the global dimensions of life into each nation's economy, politics, and culture. As a result, human beings now live in a world where the umbrella of globalization continues to expand, covering new cultures each day. Under this umbrella, cultural peculiarities (e.g., the national cultures of China and the United States, German economic practice, Italian fashion, French cuisine) are what they are because of their participation in a global system. Such differences cannot be understood beyond this global context.

In this scenario, the culturally distinct societies of the world are being overrun by globally available goods, media, ideas, and institutions. In a world where people from Vienna to Sydney eat Big Macs, wear H&M clothes, watch MTV or CNN, listen to music on their iPods, talk about human rights, and work on their IBM-Lenovo computers, characteristics that make cultures more distinctive from one another can become endangered. These internationally distributed commodities that create a kind of commonality across cultures have been used and ideas have been discussed daily around the world as a part of globalization.

This new global economic, political, and social order is made possible by computers and telecommunications. But equally important has been the spread of free-market capitalism, deregulation, global investment, privatization, the pursuit of human rights, and the recognition of the value of an open society. In combination with the dissemination of these values, globalization has created the need for international leaders to identify, study, and understand the worldviews, mindsets, and habits of their global publics in order to effectively communicate.

If globalization is economic, political, and social, it is also cultural. To say this, however, is only to raise the question of what such a phenomenon amounts to. As this chapter explains, there can be no doubt that culture plays important role in globalization and that communication is the key to success in a range of international activities—from business to political and social. Communication styles and meaning, as well as the realities perceived by individuals, are culturally constructed. Adequate knowledge of language and culture is needed for effective communication in any society.

Even in countries where English is spoken, the pattern and meaning of the English language may be different because of cultural influence. Therefore language fluency alone may be inadequate for practicing business abroad; fluency must be combined with knowledge of the culture of the native speakers. Words often do not have common meaning, especially between native and nonnative speakers of a language; English words are often associated with mental images, subtleties, and nuances closely tied to the speaker's native language. According to Beeth (1997), one who learns a language and not the related culture is akin to an elephant attempting to move through a dainty chinaware shop: No matter how carefully the elephant tries to move, each step sends fragile dishes crashing to the floor.

A lack of cultural awareness can lead to communication devoid of essential emotional content, content that might be needed in order to effectively communicate in some societies. Recognition of one's own culture and an awareness of how it differs from other cultures are needed to successfully carry out international business and political functions abroad.

The effects of globalization occur on a much broader scale today than they did in the past and have been most prominent in the last few decades.

To survive the storm winds of globalization, those who participate in the modern global economy must carefully watch the rapid changes taking place and in order to successfully adapt to the times. There is no option but to face this "new world" challenge. Although many aspects of the new global reality are not yet fully understood, success in the face of these changes depends on a sound understanding of culture's importance to effective communication and mutual understanding, principles on which the future depends.

References

Albrow, M. (1996). *The global age: State and society beyond modernity.* Stanford, CA: Stanford University Press.

Beeth, G. (1997). Multicultural managers wanted. *Management Review, 86*(5), 17–21.

Cooper, K. J. (1996, November 4). It's a lamb burger, not a hamburger at beefless McDonald's in New Delhi. *The Washington Post*, p. A14.

Friedman, T. L. (1999). *The Lexus and the olive tree.* New York, NY: Farrar, Straus Giroux.

Graham, J. L. (1996). Vis-à-vis: International business negotiations. In P. N. Ghauri & J.-C. Usunier (Eds.), *International business negotiations* (pp. 69–90). Tarrytown, NY: Pergamon.

Hall, E. T. (1976). *Beyond culture.* Garden City, NY: Anchor Press.

Hall, E. T., & Hall, M. R. (1987). *Hidden differences: Doing business with the Japanese.* Garden City, NY: Anchor/Doubleday.

Herberger, R. A. (1980). Some beliefs of Americans can lead to wrong conclusions. *Nihon Keizai Shimbun/Japan Economic Times*, pp. 19–24.

The importance of the language in the intercultural business communication. (2010). *Barackoli.com.* Retrieved June 1, 2010, from http://barackoli.com/the-importance-of-the-language-in-the-intercultural-business-communication/.

The influence of U.S. corporations on local mores. (n.d.). *Globalization101.org*. Retrieved February 21, 2011, from http://www.globalization101.org/htmlsite/index%28385%29.htm.

Klopf, D. W. (1991). *Internet encounters.* Englewood, CO: Morton.

Lewis, R. D. (2006). *When cultures collide: Leading across cultures* (3rd ed.). Boston, MA: Nicholas Brealey.

McDonald's Corporation. (2011). Our company. Retrieved February 21, 2011, from http://www.aboutmcdonalds.com/mcd/our_company.html.

Mittelman, J. H. (2000). *The globalization syndrome: Transformation and resistance.* Princeton, NJ: Princeton University Press.

Ritzer, G. (1983). The McDonaldization of society. *Journal of American Culture, 6*, 100–107.

Simons, G. F., Vazquez, C., & Harris, P. R. (1993). *Transcultural leadership.* Houston, TX: Gulf.

Starbucks Corporation. (2009). Our company. Retrieved September 27, 2009, from http://www.starbucks.com/about-us/company-information.

Starbucks Corporation. (2011). *Hoovers.* Retrieved February 20, 2011, from http://www.hoovers.com/company/Starbucks_Corporation/rhkchi-1.html.

Travel through time with us. (2011). McDonald's Corporation. Retrieved February 21, 2011, from http://www.aboutmcdonalds.com/mcd/our_company/mcd_history.html.

Varner, I., & Beamer, L. (2006). *Intercultural communication in the global workplace* (4th ed.). New York, NY: McGraw-Hill/Irwin.

Waters, M. (1995). *Globalization.* London, UK: Routledge.

Why Starbucks is not present in Italy? (2006). Innovation Zen (Blog). Retrieved February 21, 2011, from http://innovationzen.com/blog/2007/01/15/why-starbucks-is-not-present-in-italy/.

CHAPTER 2

TRADITIONAL CULTURES AND THEIR EFFECTS ON GLOBALIZATION

AN AFRICAN PERSPECTIVE

Kehbuma Langmia

Traditional cultures have defined and differentiated people over the years, and globalization has offset this diversity by creating confusion. Indigenous cultures, especially in the developing world, are gradually being eroded by the force of so-called global culture. This global culture is a whirlwind that is crushing development and threatening burgeoning traditional modes of expressions, particularly in Africa. For global culture to be considered a positive thing in Africa, the theoretical concepts of Africana critical theory and Afrocentricity should be the starting point. Eurocentrism, the dominant conceptual framework, is used repeatedly with respect to Africa, and this practice affects globalization and the digital divide as it relates to the continent. This chapter examines in detail the problems resulting from a Eurocentric view of Africa; it demonstrates the importance and value of local cultures in Africa, and specifically in Cameroon. The study examines how the related cultures have been ignored by global technology and how globalization can succeed in addressing issues of technology use.

> Globalization … has become its own "meta-narrative," implying an unrealistic degree of homogenization and inevitability. (Lister, Dovey, Giddings, Grant, & Kelly, 2003, p. 182)
>
> The divide between the income rich and the income poor, the technology haves and the technology have-nots, the information rich and the information poor, has become the most serious political economic problem facing the world today. (Parayil, 2005, p. 42)

INTRODUCTION

The culture of a people is the hallmark of its human essence and identity. When this culture fuses with outside elements, change is bound to occur. Before the era of colonialism, African culture was unique. It was relatively untainted by outside forces that could destroy it. With the advent of colonization, the people of Africa witnessed something new, intrusive, and overbearing. Rodney (1972) observed that "because of the impact of colonialism and cultural imperialism, Europeans and Africans themselves in the colonial period lacked due regard for the unique features of African culture" (p. 34).

This lack of regard, which colonialism created in terms of how Africans and Europeans view African culture, has continued for almost half a century with the emergence of globalization. Rodney (1972) asserted that "in Africa, both the formal school system and the informal value system of colonialism destroyed social solidarity and promoted the worst form of alienated individualism without social responsibility" (pp. 254–255). This chapter seeks to answer the following question: In what way has globalization become another force stripping Africa of its culture?

The process of the global integration of value systems and cultural mores through communication has created the "global village" (Green, 2001; Perrons, 2004). Local peasants now use computers to sell their produce electronically in the international markets (Moodley, 2002); local artists in Africa now download rock-and-roll and hip-hop music and use QuickTime software on their computers to fashion their own songs' beats. On the negative side, cellular phones now send bank account numbers via text messages from city youths in Africa to "potential investors" in some Western countries. Nyamnjoh (2004) described this reality in Africa succinctly:

> Criminal rackets promising effortless immigration and work permits have sprung up to take advantage of the burning desire in ordinary people to succeed. Similarly, Nigerian 4-1-9 and Cameroonian Feymen fraudsters have equally used the Internet and cell phones creatively to access more people with their letter scams and fraudulent business deals that have brought some of them dazzling riches. (Nyamnjoh, 2004, p. 52)

Without heed for cultural diversity, therefore, so-called global technology has come to signify both the good and the ugly, especially in Africa. Only a few, mostly urban, youths are privy to some of the technological gadgets that globalization has brought to Africa. This chapter, using the scholarly literature, discusses whether globalization has ushered in new cultural systems that will work side by side with existing African cultural value systems in a symbiotic relationship—or overshadow them. If the digital cultural divide between Africa and the West is to be narrowed, the primary role and function of African cultural identity must be addressed. Africans cannot continue as passive consumers of foreign cultures in the name of globalization.

BACKGROUND AND LITERATURE REVIEW

Several attempts have been made by scholars from various academic disciplines to define globalization. These attempts have polluted the field, hindering a consensus definition. Though some have viewed globalization as a process of bringing people together through new means of communication and transport (Giddens, 2006; Richmond, 2002), others have labeled globalization "a process that encompasses the causes, coursc, and consequences of transnational and transcultural integration of human and non-human activities" (Al-Rodhan, 2006, p. 2).

Of all the definitions provided for globalization, the one that fits the purpose of this chapter is Sholte's: "Globalization is a dynamic whereby the social structures of modernism (capitalism, rationalism, industrialism, bureaucratism, etc.) are spread the world over, normally destroying pre-existent cultures and local self-determination" (2000, p. 16). So modernism—the extended version of globalization—has affected preexistent cultures in Africa. It presupposes that the rest of the world is obliged to imitate economic, social, and cultural movements that are being spread by the dominant forces of Western ideology. These ideologies are diffused through modern media channels, such as the Internet, television, radio, and more recently, cell phones.

Today's global culture has become the way of adopting Western modes of life and Western value systems at the expense of local oral and written cultures. As Ess and Sudweeks explained:

> The world is getting smaller. This common metaphor is at work in the term "global village," which derives its oxymoronic appeal from the typically small size of village in contrast to the vastness of the "globe" ... Moreover, increased contact has led to the spread—sometimes through imposition, sometimes through voluntary adoption—of Western (especially US) cultural practices. Traditional dress has been replaced by suits in business settings in every country in the world; young people in urban areas everywhere watch films made in Hollywood, listen to Rock and Roll, play video games, talk on cell phones, wear jeans, drink

> Coke, eat pizza (or McDonald's hamburgers), speak English, and increasingly frequent cybercafés. Part of what makes the world "smaller" today is that one is more likely to encounter familiar symbols and practices in geographically distant places than was the case one hundred years or even fifty years ago. (Ess & Sudweeks, 2001, p. vii)

Nowhere in Europe or America does one notice a significantly large population of Westerners adopting the communal lifestyles of Africans as a sign of global togetherness. How many universities in Europe and America have language departments that teach African languages like Lingala, Hausa, Swahili, and Yoruba—or indeed, any languages from Africa at all? Only a handful of educational institutions offer these studies. But most universities in Africa have English, French, German, and Spanish departments. If the globalization of technology is really meant to be global, why are the aforementioned popular African languages not among the plethora of languages available on modern computer systems like PCs (personal computers), PCSs (personal communication services), and PDAs (personal digital assistants)? It is as if the West dictates the rhythm of life on earth. If that is the case, the very notion of making the world a global village is a painfully one-sided ideology.

This situation is unfortunate. When African youths dance and dress like Hollywood stars, the future of African culture appears very bleak indeed. The vexing issue is that these Western cultural styles are assimilated in young Africans' ontological "culturescape." The original cultural forms—for instance, folk tales, music, dance, rituals, divinations, incantations, and festivals—tend to lose their uniqueness and, in some cases, are called "uncivilized" practices. These youth are assimilated—not integrated—into the "acceptable" Western patterns.

Diversity has become the cliché, the catchphrase for—seemingly—integrating minority cultures into the mainstream. The marriage between diversity and Westernization constitutes what should be a globalization of cultures. But the reality is that some cultural norms, particularly in

Africa, have been dubbed primitive and uncivilized by pro-Western scholars and neocolonialists:

> The combine and the gun originated in the sphere of Western or Christian civilization. Therefore, those who wish to give up hoe, machete, bow and arrow and to have combines and guns must also give up healing by witchcraft, polygamy, and superstition … how can primitive peoples survive contact with the scientific-technological age? (Jahn, 1990, p. 12–13)

Therefore, if these traditions, customs, oral culture, and religious rites are to be transported into the international spheres to function alongside Western cultures and value systems, clash is eminent.

This conflict, however, defeats the purpose of global culture or the global village. The advent of technology has further compounded the notion of global culture, facilitating the one-way flow of ideas:

> [W]hen it is possible to find your McDonalds [*sic*], Coca-Cola, Fish and Chips, Mars Bar, English or Continental breakfast and five course meal, John Lennon, Elvis Presley, Spice Girls or Madonna tune, Barbie, Batman or Mickey Mouse even in the remotest corners of the Dark Continent? It is largely thanks to facilitation by the African leadership (in the broadest sense of the word), that such unmitigated one-way flows are perpetuated, and everyone becomes trapped by the neo-liberal consumer web in one way or another, at one level or the other. (Nyamnjoh, 2004, p. 48)

This kind of situation represents what globalization has come to signify to rural populations all over the African continent. They might prefer Western movies to African movies that are not yet popular in the West. African films shot and directed by African producers can only have mainstream appeal in the United States during African or black film festivals. But why would mainstream African television channels or theaters not advertise or screen these films as regularly as they do Hollywood films in all the cities in Africa? American films and American ways of life have transformed young people, many of whom have come to think, act, and behave like Americans. This is the reason some scholars have associated globalization with Americanization (Sorge, 2005).

Numerous studies over the last decades have explored the globalization debate as it affects local or indigenous cultures. Using quantitative as well as qualitative research strategies, these studies have varying results, but all of them seem to agree that Westernization has affected, in one way or another, the growth of local cultures in non-Western countries.

A study by Chong (2006) titled "Ethnic Identities and Cultural Capital: An Ethnography of Chinese Opera in Singapore" found that multiculturalism in Singapore has affected the way Chinese opera is performed. Chong conducted semistructured interviews with a representative sample of 32 Chinese opera practitioners and some government representatives. His study affirms that "the national policies on multiculturalism, English language, and discouragement of Chinese dialects effectively reduced the symbolic and cultural capital of Chinese opera and, by extension, Chinese identity" (p. 291). This finding implies that Chinese opera would henceforth imitate Western-style opera because the performers would be speaking a Western language (i.e., English) and, in most cases, limiting their use of Chinese.

Another approach to globalization as it affects local culture has been examined by Parameswaran (2008). She discussed the ways that outsourcing American phone services to India has affected the cultural life patterns and attitudes of some Indian youths. Many young Indian workers are trained to answer phone calls from the United States using American or British accents; they work long hours at night, leading to abnormal schedules and the deprivation of daytime social interactions:

> The lack of daytime social life for those who sleep during the day and the packed schedules of those who forgo sleep to maintain ties with family and friends have led to "complaints of stress, panic attacks, depression, relationship troubles, alcoholism, and eating disorders." (Parameswaran, 2008, p. 120)

Parameswaran likewise stressed the negative effects of globalization on the importation of foreign value systems to the Indian community; one example is the celebration of Valentine's Day, a Western convention that has become common in India, as well. Parameswaran maintained that the age-old traditional notions of fidelity and the code of behavior for love that characterize Hindu religious doctrine in particular are being affected by Valentine's Day rituals. This cultural importation is not only affecting the culture per se of the people but also endangering the formation of national identities, in both the short term and the long term.

A study by Arnett (2002) titled "The Psychology of Globalization" documents the effects of Western influences on local cultures in developing countries, particularly sub-Saharan Africa: "The people of Africa are facing the challenge of maintaining their traditions while adopting many of the ways of the global culture" (p. 776). The adoption of the new ways of life—in this case European or American ways—often causes local cultures to be despised by the local youth and, in most cases, "modernized." Arnett placed the blame squarely with Western media, which have contributed to local cultures' losing ground and losing "relevance in the eyes of the young" (p. 776). The charges levied against the Western media are legitimate, considering the volume of Westernized music, film, and videos in local markets in Africa.

Arnett's research is exploratory in nature and poses questions for future researchers to consider: "How should the effects of globalization be measured for a given population, and how should exposure to globalization be measured at the individual level?" (p. 775). The article concludes with the supposition that globalization will, in the end, "alter and erode traditional ways" (p. 781). If globalization erodes traditional norms and customs and replaces them with artificial or imported modes of life, then the world will be left with a crop of human beings who are striving to be homogenous, thereby destroying the beauty of cultural diversity (Adu-Febiri, 2006).

Pieterse (2009) focused on the homogenization of culture because of downward globalization as a setback. Cultural differences, which should be the hallmark of ethnic identity, are in a danger of fading away because of the strong forces of globalization. Various communities and groups that maintain local cultures and adhere to unique ways of life may have to struggle for survival. Pieterse went further:

> Modernization has been advancing like a steamroller, erasing cultural and biological diversity in its way, and now not only the gains (rationalizations, standardization, control) but also the losses (alienation, disenchantment, displacement) are becoming apparent. (Pieterse, 2009, p. 43)

If rural communities are losing their identities, their uniqueness, and their cultural essences to globalization, traditional entities will by no means be restored if the trend continues unchecked. Instead, everyone will be forced from birth to act, speak, write, and perform through the lens of the West. Adu-Febiri (2006) affirmed that "flourishing cultural diversity or egalitarian cultural pluralism is critical to the development of sustainable globalization that would benefit all stakeholders in a globalize world" (p. 57).

Globalization and Cameroon

Cameroon, like most African countries, possesses rich cultural forms that predate contact with Western cultures—dance, music, folk tales, rituals, festivals, and dirges—traditional riches that are disappearing mainly because of globalization. These cultural forms represent, by their very essence, the identity of the citizens; their erosion under the influence of foreign cultures by way of globalization creates a disconnect between people and their own cultural heritage. In this situation, the media play a significant role in shaping the national culture. As a result of the influx of foreign media, progressively more non-Cameroonian programs are being aired on Cameroon media, and therefore more Cameroonians are turning to cable and satellite broadcasts by foreign companies like CNN, the BBC, Canal France Horizon, Eurosport, and others. This is what Nyamnjoh observed about these media's effects on the Cameroonian youth:

> Not only do young Cameroonians appropriate media representations never intended for them, they use these representations

> to construct fantasies about whiteness, which in turn serve as a standard of measure in encounters with actual whites. The media reinforce the ideas of western superiority and allure, thus buttressing fantasies that deny the reality of actual experiences with the modest circumstances of the white tourists, volunteers, researchers or clergy often encountered by the Cameroonian youth. (Nyamnjoh, 2002, p. 45)

This quotation captures this chapter's thesis on the issue Western culture's "superiority" over African culture. The African media have perpetuated this phenomenon, in part because of the cheap importation of Western products into African society and its market and in part because of Africa's lackluster effort to dedicate the necessary resources to creating homemade programs and products that highlight the richness of African culture. This lack of zeal and courage on the part of decision makers is creating a gulf of disparity between foreign cultures and indigenous cultures in Africa. Nyamnjoh (2002) corroborated this: "If globalization is a process of accelerated flow of media content, to most African cultures and children it is also a process of accelerated exclusion" (p. 43).

During this era of globalization, technology should be a force to bring developed and developing countries together. It should facilitate mutual exchange whereby the developed countries benefit from raw materials coming in from Africa, Southeast Asia, Latin America, and the Caribbean even as developing countries benefit from the finished products arriving from Europe and America—through exchange in which neither party exploits the other. Otherwise, the race for superiority will widen and create a still larger divide.

THE DIGITAL DIVIDE AND AFRICAN CULTURES

The term *digital divide* was coined to denote the exclusion of some part of the world's population from fully enjoying the fruits of information superhighway technology (Conradie, 2001; Lister et al., 2003; Schiller, 1999). The concept that the digital divide is a problem to be overcome implies that software and hardware are designed with every culture in mind; the truth, however, is that these new media technologies favor the spread of Western cultures and ideas. Most computer software used in Africa is conceived and produced in the West and is then shipped. Or if advanced technological infrastructures are to be installed in Africa, Africans are the backbenchers rather than the leaders in the initiative. Lister, Dovey, Giddings, Grant, and Kelly (2003) concurred, relating the case of the installation of the Africa One undersea fiber-optic communication cable: "Not one single African nation was involved in its development, and its operational structures will be oriented to those who can pay for access" (p. 206).

Within this framework, the languages, religions, rituals, values, customs, and traditions of the local people are almost never included in the conceptualization process associated with the developments of communication-related technologies. For example, a Cameroonian individual who wishes to send an e-mail to a relative in Europe must translate the message from his or her native language into English or French in order to use a language or a character system recognized by an e-mail program. Although English and French are the two official languages of Cameroon, they are written and spoken only by the educated few. In fact, there are over 200 ethnic languages in Cameroon, yet none of those languages enjoys the status English and French do as recognized languages of instruction in the country's schools.

From primary education to the university level, children in Cameroon are taught to read and write in these two foreign languages. As a result, these children now often find themselves acting as translators and interpreters for their parents at home when these family members encounter foreign cultural products, such as television programs. When they wish to send e-mail to their children living in Western countries, less educated individuals have to pay someone to translate their native languages into either English or French before the message can be sent because the language of the Internet or the encryption on the keyboards is either in French or English. This situation contributes to the digital divide, but it is not irreversible. If sound features, for example, were incorporated into the keyboard and the mouse through specially designed software packages, individuals who are not literate in either English or French could use technology—especially to access the audio components that are available in some of the main indigenous African languages on the Internet.

In terms of culture, design, and online communication, consider the emoticons in Yahoo's instant messaging. These image-based items do not have faces of people wearing masks, head ties, or hair styles resembling people in Cameroon or any other African country. Similarly, most sound bites and audio files available for new technology platforms represent famous Western artists, especially in the case of songs available for downloading to cell phones. If one wished to send an image of, say, a traditional cow-horn basket to a receiver in Europe, the sender would have to self-design that image, photograph it, or look for an approximate image from the Western clip-art features in his or her Microsoft Office program. These examples illustrate that the whole notion of digital divide is not solely a matter of access to functional technology that can serve people. Rather, it is also a matter of rejecting the "other" in the very process of conceiving technology. Stakeholders—the local cultural groups that will use a particular technology people and groups invested in the local culture—ought to be involved in decision making related to the design and use of technologies. The value systems and worldviews of these individuals should be incorporated in the process of developing new technologies so that their way of life is not neglected as this new way of life progresses.

Another issue affecting the global digital divide as it relates to culture is that Africans continuously flood themselves with the luxury goods of Western cultures: satellite television, wireless telephones, fax machines, smart phones, and MP3 players, to name a few. As a result, Africans are gradually becoming stooges of Western cultural imperialism; their cultures are being relegated to the background in favor of Western ways of life (Arnett, 2002). Had African cultures been considered in the promotion of digital technology, such as cell phones and laptops, the issue of global culture would not be as problematic as it is today.

Most African scholars (whether trained in the West or not) now speak their native languages with foreign accents. Their African accents are fast disappearing; their mannerisms are now mostly Western. Cameroon-made films like *Potent Secrets* (directed by Ako Abunaw, 2004)—or any other film made jointly with Nigerian actors and actresses—imitate American-style movies: The actors want to speak like Europeans, dress like Europeans, and use the same European and American props. A newly released Nigerian film titled *Beyonce* (directed by Frank Rajah Arase, 2006) is a classic example of an African film made using an American format; this is done for the sake of global marketability but at the expense of African culture.

In this context, the new digital products on the world market are new forms of Western domination of the market in disguise. These technologically advanced gadgets for sale in Cameroon or any other sub-Saharan African country are not only expensive for economically disadvantaged individuals to obtain and use but are also programmed in languages that they hardly understand. A case in point is e-mail. If a typical African mother of adult children, for example, wishes to send an electronic message, the only option available is to communicate through a Western-educated person who transmits her message to her son in Europe or America. She has not been provided with tools needed to use a PC or a smart cellular phone (although she owns one, bought by her son in the capital city or in Europe and given to her to facilitate quick and easy communication). She has no understanding or experience of text messaging, blogging, chatting, downloading sounds and images, or choosing wallpaper. The camera on her cell phone has never been used, and her ailing eyes cannot make out the tiny numbers and letters on the digital keyboard. The mother's cellular phone, moreover, speaks a language entirely different from her own, and when it turns off, she needs to navigate the new language of rebooting or recharging. If she does not know this language, her Western-literate son or daughter must help in the translation and interpretation. Exclusivity, as opposed to inclusivity, is the engine creating digital divide.

Africana Critical Theory and Afrocentricity

Both Africana critical theory, presented by Rabaka (2002), and Afrocentricity theory, presented by Asante (1987), form the core ideology for understanding digital divide as it relates to Africa. Rabaka (2002) argued that domination and discrimination are the key factors responsible for relegating Africa to the background. When major decisions about Africa are being made in the halls of power in the West, colonial perspectives and superior attitudes seem to be primary motives. Africa has the world's lowest GDP and has increasing rates of poverty, malnutrition, and death, and Western democracies often use piecemeal measures to address such situations. These approaches, however, often end in disaster. Rabaka and many other theorists believe these problematic piecemeal approaches stem from the domination and discrimination that Africa has suffered since the 1884 Berlin Conference, which partitioned the continent among European powers. Asante (1987) strongly argued that for any initiative to bear fruit in Africa, the total epistemology and ontology of Africa need to be adhered to. Africa is not Europe, nor is it America. The continent has its own ways of life, and Western powers need to thoroughly, completely understand these ways of life before implicating Africans in decisions.

Asante (1987) defined Afrocentricity as "the most complete philosophical totalization of the African being-at-the center of his or her existence" (p. 125). It is a concept that professes to highlight the importance of Africa in any given cultural discourse. In this context of examining Africa, Afrocentricity constitutes the first step toward the holistic understanding one needs in order to be cognizant of blackness and its value systems. This idea should be applied to the idea of a global culture in which Africa is included. Concepts and ideologies, whether of Western origin or not, should be able to include the African continent in all of its ramifications. With little or no proper grasp of the African experience, Western cultural scholars continue to view black studies as barbaric and primitive. In order to thwart this antithetical stance by Western scholars toward black culture, a dialogue must take place between the two opposing ideologies.

Another theoretical framework that should inform Western thought when dealing with issues related to Africa is Africana critical theory, which Rabaka (2002) defined as a "theory critical of domination and discrimination in continental and diasporan African life-worlds and lived experiences" (p. 147). Like Afrocentricity, this theory stands against the tide of dominant forces that seem to have taken Africa hostage. Africa is now in last place in terms of world technological growth. Because of Western domination, Africa is also in last place in terms of technological innovations: "The Western powers need to stop manipulating Africa as an ancillary continent that must succumb to Western models of modernity. Africa's cultural, economic, and social worth ought to be recognized as vital for her development" (Langmia, 2006, p. 153).

Black cultural scholars see Afrocentric ideology as a weapon to combat Europeanized hegemonic influences. Faced with the increasing threat of globalization, black cultural studies as championed by scholars like Asante (1987), ben-Jochannan (1997), and Allen (1991) needs to defend African values, beliefs, and traditions. If Westernization gains a foothold in the cognitive sphere of Africans and African Americans, the chances for resistance will be slim. But resistance is the solution. African languages, history, and culture occupy a limited space in most Western universities, whereas European and American cultures exert a great influence in most African universities and institutions. It was this seeming lack of interest from the West that gave rise to derogatory terms like *minorities*, *third world*, *developing countries*, and *aliens* that are applied to the black race and the African continent.

For the ideological success of globalization, especially as it relates to African culture, Afrocentric tenets must be considered. These tenets, Asante (1987) explained, include *Nommo* (the power of the spoken word), call and response, communal essence, rituals, music, and philosophy. The power of the spoken word, for instance, does not correspond with the culture of most new technological communication devices on the world market today. It is no secret that Africans enjoy talking loudly with each other, but cell phones, laptop computers, PalmPilots, and Blackberries encourage the silence and individualism that characterizes Western culture. These technologies have the same silencing or muting effect on communal essence, which forms the cornerstone of understanding African culture. Asante (1987) described communication from the Afrocentric ontological perspective:

> [I]nteraction in African society proceeds from different bases than interaction in European society … the speech is a functioning and integral part of the society and cannot be separated from the entire world view because the word-power is indeed the generative power of the community. (pp. 62–66)

This perspective is what defines the African identity. Therefore any discussion about including Africa in the notion of globalization must take into consideration the issue of interpersonal and group communication dynamics. As the cell phones' promotion of individualism shows, there is every reason to suppose that Africa was not taken seriously in the conceptual framework of global technology, thereby making the issue of digital divide more compelling.

RESOLVING THE DIGITAL DIVIDE IN AFRICA

To narrow the digital cultural divide between Africa and the West, both sides must address the primary role and function of African cultural identity. Africans cannot continue to be passive consumers of foreign cultures in the name of globalization; this is a form of political and psychological technology divide. African intelligentsia, philosophers, theorists, and policy determiners must be summoned to the table for any decision making that will affect the continent in any possible way. Africans need to mentally bypass the era of colonial domination and the modernization bonanza through decolonization of the mind (Wa Thiong'o, 1986). They should not be coerced by neoliberalism and neoimperialism as if their role were that of passive citizens who must be dictated to. Traditional African cultural elements that define and uniquely categorize Africans should be integral to the new media technology, as they are not today—I have yet to come across computer keyboards or cell phones, for instance, with any of the prominent African language symbols or icons, even when these items are being marketed to African consumers.

Africans themselves need to do more to counter the tide of digital divide on the continent. African scholars with Western education ought to use their expertise to push for more recognition of African cosmology and values in the conceptualization and production of those technological accessories that fill the African markets. When this has been achieved, those same individuals should be at the forefront of fostering education and training for both the young and the old in the uses of those technologies. Educational establishments in Africa should be encouraged to integrate elements of indigenous traditional cultures into the curriculum. Students should be taught to respect and admire their traditions and customs and encouraged not to be ashamed of them or to ignorantly imitate the West. Western culture that is transmitted through the media should not be shunned or castigated; rather, such transmissions should be viewed as representing other ways of life that are intrinsically embedded in foreign cultures—ways of life that Africa does not relate to. Any similarities such foreign transmissions exhibit to elements in the African culture could be shown by the broadcaster of the transmission, but these areas of overlap should not be considered reflections of a superior entity that Africans must emulate in order to become "globalized" or "civilized."

Some scholars have argued that, to close the gap of digital divide, technological products shipped to Africa (e.g., personal computers) should not be sold at excessively high prices. Rather, they should be inexpensive enough that everyone can afford them. That argument is particularly strong from the economic supply-and-demand perspective. But I argue that the politics of economic profiteering has dug a deep hole in the cultural identity of Africa. The demand for personal computers in a country like Cameroon will rise if (a) the computer is user-friendly and economically or culturally beneficial, (b) the user can identify the keyboard markings and icons or symbols attached to the software, and (c) the user has been theoretically trained to face the challenges of the product updates. In most cases, people are at ease with technology when it allows them to find answers to problems plaguing their lives.

CONCLUSION

The idea of traditional value systems in Africa acting as an impediment to technological progress is anachronistic; traditional values show the rich, colorful paraphernalia of Africa's cosmic essence. Erstwhile, missionaries in Africa branded such values as backward and evil and antithetical to Christianity. Now, globalization is eroding the traditional cultures by implanting Western ideas and value systems into the psyche of non-Western peoples. The same process of destabilizing African ways of life used by earlier colonizers is again being used by detractors. This situation must not be allowed to progress. Rather, policy makers and technology developers should seek to be inclusive and not exclusive. In my view, using the tenets of Africana theory and Afrocentricity to form the bases for Africa's meaningful involvement on the global stage is the solution to resolving digital divide in the near future.

Including African ways of life in a broader and more informed understanding of global initiatives in a global perspective without aspirations of domination or marginalization by the West (in its drive toward the global village) seems to be the solution for a meaningful technological revolution in Africa. Africa cannot survive a third wave of colonization, for it would be devastating to the continent. The West has much to gain (economically) from Africa through mutual collaboration, from learning how to integrate African cultural artifacts into the production and distribution of goods and services that are shipped to the continent. A careful reading of Asante and Rabaka's theoretical postulations will provide individuals from outside of Africa with a framework for mutual dealings with Africa. When this is done, incidents like the shameful Africa One affair—in which Africa was never invited to the decision-making table to contribute to the telecommunications development that would ultimately affect the lives of generations of Africans (Lister et al., 2003, p. 206)—will cease to occur in the future.

References

Adu-Febiri, F. (2006). The destiny of cultural diversity in a globalized world. *Review of Human Factor Studies, 12*(1), 30–64.

Allen, N. (1991). *African American humanism.* Amherst, NY: Prometheus Books.

Al-Rodhan, N. R. (2006). Definitions of globalization: A comprehensive overview and a proposed definition. *Program on the Geopolitical Implications of Globalization and Transnational Security.* Geneva Centre for Security Policy (GCSP). Retrieved February 25, 2009, from http://www.gcsp.ch/e/publications/Globalisation/Publications/Pillars/definitions-of-globalization.pdf.

Arnett, J. (2002). The psychology of globalization. *American Psychologist, 57*(10), 774–783.

Asante, K. M. (1987). *The Afrocentric idea.* Philadelphia, PA: Temple University Press.

ben-Jochannan, Y. (1997). *Africa: Mother of Western civilization.* Baltimore, MD: Black Classic Press.

Chong, T. (2006). Ethnic identities and cultural capital: An ethnography of Chinese opera in Singapore. *Global Studies in Culture and Power, 13*(2), 283–307.

Conradie, P. (2001). Using information and communication technologies for development at centres in rural communities: Lessons learned. In G. Nulens, N. Hafkin, L. Van Audenhove, & B. Cammaerts (Eds.), *The digital divide in developing countries: Towards an information society in Africa* (pp. 237–263). Brussels, Belgium: VUB Brussels University Press.

Dunn, H. S. (1988). Broadcasting flow in the Caribbean. *Intermedia, 16*(3), 39–41.

Ess, C., & Sudweeks, F. (Eds.). (2001). *Culture, technology, communication: Towards an intercultural global village.* Albany, NY: State University of New York Press.

Giddens, A. (2006). *Sociology.* Cambridge, UK: Polity Press.

Green, L. (2001). *Communication, technology, and society.* Thousand Oaks, CA: Sage.

Jahn, J., (1990). *Muntu: African culture and the Western world* (Marjorie Grene, Trans.). New York, NY: Grove Press.

Langmia, K. (2006). The role of ICTs in the economic development of Africa: The case of South Africa. *International Journal of Education and Development using Information and Communication Technology, 2*(4), 144–156.

Lister, M., Dovey, J., Giddings, S., Grant, I., & Kelly, K. (2003). *New media: A critical introduction.* New York, NY: Routledge.

Moodley, S. (2002). E-business in the South African apparel sector: A utopian vision of efficiency? *Developing Economies, 40*(1), 67–100.

Nyamnjoh, F. B. (2002). Globalization, boundaries, and livelihoods: Perspectives on Africa. *Identity, Culture, and Politics, 5*(1–2), 37–59.

Parameswaran, R. (2008). The other sides of globalization: Communication, culture, and postcolonial critique. *Communication, Culture, and Critique, 1*, 116–125.

Parayil, G. (2005). The digital divide and increasing returns: Contradictions of informational capitalism. *Information Society, 21*(1), 41–51.

Perrons, D. (2004). *Globalization and social change.* New York, NY: Routledge.

Pieterse, J. N. (2009). *Globalization and culture: Global mélange.* Lanham, MD: Rowman & Littlefield.

Rabaka, R. (2002). Malcolm X and/as critical theory: Philosophy, radical politics, and the African American search for justice. *Journal of Black Studies, 33*(2), 145–165.

Richmond, A. (2002). Globalization: Implications for immigrants and refugees. *Ethnic and Racial Studies, 25*(5), 707–727.

Rodney, W. (1972). *How Europe underdeveloped Africa.* Washington, DC: Howard University Press.

Schiller, D. (1999). *Digital capitalism: Networking the global market system.* Cambridge, MA: MIT.

Sholte, J. A. (2000). *Globalization: A critical introduction.* London, UK: Palgrave Macmillan.

Sorge, A. (2005). *The global and the local: Understanding the dialectics of business systems.* Oxford, UK: Oxford University Press.

Wa Thiong'o, N. (1986). *Decolonising the mind: The politics of language in African literature.* London, UK: Heinemann.

West, C. (2004). *Democracy matters: Winning the fight against imperialism.* New York, NY: Penguin Press.

Chapter 3

The Role of Appropriate ICT in Bridging the Digital Divide

Theoretical Considerations and Illustrating Cases

Victor van Reijswoud and Arjan de Jager

The importance of bridging the global digital divide is no longer discussed; the focus has shifted to the design and the implementation of programs that aim to close the information and knowledge gap between developing and developed nations. Unfortunately, the majority of these programs mimic what has been successfully implemented in the developed world, and it is becoming increasingly clear that these successes cannot necessarily be transferred wholesale to the context of developing nations. This chapter develops the hypothesis that information and communication technology (ICT) projects in developing countries will become more successful when they adapt to local conditions. The chapter also examines the concept of appropriate technology (AT), which has already been embraced by fields like architecture, building technology, and agriculture but has not yet taken root in the area of ICT.

INTRODUCTION

It sounds reasonable: When one prepares for a mountain hike, one wears good boots and a sweater against the cold at higher altitudes. When one goes to the tropics, one chooses a lightweight outfit and a hat or a cap to shield against the merciless sun. People have been taught the need to adapt to the local circumstances. In sectors such as architecture, civil engineering, and industrial design, the discipline of identifying suitable and appropriate technology (AT) is an important component. However, in the field of information and communication technology (ICT), which is a young discipline, this concept is still in its infancy.[1]

Computer hardware, software, and the methods and techniques for the design and the implementation of information technology are almost all invented or developed in the West (Europe and North America). Environmental requirements and conditions become an integral part of the design of these technologies, and this factor limits the transferability of the technology to other, different environments. Designers are often not aware of the contextual elements that become part of the design (Collins, 1992; Evans & Collins, 2007). Embedded assumptions become clear in cases of a breakdown of operations (Winograd & Flores, 1986) and will initiate problem-solving discussions or discourse (Habermas, 1985). In the field of ICT for development (ICT4D), a discussion about the limitations of commercial off-the-shelf ICT tools, software, and methodologies in the context of less developed countries has been initiated (Dymond & Oestmann, 2004; Gairola et al., 2004; Gurstein, 2003; Reijswoud & Topi, 2004).

The field of ICT4D has grown dramatically in size and importance over the past decade (Levey & Young 2002; McNamara, 2003). ICT4D is based on the premise that ICT is able to bridge the global digital divide between the West and less developed countries and is thus able to contribute to equal distribution of wealth. ICT is considered vital for the improvement of governance and production resources (Sciadas, 2003). The importance of ICT for poverty alleviation was recognized at the highest international levels when the United Nations Development Program (UNDP) dedicated its annual *Human Development Report* to the role of information and communication technologies (UNDP, 2001). At present, most large development organizations have substantial ICT programs, and a large number of smaller development initiatives have started projects in the field of ICT.

Many individuals who are not familiar with ICT4D wonder if ICT is relevant to the poor. They argue that poor people in the southern hemisphere not only have less access to ICT but also do not have access to sources of stable income, education, and health care—and at a first glance, these issues might seem more relevant than access to ICT. But ICT is increasingly important in the creation of economic opportunities and for the delivery of services such as health and education. When it comes to health care, for example, the critical issue is choosing between ICT or health services. Rather, it is a matter of choosing the most effective way to improve health-care delivery. ICT is just one of the tools that can realize improvement in overall services.

In spite of widespread efforts, the global digital divide has not been bridged, and well-documented success stories of the application of ICT for poverty alleviation are hard to find (Curtain, 2004; Osama, 2006). There are many reasons why ICT projects in less developed countries fail (Heeks, 2003), and these problems have been reported from the start (Moussa & Schware, 1992). Evaluations of ICT projects often reveal underutilization of resources because the newly introduced ICT has not been well integrated within the local context (Kozma, 2005). The worst cases result from "dump-and-run" approaches (van Reijswoud, de Jager, & Mulder, 2005; Vosloo, 2006) and lack of local ownership in the receiving communities (Vaughan, 2006). In addition, technical (hardware and software) problems resulting from the "hostile" conditions (e.g., dust, heat, and humidity) in which the ICT was introduced reduce the technology's impact (Gichoya, 2005).

High rates of breakdown combined with the low technical problem-solving skills of many users have led to underutilized and even abandoned projects. Moreover, recurring high maintenance costs for hardware, software, and Internet connectivity put a financial burden on projects, making them fiscally unsustainable. Finally, the change-management process (i.e., the approach by which the new technology is introduced and integrated into the new environment) does not take into account local conditions, values, and cultural requirements.

To address these issues, we have created a theory for the design and implementation of ICT projects in less developed countries. We developed this theory along the lines of existing theories of AT in other fields of science. As in other disciplines, the design and implementation of ICT solutions must be carried out in relation to culture, environment, organization, available resources, economic and political circumstances, and desired impact. We propose an integration of the AT discipline, which aims at devising suitable technological solutions. Our theory identifies principles to do so on three levels: hardware, software, and ICT change management. We first describe the theory; next, we illustrate the guiding principles of appropriate ICT through real-life cases of ICT4D in Africa. In the final section, we conclude with an agenda for further research.

Appropriate Technology

In order to better understand how to improve the design and implementation of ICT projects in less developed countries, one must first become familiar with the field of appropriate technology (AT). Because AT has not yet gained ground in the area of ICT, our exploration starts with other fields of application. As a general definition, we adopt the idea that AT is technology suitable for the environmental, cultural, and economic conditions in which it is intended to be used. At the other end of the spectrum is the one-size-fits-all concept, also known as the universal model, which builds on the premise that well-designed technology can be used under all circumstances.

Darrow and Saxenian (1986) provided ten criteria that provide a starting point. These criteria have been formulated to act as a basic set of guidelines for a broad spectrum of several technologies. Darrow and Saxenian did not explicitly consider ICT; however, their criteria can serve well as a reference for devising and evaluating ICT-supported programs in less developed countries. The following are criteria for an appropriate technology as proposed by Darrow and Saxenian (1986):

- It should be possible to implement and realize technological solutions with limited financial resources.
- The use of available resources must be emphasized to reduce the costs and to guarantee the supply of resources (e.g., for maintenance).
- Technologies may be relatively labor-intensive but must have a higher output than traditional technologies.
- The technology must be understandable to people without specific or academic training.
- Small rural communities should be able to produce and maintain the technology.
- The technology must result in economic or social progress.
- The technology must be fully understandable for the local population, and the end-use should offer locals opportunities to become involved in the possible innovation and extension of the use of the technology.
- The technological solutions must be flexible and easily adapted to changing circumstances.
- The technology must contribute to the increase of productivity.
- The technology should not have a negative effect on the environment.

The guiding idea behind these criteria is that technologies have a good chance of being effective if they are appropriate to the needs, expectations, and limitations of the surroundings in which they will be applied. In other words, the selected solution must be in harmony with local standards and values and build on existing skills and techniques. A new technology will not be embedded in a sustainable manner into an organization or community if dependence on the developers of the solution is high and if the available resources (financial and human) for maintenance are expensive and unavailable or difficult to obtain.

Finally, it is important that the benefit of a new technology is visible not only to the policy makers and the implementers but also to the potential end-users. The introduction of new technologies is often done through a push mechanism; with a larger agenda in mind, governments and national or international nongovernmental organizations (NGOs) tend to impose the use of new technologies on communities. The introduction of ICT is doomed to fail when its added value is not clearly understood by the potential end-users.

The criteria proposed by Darrow and Saxenian delineate an appropriate design of the technology, but they fail to highlight the implementation process. Even appropriate technology can be abandoned by the potential end-users if the implementation process does not align with the needs, expectations, and limitations of the community. Appropriate technology can also fail when the invoked changes are not guided in an appropriate manner.

Appropriate ICT

The large-scale use of ICT in less developed countries is new and a work in progress (McNamara, 2003). Until recently, the use of ICT in Africa had been limited to large international organizations and foreign NGOs. Foreign ICT experts had to be brought in for installation and maintenance (Bruggink, 2003) and for training beyond basic-level office applications (Heeks, 1998). Implementers had to fly to Europe or North America to receive training. Only one in 130 people in Africa owns a personal computer (Jensen, 2002), and most people have never seen a computer. Over the last several years, this situation has begun to change rapidly (Levey & Young, 2002). The digital gap appeared on the international agenda—and is often strongly linked to, among other things, the eight Millennium Development Goals (MDG)[2]—and with foreign support, the first programs and projects have been set up.

In order to bridge the global digital gap, information technology must be available to and affordable for the "ordinary person." The goal is to provide European and North American levels of access to computers and information to almost all users around the globe. Such access should not be restricted to individuals in the large cities or to the privileged class of a nation. Rather, information technology must also be made available to the populations in the rural areas and to people with lower levels of education in those nations. This goal creates formidable challenges for the developers and implementers of ICT solutions.

Availability in this context is multifaceted; it depends not only on the existence of infrastructure and access but also, to a large degree, on the existence of human capacity. These capacities can be divided into three main groups. The first group involves affordability: ICT can be appropriate only where ICT systems and infrastructure can be procured at a reasonable price in economic settings that are different from those in the West. The second group addresses usefulness: ICT becomes valuable to people only when useful local content is available. Therefore the capacity to create and maintain useful content for different sectors in appropriate language must be available. The third group covers end-user capacity: Users must develop the capacity needed to understand and use the applications and the infrastructure (i.e., the technology).

Appropriate ICT should be perceived from two perspectives: that of the product and that of the process. The product perspective is concerned with the design of the ICT systems that will be used to offer information and communication services. This perspective covers all aspects of the setup individuals use, and it includes computers (and other connected electronic equipment), servers, networks, and connections. For example, in our approach, a computer setup that is to operate in a community in the

African desert is not considered appropriate when it is not well protected against heat, sand, and dust. The product perspective is very much in line with the guidelines developed by Darrow and Saxenian (1986).

The process perspective is vital during the implementation stage and has, up to now, received less attention. However, we are convinced that a mere technology-centric approach, even when rooted in the principles of AT, will not deliver suitable ICT solutions that are embedded in the community and will not be exploited by the potential end-users. We refer to the emerging, interdisciplinary fields of social informatics (Kling, 1999) and community informatics (Gurstein, 2000; 2003) to address the process perspective of our appropriate-ICT approach. Social informatics concentrates on three areas of research:

- Theories and models: The development of models and theories that explain the social and organizational uses and impacts of ICT.
- Methodologies and approaches: The development of methodologies that address the social effects of the design, implementation, maintenance, and use of ICT.
- Philosophical and ethical issues: The study of philosophical and ethical issues that arise in the use of ICT in social and organizational contexts.

Community informatics constitutes a subset of social informatics with a focus on communities (McIver, 2003). Whereas social informatics has a stronger research focus, community informatics is more suitable for the development and implementation of ICT in less developed countries (e.g., Vaughan, 2006). The community itself is involved in the adaptation of ICT to its members' purposes through advocacy, local information on available community resources and services, and community mapping for community planning and development (e.g., demographics and geography; Gurstein, 2000).

The process perspective of appropriate ICT needs to encompass a community-oriented and participatory focus in order to address the needs, expectations, and limitations of the community in which the technology is to be used. So if computers are introduced in the African context, the process of introduction should address the expected changes in the working practice, the impact of ICT on knowledge levels, and the ways this might affect relations in the community. To summarize, we define appropriate ICT as the integrated and participatory approach that results in tools and processes for establishing ICT that is suitable for the cultural, environmental, organizational, economic, and political conditions in which it is intended to be used.

A Framework for Appropriate ICT

In this section, we propose a framework for AT that enables the design and implementation of ICT in less developed countries. The framework is based on the traditional *systems development life cycle* that is used in computer system development but also extends to the system tools and approaches that will guide the ICT solution to appropriateness.

The systems development life cycle (SDLC) comes in many types and variations (Brandon, 2006), but we adopt a basic five-phase model (Dennis & Wixom, 2000; Hoffer, George, & Valacich, 2006; Laudon & Laudon, 2005):

- *Definition*: Determination of the goals, scope, and requirements of the ICT solution.
- *Design*: Resolution of technical issues; selection of architecture and standards.
- *Construction*: Implementation of the design; testing and documentation of the system.
- *Installation*: Roll-out of the services offered by the systems to the end-users; training.
- *Operation/maintenance*: Problem solving, user support, and incremental improvement through monitoring and evaluation focusing on use of the services by end-users.

In the appropriate-ICT framework, the SDLC is supplemented with five specific focus areas that guide the ICT tools and approaches to appropriateness:

- *Culture*: Societies, or groups in a society, vary in their sets of shared attitudes, values, goals, and practices. Culture deserves careful attention when ICTs are introduced in the development context (Westrup, Liu, El Sayed, & Al Jaghoub, 2003). We consider culture a central variable.
- *Environment*: Physical conditions (e.g., heat, cold, dust, humidity) must be considered in order to establish an important ICT solution design.
- *Organization*: The structure of the organization (in the broadest sense of the word) determines the implementation strategy of systems in both the developed and the developing world.
- *Economy*: The current and future economic situation of a country, sector, or organization should serve as a determinant in the ICT investment decisions.
- *Political climate*: Some governments are more restrictive in their ICT guidelines than others. Openness is not always appreciated, and some governments have "partnerships" with hardware and software suppliers.

Figure 3.1 displays the foundation of the appropriate-ICT framework, the SDLC on the outer ring and the five criteria that should be considered to design and implement appropriate-ICT solutions on the inner ring. Culture is displayed in a central role.

Most of the methods to support the development of appropriate-ICT solutions are still under development or taken from traditional system-development approaches. An integrated approach needs to be developed further. Figure 3.2 includes some tools on the outer ring that have proved helpful in the development of appropriate ICT. More tools and methods can be included as long as they are able to address cultural, environmental, organizational, economic, and political aspects of the ICT project.

Figure 3.1. The core of the appropriate-ICT framework: SDLC combined with focus areas.

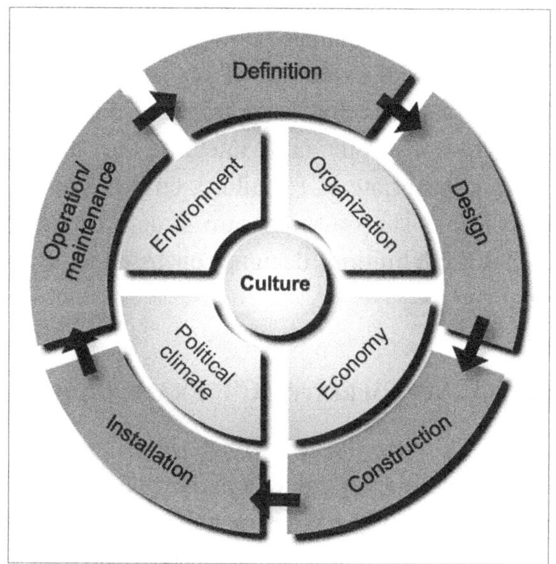

Figure 3.2. Some tools used in the appropriate-ICT framework.

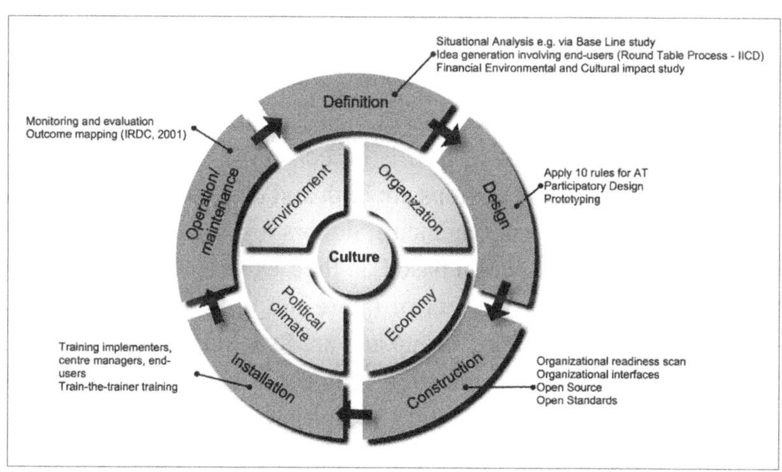

As mentioned earlier, appropriate ICT should be perceived from two angles, in terms of the product and in terms of the process. Therefore the appropriate-ICT framework needs to address three aspects—hardware, software, and change management—that affect both product and process. Table 3.1 provides examples of key questions that need to be answered in order to address the issues relevant in the appropriate-ICT framework. The questions in the table integrate the 10 rules for AT and the focus areas of appropriate ICT: culture, environment, organization, economy, and politics. The questions are structured according to the phases of the SDLC: definition, design, construction, installation, and operation/maintenance.

EXAMPLES OF THE APPROPRIATE-ICT FRAMEWORK

In this section, we illustrate the appropriate-ICT framework with some examples. We also describe the situation and explain how an appropriate-ICT perspective would change the design and implementation of the ICT solution. The examples are based on the authors' own experiences and respective activities in Africa.

Determining Appropriate-ICT Requirements

Determining requirements for ICT solutions has been a challenging issue in ICT4D projects. The most important reason is that most users and policy makers in less developed countries have never been exposed to the actual use of computers to support their work processes; their understanding of the capabilities of ICT is based on the media and on hearsay in other projects. Expectations are high and often unrealistic. Project managers from development agencies, donors, or ICT consultants often end up prescribing the solution based on their experiences in other projects. As a result, a larger number of the resulting ICT solutions do not address the needs of the target group and are thus not appropriate.

A lack of proper communication and coordination of instruments results in the initiation and execution of multiple, similar ICT4D projects in the same geographic area or the same thematic field. For example, in

TABLE 3.1. Key guiding questions for appropriate-ICT development.

Phase	Hardware	Software	Change Mgnt
Definition	Specific requirements in terms of climatological and environmental conditions? What are the enabling factors (Internet connectivity, electricity)?	What are the needs? What are the expectations?	What are the ICT knowledge levels? What are the financial constraints? What is the cultural context? What added value is created? How is the economic equilibrium affected? What new ways of working are introduced? What will be the impact in terms of organizational change? What is the involvement in the idea generation of key decision makers (political and religious leaders)?
Design	What is offered on the local market? What are the physical constraints? What are the financial constraints?	What interoperability is needed? What localization is needed? What flexibility is expected?	What are the information needs of the various target groups? How will these needs and expectations evolve?
Construction	What local skills are available? Is the equipment protected against physical conditions?	What local skills are available? Are features in line with skills? Are free and open-source alternatives considered? Is the system well documented?	Are local skills and knowledge being developed? Are stakeholders actively involved? What new ways of working are introduced? What will be the impact in terms of organizational change?
Installation	Is the equipment protected against physical conditions?	Has the system been tested with all stakeholders?	Are all stakeholders involved in the training program? Is the added value made clear?
Operation / maintenance	Is local capacity sufficient? Are spare parts easily available?	Are software maintenance skills available?	Is a support organization in place? Is the support organization able to support all stakeholders (e.g., address gender issues)?

Kampala, Uganda, several organizations are supporting the setup of telecenters or information centers to improve access to information and communication in poor neighborhoods. At the same time, many of these initiatives fail to deliver services that are appreciated by the target group. Moreover, most of these centers suffer from operational problems because of limited technical maintenance skills. An appropriate-ICT framework can identify and address these problems.

ICT for Health in Tanzania: Determining Appropriate-ICT Requirements in the Definition Phase

In recognition of the facts that ICT can offer important advantages to the health sector in less developed countries and that large numbers of projects have been initiated over the past decade, a new ICT for health program in Tanzania initiated by the International Institute for Communication and Development (IICD) encountered challenges. The chances of unwanted duplication of initiatives were high, and the need gaps for the sector were unclear; at the same time, the local ICT skills were minimal, especially in the suburban and rural areas. In order to address these problems, it was decided to start the program with a health-sector-wide initiation phase.

In order to determine the needs and expectations of the sector and to avoid duplication of projects, a participatory idea-generation process was initiated.[3] This process goes beyond that traditionally used in consultation processes and is more suitable for generating the requirements in the context of an appropriate-ICT framework. It uses the scenario-development method to allow participants to identify priority areas for the development of their sector or their organization. This approach avoids a technology focus. To bring all participants to the same starting level, a baseline study (a situational analysis) is produced on the status of the sector prior to the workshop. Thus this process is a useful method of allowing participants to answer questions at the initiation phase. The workshop is only one part of the overall process, and a follow-up meeting is later conducted in order to allow participants to develop and implement their own ICT projects.

During the workshop in Tanzania, the stakeholders were not only asked to express their needs and expectations for the program but were also assisted in the generation of preliminary project and policy proposals that were shared with all the stakeholders involved. Through a process of feedback and support, the stakeholders were able to generate ideas (e.g., using ICTs to create more opportunities for in-service training, access to information on outbreaks of diseases) that were new, in line with the needs of the sector, and feasible in the context of the available skills.

Through the participatory idea-generation approach, the stakeholders have been able to generate a coherent ICT program for the health sector of Tanzania. The program now includes the following interrelated project areas:

- ICT policy for the health sector, supported by all stakeholders in the sector to create an environment conducive to information exchange.
- Capacity development for health workers through a continuing medical education program.
- Development of management capacity in both the public and private health sector.
- Development of ICT tools based on free and open-source software[4] and open standards to maximize cost-effectiveness, to enable the development of national standards, and to avoid duplicating earlier efforts.
- Information portal and low-cost Internet connectivity services to enable health units up-country, especially to access the latest information on outbreaks, available treatments, and so forth.

In fact, the projects are classified according to their target groups, and the ICT strategy is obviously targeting the level of technical expertise and the donor community. The other projects are focused on capacity development. The health management information system (HMIS) and continuing medical education projects aim to improve the access to and management of information and knowledge for better health-care delivery by staff, and grassroots projects such as Health Child Uganda (see www.iicd.org/projects/uganda-health-child/) focus on improving access to information for people in the community.

This participatory idea-generation approach naturally structured the definition phase of SDLC, which takes into account the needs and expectations of the stakeholders. Political, cultural, and organizational issues were addressed in the process through elaborate peer and reality checking of the preliminary project proposals that were generated. Economic issues were covered less in the initiation phase, but financial feasibility studies were conducted before the design phase of the projects. Environmental issues were insufficiently covered in this initiation phase but were addressed in the construction phase.

DESIGNING APPROPRIATE ICT

Designing hardware, software, and network configurations that fit the development context has been a major challenge over the past years. Unfortunately, in most cases, the solutions are grounded in the European or American contexts and are not necessarily suitable for the development environment of emerging economies. For example, hardware is not protected against the dust, sand, and heat of African countries; likewise, some software needs an Internet connection to be activated or does not support local languages. In addition, theories and tools for system development, such as the unified modeling language (UML), have proved difficult to use in an African context.

UML is a software specification tool, essentially a graphical tool to support a specification of software. The symbols used are understandable for the target groups and in this way support the refinement of the requirements. Amongst Western developers, there seems to be a strong preference for using UML as a communication tool rather than as a basis for partial or full code generation. Many developers in the global south complain that the graphical notations used by UML do not solve communication problems at all. In various projects (by the IICD, the University of Dar-es-Salaam in Tanzania, and by Makarere University in Uganda), we experienced resistance while talking prospective users through the use cases of a simple information system. This problem arose in large part because the graphical notations in the use cases were not associated with anything serious.

A carefully conducted project definition phase results in an outline of the needs, expectations, and possibilities for the ICT solution. In the design phase, creativity is needed to determine the specifications of the new ICT tool. The specifications need to address the context, not the other way around. Implementing a complex program like Microsoft Word is unnecessary when the characteristics of a simple word processor like AbiWord meet a community's needs. Likewise, Wi-Fi equipment that is suitable for the European context, in which large numbers of people operate in a large area, is not a suitable choice for Timbuktu, where a very limited number of people are using the connection across a large geographical area (Wireless Internet Institute, 2003).

Designing a Campus-Wide ICT Infrastructure in Rural Uganda[5]

Uganda Martyrs University is located 80 km from Kampala, the capital of Uganda. The university operates on a relatively small budget but has developed itself as the leading private university in the country. In spite of financial limitations, the university's administration decided that access to information technology and to the Internet was essential for the students and the staff. Against this background, the university requested an ICT infrastructure that is low cost (both in terms of initial and recurrent costs) and easy to maintain but that allows staff and students to access academic information and that equips students with good ICT skills.

With these requirements in mind, the university's ICT department, in collaboration with external expertise, developed a plan for an ICT infrastructure based on the following items:

- Open-source software and open standards to keep software costs low and avoid future licensing costs.
- Reuse of and upgrade of existing infrastructure through the implementation of a Linux terminal server project (Martindale, 2002).
- Elaborate capacity development to train knowledgeable ICT support staff and well-informed students and lecturing staff.

- Bandwidth management to provide maximum access to research information while limiting access to nonacademic material and functions (e.g., pornography, music and film downloads, sports matches, chat rooms).

The ICT infrastructure was successfully implemented over the period 2003–2005, and this implementation serves as a point of reference for other East African universities that operate under similar conditions. The infrastructure has proved to be low cost, and through the capacity-development program, it is sustainable. In addition, the managed Internet connection provides important information for staff and students.

The project is a good example of the design phase of appropriate ICT because it has taken into account the specific local conditions of the university and the context in which ICT was to be implemented. The economic requirements and the organizational aspects were also addressed. Moreover, the academic culture that was considered important for the project was covered in the design of the network.

IMPLEMENTING APPROPRIATE ICT

Introducing ICT in a rural setting has challenges from both a production perspective (e.g., ensuring the robustness of hardware and software) and a process perspective. For example, introducing a system up-country without the consultation and the participation of local and religious leaders is doomed to failure. Whereas citizens of urban centers are more or less accustomed to modern ICTs, the rural population of sub-Saharan Africa (SSA) is not. Rather, this population requires the framework of a step-by-step approach when ICT solutions are introduced in a rural setting.

Constructing and Implementing a Health Management Information System in Uganda

The Uganda Catholic Medical Bureau (UCMB) is the health office of the Roman Catholic Church in Uganda, and it is amongst others in supporting

27 rural hospitals. In 2004 the UCMB established a system aimed at improving the use of the national Health Management Information System (HMIS). The introduction of the HMIS is an example of an initiative in which ICTs are being used to improve management. Improved management is a necessity in a situation in which health-sector funding in the global south is decreasing and, at the same time, health-care delivery funding is changing from lump-sum financing (in which hospitals simply receive a fixed sum from central government) to a cost-based system (hospitals receive funding from government based on data such as number of patients, number of treatments, etc.). Therefore, more effective and efficient management procedures were the only way to keep health services at an acceptable level.

The project addressed five prominent problems. First, unreliable information collection created problems. Using the lengthy, labor-intensive HMIS forms was an unreliable, incomplete, and inaccurate system. The hard-copy forms had to be filled in manually, obligating hospital managers to spend hours correcting mistakes. Then the data from the 27 hospitals had to be typed at the UCMB in order to create a digital record. Second, slow feedback from the UCMB concerning the inaccurate information in hard-copy form provided by the hospitals caused delays. Backlogs of three to six months were not uncommon. Third, insufficient human capacity (technical as well as managerial) caused problems for the implementation and use of a proper HMIS. Fourth, an HMIS system at the hospital level, in fact, supports decentralization. Therefore it is essential that project organizers include users in the planning and the implementation of the system—particularly when deciding who is responsible and deciding whom to train. It is also vital to show these users the results of their involvement (e.g., through creative feedback loops for data typists). Finally, change management is essential to success. Changes will always threaten individuals' status; therefore medical staff must, crucially, receive recognition for their important role in the organization and realize that their importance will not change.

The proposed technical solution was simple and straightforward. The problem of unreliable information collection was addressed first, and hard-copy forms were replaced by standardized spreadsheets (which were sent to the UCMB by post). The organizational impact of this step was still small, but the introduction of ICTs in an organization often starts by supporting manual processes with ICT applications. After this step, communication links between the up-country hospitals and the UCMB were set up to address the problem of slow feedback from the UCMB. The issue of insufficient human capacity was, in turn, addressed throughout the lifespan of the project by a massive training program targeted at administrators and managers.

The percentage of hospitals submitting complete and accurate HMIS forms eventually rose from 48% to 96% during project implementation. Moreover, the UCMB can now work much more efficiently because it is no longer responsible for digital recording; the organization has more time for analysis and feedback to hospital managers, thus enabling informed decision making. The feedback mechanism enables hospital managers to finalize their planning and budgeting processes in a timely manner. The effect of these steps from an organizational perspective was much bigger than what had been expected. For example, because of the timely, high-quality feedback from the UCMB, managers can now base their decisions on an activity-based cost analysis.

At the start of the project, the rural hospitals had virtually no experience with ICT, and the offerings of the different ICT suppliers were meager. The implementers constructed the project acknowledging the huge changes that would it would produce and chose a careful, systematic approach. The data collection and transformation went through the following phases over a period of three years:

- Data quality: Shift from using hard-copy forms to using standardized Excel spreadsheets that could be filled in using a computer.
- Data timeliness: Shift from sending these Excel forms via the postal service to sending them as e-mail attachments.
- Managerial-level data use: Implementation of a system that made it possible to link and analyze the HMIS output with a cost-based

financial system, allowing hospital managers to implement an activity-based cost model in their hospitals.
- Macro-level data use: Change from sending Excel forms as e-mail attachments to filling in online forms to allow UCMB and the 27 hospitals to generate quality information on trends, statistics, and so forth.

This project is a good example of the construction and the installation phases of appropriate ICT because it took into account the enormous changes in the organizational structures and applied a step-by-step approach over a three-year period. The economic requirements were addressed (i.e., the hospitals took over the recurrent costs after a period of two years), as were the political aspects (i.e., religious leaders and the Ministry of Health were involved in the process).

Conclusion

The need to bridge the global digital divide is evident. No organization or individual will deny this fact, and donor support has been significant during the past decade. At the same time, although progress is being made, it is being made too slowly, and in many cases that progress has a very fragile basis (United Nations Conference on Trade and Development [UNCTAD], 2007). Other media like radio, television, and printed sources also play a role in bridging the information gap, but ICT and the Internet offer the largest source of free information and allow easy distribution of local information. Offering widespread access to shared information on a global level can have far-reaching emancipatory effects in developing countries.

The biggest challenge now is to develop ICT infrastructure, knowledge, and skills that provide opportunities for sustainable development; this goal requires a change in perspective. The ICT4D community should shift away from traditional off-the-shelf solutions to an approach that develops and uses appropriate ICT that suits the context in which it is to be implemented. ICT hardware, software, and change management need to align with the local cultural, environmental, organizational, economic, and political contexts in order to realize sustainable development.

The appropriate-ICT framework, as presented in this chapter, provides a guiding model for designing suitable ICT for less developed countries. The model is based on existing theories in appropriate technology, on social and community informatics, and on the system development life cycle. As illustrated by the examples in this chapter, an appropriate-ICT framework can increase a project's effectiveness and sustainability by shifting the project's focus to solutions that are designed, developed, and implemented according to the context in which technologies are used.

More expertise is needed in the design and implementation of ICT projects in developing countries. The complexity of ICT is often underestimated, and ICT4D projects are often designed and implemented by general project managers who have limited understandings of ICT's possibilities. These individuals often resort to the implementation of standard solutions that have proved effective in the developed world. As a result, ICT project recipients in the developing world are often left with hardware that is not designed for harsh environmental conditions, without sufficient skills to maintain the software, or facing users who do not see the value of the ICT. In such cases, the initial success and euphoria dissipates as soon as the donor retreats. Donor agencies need to recognize that ICT projects require qualified expertise and cannot be left to general project managers. Ultimately, failing to implement sustainable ICT solutions will slow efforts to bridge the digital divide.

With respect to the private sector, suppliers of software and hardware should be questioned critically about how their products fit different local contexts. The private sector, moreover, should acknowledge the business potential of developing specific hardware and software for the ICT market in less developed countries. The success of companies like Cell Tell shows that a viable ICT market emerges once the products align with local needs and local circumstances. In addition, governments need to continue their efforts to increase the penetration of ICT skills and infrastructure among their citizens and should concentrate more on rural areas. Development partners, in turn, should support more research.

We recommend more research on this topic. So far, the academic world has shown very little interest in the development of theories and models that suit the developing world. Too often, academics seem to believe that they are developing universal theories and models. Experience with the applications of these theories and models in the developing world, however, shows that they are often far from universal and generally do not guarantee success. In other words, we challenge the academic world to create a system-development theory that covers both production and process dimensions. We also hope that the academic world will further develop the model of the appropriate-ICT framework as presented here.

The appropriate-ICT framework in this chapter forms the foundation for a larger project that aims to provide a flexible approach to the design and implementation of ICT in developing countries. This project will provide a more detailed inventory of tools, develop methodologies, and review case studies more thoroughly. The appropriate-ICT framework discussed here will need to be tested as a prescriptive methodology; initial tests of the framework have started in a project that focuses on the design and implementation of a nationwide academic registration information system in Mozambique (Pscheidt, van Reijswoud, & Van Der Weide, 2009).

ENDNOTES

1. A good attempt to adapt hardware design to the requirements of the environment is the XO-computer (One Laptop Per Child project; http://laptop.org). See also Kraemer, Dedrick, & Sharma (2009) on the challenges of the project.
2. For more details on the role of ICT in realizing the MDG, see the World Bank Group's *ICT and MDGs: A World Bank Group Perspective*, http://www-wds.worldbank.org/servlet/WDSContentServer/WDSP/IB/2004/09/15/000090341_20040915091312/Rendered/PDF/278770ICT010mdgs0Complete.pdf.
3. The process was facilitated by the International Institute for Communication and Development (IICD). The organization uses the term *round table* to label a participatory idea-generation process. For more details on ideas behind this process, see IICD (2004).
4. See Dravis (2003) and van Reijswoud & Topi (2004) on the advantages of the use of free and open-source software in the developing world.
5. For an in-depth discussion of this case study, see van Reijswoud and Mulo (2007). Evaluating the potential of free and open source software in the developing world. In K. St. Amant & B. Still (Eds.), *Handbook of Research on Open Source Software: Technological, Economic and Social Perspectives* (pp. 79–92), Hershey, PA: IDEA Group.

References

Brandon, D. (2006). *Project management for modern information systems.* Hershey, PA: IRM Press/IDEA Group.

Bruggink, M. (2003). *Open source in Africa: A global reality: Take it or leave it?* International Institute for Communication and Development [IICD]. IICD Research Brief, no. UICT01. Retrieved August 10, 2010, from http://www.iicd.org/articles/IICDnews.import2172.

Collins, H. M. (1992). *Artificial experts: Social knowledge and intelligent machines.* Cambridge, MA: MIT Press.

Curtain, R. (2004). *Information and communication technologies and development: Help or hindrance?* Australian Agency for International Development [AusAID]. Retrieved August 11, 2010, from http://www.developmentgateway.com.au/jahia/webdav/site/adg/shared/CurtainICT4DJan04.pdf.

Darrow, K., & Saxenian, M. (1986). *Appropriate technology sourcebook: A guide to practical books for village and small community technology.* Appropriate Technology Project/Volunteers in Asia. Retrieved August 10, 2010, from http://www.villageearth.org/pages/Appropriate_Technology/ATSourcebook/index.php.

Dennis, A., & Wixom, B. (2000). *Systems analysis and design: An applied approach.* Hoboken, NY: Wiley.

Dravis, P. J. (2003). *Open source software: Perspectives for development.* Washington, DC: World Bank. Retrieved August 10, 2010, from http://www.infodev.org/en/Document.21.pdf.

Dymond, A., & Oestmann, S. (2004). *Rural ICT toolkit for Africa.* Washington, DC: World Bank. Retrieved August 10, 2020, from http://www.infodev.org/en/Publication.23.html.

Evans, R., & Collins, H. M. (2007). Expertise: From attribute to attribution and back again? In E. J. Hackett, O. Amsterdamska, M. Lynch, &

J. Wajcman (Eds.), *The handbook of science and technology studies* (3rd ed.). Cambridge, MA: MIT Press.

Gairola, B. K., Chandra, M., Mall, P., Chacko, J. G., Sayo, P., & Loh, H. (2004). *Information and communications technology for development: A sourcebook for parliamentarians.* New Delhi, India: Elsevier.

Gichoya, D. (2005). Factors affecting the successful implementation of ICT projects in government. *Electronic Journal of e-Government, 3*(4), 175–184.

Gurstein, M. (2000). *Community informatics: Enabling communities with information and communications technologies.* Hershey, PA: IDEA Group.

Gurstein, M. (2003). Effective use: A community informatics strategy beyond the digital divide. *First Monday, 8*(12). Retrieved August 10, 2010, from http://firstmonday.org/htbin/cgiwrap/bin/ojs/index.php/fm/article/wivew/1107/1027.

Habermas, J. (1985). *The theory of communicative action, volume 1: Reason and rationalization of society*. Boston, MA: Beacon Press.

Heeks, R. (1998). *Getting the most from IT training courses for Africa.* Manchester, UK: Institute for Development Policy and Management, University of Manchester.

Heeks, R. (2003). *Most eGoverment-for-development projects fail: How can risks be reduced?* Manchester, UK: Institute for Development Policy and Management, University of Manchester.

Hoffer, J. A., George, J. F., & Valacich, J. S. (2006). *Modern systems analysis and design.* Upper Saddle River, NJ: Prentice Hall.

International Institute for Communication and Development [IICD]. (2004). *The ICT round table process: Lessons learned from facilitating ICT-enabled development.* The Hague, The Netherlands: IICD.

Jensen, M. (2002). *The African Internet: A status report, July 2002.* Retrieved August 10, 2010, from http://demiurge.wn.apc.org/africa/afstat.htm.

Kling, R. (1999). What is social informatics and why does it matter? *D-Lib Magazine, 5*(1). Retrieved August 10, 2010, from http://www.dlib.org/dlib/january99/kling/01kling.html.

Kozma, R. B. (2005). Monitoring and evaluation of ICT for education impact: A review. In D. A. Wagner, B. Day, T. James, R. B. Kozma, J. Miller, & T. Unwin (Eds.), *Monitoring and evaluation of ICT in education projects: A handbook for developing countries.* Washington, DC: World Bank. Retrieved August 10, 2010, from http://www.infodev.org/en/Publication.9.html.

Kraemer, K. L., Dedrick, J., & Sharma, P. (2009). One laptop per child: Vision vs. reality. *Communications of the ACM, 52*(6), 66–73.

Laudon, K. C., & Laudon, J. P. (2005). *Essentials of management information systems.* Upper Saddle River, NJ: Prentice Hall.

Levey, L., & Young, S. (Eds.). (2002). *Rowing upstream: Snapshots of the pioneers of the information age in Africa.* Johannesburg, South Africa: Sharp Media. Retrieved August 10, 2010, from http://www.piac.org/rowing_upstream.

Martindale, L. (2002, November 1). Bridging the digital divide in South Africa. *Linux Journal.* Retrieved August 10, 2010, from http://linux-journal.com/article/5966.

McIver, W. Jr. (2003). A community informatics for the information society. *United Nations Research Institute for Social Development briefing paper.* Retrieved August 10, 2010, from http://programs.ssrc.org/itic/publications/civsocandgov/mciver.pdf.

McNamara, K. (2003). *Information and communication technologies, poverty, and development: Learning from experience.* Washington, DC: World Bank. Retrieved August 10, 2010, from http://www.infodev.org/files/1041_file_Learning_From_Experience.PDF.

Moussa, A., & Schware, R. (1992). Informatics in Africa: Lessons from World Bank experience. *World Development, 20*(12), 1737–1752.

Osama, A. (2006, November 9). ITC for development: Hope or hype? *Science and Development Network*. Retrieved August 10, 2010, from http://www.scidev.net/Opinions/index.cfm?fuseaction=readOpinions &itemid=537&language=1.

Pscheidt, M., van Reijswoud, V., & Van Der Weide, T. (2009). Assessing appropriate ICT with the ARIS case in Mozambique. In *Proceedings of the 5th Annual International Conference on Computing and ICT Research SREC09*. Kampala, Uganda: Fountain Publishers.

Sciadas, G. (Ed.). (2003). *Monitoring the digital divide and beyond*. Montreal, Canada: NRC Press.

United Nations Conference on Trade and Development. (2007). *The least developed countries report 2007: Knowledge, technical learning, and innovation for development*. New York, NY: United Nations. Retrieved August 10, 2010, from http://www.unctad.org/Templates /webflyer.asp?docid=8674&intItemID=4314&lang=1&mode= downloads.

United Nations Development Program. (2001). *Human development report 2001: Making new technologies work for human development*. New York, NY: United Nations. Retrieved August 10, 2010, from http://hdr.undp.org/en/reports/global/hdr2001/.

van Reijswoud, V. E., de Jager, A., & Mulder, J. B. (2005). 8 lessen voor ICT in de derde wereld: Raamwerk voor ICT projecten [Lessons for ICT in the third world: Framework for ICT projects]. *Informatie, 47*(4), 18–22.

van Reijswoud, V. E., & Mulo, E. (2007). Evaluating the potential of free and open source software in the developing world. In K. St. Amant & B. Still (Eds.), *Handbook of research on open source software: Technological, economic and social perspectives* (pp. 79–92). Hershey, PA: IDEA Group.

van Reijswoud, V. E., & Topi, C. (2004). Alternative routes in the digital world: Open source software in Africa. In P. Kanyandago &

L. Mugumya (Eds.), *Mtafiti Mwafrika* [African researcher] (pp. 76–94). Nkozi, Uganda: African Research Documentation Centre.

Vaughn, D. (2006). Linking policy to community outcomes. *Partners in Micro-Development*. Retrieved August 10, 2010, from http://www.microdevpartners.org/documents/ICT4DLinkingPolicytoCommunityOutcomesPDF.pdf.

Vosloo, S. (2006, December 20). A quick guide to implementing ICT for development projects. *Digital Divide Commons*. Retrieved August 10, 2010, from http://www.digitaldivide.net/articles/view.php?ArticleID=742.

Westrup, C., Liu, W., El Sayed, H., & Al Jaghoub, S. (2003). Taking culture seriously: ICTs, cultures and development. In S. Madon & S. Krishna (Eds.), *The digital challenge: Information technology in the development context* (pp.13–28). Hampshire, UK: Ashgate.

Winograd, T., & Flores, F. (1986). *Understanding computers and cognition: A new foundation for design*. Norwood, NJ: Ablex.

Wireless Internet Institute. (2003). *The wireless Internet opportunity for developing countries*. United Nations ICT Task Force/Wireless Internet Institute (W2i). Retrieved August 10, 2010, from http://www.infodev.org/files/1061_file_The_Wireless_Internet_Opportunity.pdf.

Chapter 4

Wireless Networking Bridges the Digital Divide in Africa

Anas Tawileh

The emerging global information society is enabling more people than ever to work, learn, and interact together regardless of their geographical locations and cultural backgrounds. Unfortunately, during recent periods of technological explosion, significant parts of the world—particularly the developing regions of Africa, Asia, and Latin America—could not afford to build the telecommunications infrastructure needed to allow people there to participate in the evolving knowledge revolution. This chapter uses two case studies to explore the potential of low-cost wireless networks to bridge this global digital divide. The first case study focuses on the implementation of wireless networks at a community center in Tanzania. The second case study examines a project involving the use of low-cost wireless networks and free and open source software (F/OSS) to support teaching and learning at several schools in South Africa.

INTRODUCTION

The emerging global information society is empowering people all over the world to actively apply knowledge in order to solve complex problems and challenges. The unprecedented global growth of the Internet is making massive repositories of information available to anyone, anytime, anywhere. Though these developments have certainly had a positive effect on societies, the availability of appropriate communications infrastructures is a prerequisite for their exploitation. Unfortunately, not all parts of the world are well prepared to make use of this information revolution; rather, billions of people live in areas that lack any means of connectivity. The term *digital divide* (Harmon, 1996) was coined to refer to the expanding difference between those who enjoy reliable access to the information sources available on the Internet and those who do not.

It is widely believed that the digital divide negatively affects disadvantaged communities and reduces their ability to tackle their development challenges (Heeks, 1999; Molina, 2003). Several initiatives address the consequences of the growing global digital divide. For example, following a call from its secretary general Kofi Annan for "a bridge that spans the digital divide" (Annan, 2001, para. 5), the United Nations established the United Nations Information Technology Service (UNITS), the World Summit on the Information Society (WSIS), and the Internet Governance Forum. The primary challenge these initiatives face involves the high costs of building and maintaining the network infrastructure required to provide Internet access for disadvantaged communities.

Building reliable, large-scale communications infrastructure requires significant investment because of the high costs of hardware, software, and training. This situation puts technology infrastructure investments in direct competition with other high-priority projects, such as providing housing, water, and electricity. Governments and organizations are usually forced to postpone the development of their technology infrastructure in favor of such other critical projects. This delay creates a negative feedback cycle—that is, low investments in technology infrastructure lead to reduced capacity to tackle complex development problems, which leads to lowered economic competitiveness of the country. Such situations, in turn, intensify the competition for even fewer resources within that nation.

Breaking out of this cycle requires alternative technological solutions that reduce the costs associated with communications infrastructure projects. Such solutions should provide lower cost hardware and communications infrastructure. They should also ease the burden of software licensing costs for developing regions and countries and offer cost-effective training and capacity-building options.

The emerging free and open-source software movement has proved itself as a viable alternative to proprietary software in almost every application. Based on the values of sharing and equality, software released under a free or open-source license grants users the right to modify, change, and redistribute it for any purpose without paying hefty licensing charges. The One Laptop per Child project, for example, uses this open-source feature to offer low-cost laptops to children in developing countries ("One Laptop per Child," n.d.). Although the project did not meet its expected potential, it proved the case that free and open-source software could reduce the costs of software licenses in portable computers. Many netbooks (small laptop computers designed specifically for general-purpose computing and rich Web applications) available on the market today use free and open-source operating systems and software applications ("Small is Beautiful," 2008).

In contrast, technological innovation in hardware development has produced extremely capable devices for progressively lower costs. Wireless networking is a remarkable example of this kind of achievement. Within the past few years, networking hardware has evolved to provide affordable wireless connectivity between sites kilometers away from each other (Pentland, Fletcher, & Hasson, 2004; Subramanian et al., 2006). Moreover, open standards and commodity hardware attracted developer communities to tinker with the available hardware and stretch the capabilities of that hardware.

In this chapter, I explore the potential of emerging alternative technologies, paying particular attention to the role wireless networking and free and open-source software can play in bridging the digital divide. To investigate such developments, I consider two projects in Africa. The first case study shows how a remote community center in rural Tanzania has successfully exploited wireless technologies to provide information services to a community of more than 400,000 people. The second case study examines a project to build a network of schools in South Africa and offer e-learning services based on wireless networking and free and open-source software. The chapter concludes with an analysis of these cases and a discussion of directions for future research in this area.

CASE STUDY 1: FADECO TELECENTER AND FM RADIO STATION

Family Alliance for Development and Cooperation (FADECO) is a small center that provides computer training, Internet services, and radio broadcasting to local communities in Karagwe, Tanzania, one of the most remotes sites in the country. The center is investing tremendous efforts in several initiatives designed to bridge the digital divide for 428,000 people in this rural part of the African continent. These undertakings include an educational program, a resource telecommunications center, and HIV/AIDS awareness activities. In its pursuit of leveraging the limited resources available and maximizing the initiatives' impact on people's lives, FADECO focuses on the consolidation of its information resources and on implementing the most effective methods of content dissemination.

The People and the Need

In this context, Internet connectivity is crucial for the center; without it, the center cannot deliver its services to the local community. The center taps into resources available on the Web in order to collect information that would benefit the local community. The center then makes this information available in alternative formats in order to reach the largest possible audience. The center also provides community members with access to electronic services that can facilitate communications beyond the perimeter of their rural community.

In several cases, such communications have enabled community members to obtain employment in other parts of the country, helped farmers find appropriate cures for animal and crop diseases, and supported the community in commanding fair prices for its produce. In addition, the Internet simplifies the distribution of locally produced content to other Swahili-speaking parts of the continent (Swahili is the official language in Karagwe). The cost of Internet connectivity is a substantial burden on the center; expenses include ongoing monthly subscriptions, electricity charges, and staffing, in addition to the fixed cost of the expensive equipment required. In order to meet the high costs of Internet connectivity, FADECO had to develop innovative solutions that could be implemented under the strict resource limitations the center faces.

The Technology and the Environment

FADECO has a very small aperture terminal (VSAT) Internet connection supplied by a service provider called SATCOM. Based in the Southeast Asian country of Brunei Darussalam, SATCOM provides FADECO with equipment and manages the center's connections and bandwidth. The VSAT, in turn, provides 128 kbps of bandwidth downstream and 64 kbps upstream through a Ku-band connection. The related link costs are USD $195 per month (an example of the radical difference in the price of Internet connectivity between the global north and the global south). Based on these factors, FADECO decided that the most viable option for sustaining its Internet connectivity would be cost sharing with other institutions. According to this scenario, FADECO could split the burden of the Internet connection costs by giving others the right to use the connection in exchange for paying a share of the cost.

The significant challenge faced by FADECO in sharing its Internet connection was the sparse geographical distribution of potential clients in Karagwe. The locations of clients' sites were many kilometers away from FADECO's building. Moreover, installing appropriate cabling links was virtually impossible because of the nature of the terrain and the prohibitively expensive cost of fiber-optic cables.

Wireless networking was considered and selected as a viable solution to address these issues. Using commoditized hardware and locally assembled antennas and masts, FADECO was able to install two dedicated connections to remote sites. The first connection (spread over 12 kilometers) linked FADECO to a school building. The school uses this link to connect more than 15 computers in its local area network to the Internet. The second wireless connection is used by an organization to connect 10 computers to the Internet (the organization's building is 10 kilometers away from FADECO). These two connections are implemented using a point-to-point topology between FADECO's building and each of its clients' sites. Wireless Internet connectivity was also extended to the local area through a hot-spot designed to provide Internet access to local community members who have wireless-equipped machines.

All the design and installation work for this network was performed by a single person—FADECO director Joseph Sekiku. This do-it-yourself approach has led to significant cost savings and, more important, has enabled the center to develop the required knowledge and expertise to maintain the network and handle potential future growth.

In another attempt to address the needs of its local community, FADECO installed a community radio station to extend its information services to communities that suffer from high levels of illiteracy. The new radio station was built entirely with low-cost materials that were sourced locally and assembled by Sekiku and his colleagues. Innovation is apparent in several components of the resulting system. For example, plastic pipes are used as antenna masts in order to prevent lightning strikes to the equipment. In addition, the equipment was designed to be portable and lightweight, so it can be easily used in the field to broadcast live events. The radio station went live on July 22, 2007, and it currently provides local content related to education and sustainable development—information that can contribute to the local government's efforts to fight and eradicate poverty.

The network hardware at FADECO includes a Pentium III personal computer (PC) running Linux as the primary operating system. This PC, which was purchased secondhand for a bargain price, acts as the main server. Because of the extremely high temperatures in the area and the lack of sufficient cooling equipment, the PC is operated with its case cover open, facilitating air circulation. The server has two network adapters to enable the network address translation (NAT) that facilitates the VSAT Internet connection sharing. The system is smartly designed to alleviate the restrictions imposed by the Internet service provider—restrictions that prevent the connection from being shared by more than three PCs. These components cost very little to acquire, assemble, and operate, and they are being successfully exploited to provide the appropriate infrastructure required to satisfy the needs of FADECO and its local community.

The Outcome

This case study provides an exemplary illustration of the potential that emerging technologies, such as wireless networking and free and open-source software, offer for bridging the global digital divide. Tackling the challenges of a global information society no longer requires significant investments. Instead, innovative solutions can be designed and built using low-cost materials and information that is freely available on the Web.

FADECO was highly successful in exploiting these trends in technology development. Its low-cost, locally designed and built network now serves the information needs of some 428,000 people and does so in ways that would never have been possible through other methods. The populations served include students, farmers, business people, livestock keepers, and homemakers. Moreover, the center is playing a crucial role in preserving local culture through participatory content production and much wider outreach potential.

To a large degree, the ability to successfully design and implement low-cost technology solutions depends on the availability of open information sources. Such sources are invaluable, for they could provide the required know-how without the excessive restrictions of traditional copyright protection regimes. Institutions in the global south, for example, do not usually possess the resources needed to train and build the capacity of their staff members in order to tackle their technology challenges. The open-content movement, however, addresses this issue by providing more people with access to information sources that are vitally important for building a global, equitable, and inclusive information society.

Sustainability

Even when equipment and information can be acquired and used at reasonable costs, other (usually hidden) expenses threaten the long-term survival of many projects. In this example, the ongoing charges for the VSAT Internet connection, its maintenance, and staffing represent the primary challenges. To sustain its ability to access the Internet, FADECO devised a cost-sharing scheme that not only eased the burden of the expensive monthly charges but also enabled other institutions to connect to the global network. The value FADECO adds for its partners, however, extends beyond the Internet connection itself, for FADECO can also offer technical support and expertise that offload the burden of managing the connection and, to a certain extent, the technology at the partners' sites.

Case Study 2: School Network in South Africa

Universal primary education was identified by the United Nations as one of the major Millennium Development Goals it aims to achieve by 2015 (United Nations, 2005). It can be argued that in today's interconnected global economy, knowledge and intellectual capital pay the highest dividends. Moreover, knowledge can also be applied to other fields of economic activity in order to increase the added value generated by these fields and to enhance efficiency and effectiveness (Harrison & Sullivan, 2000). Thus the value of proper education is critically important in the currently emerging global knowledge societies.

The People and the Need

Many initiatives have aimed to bring high-quality education to under-served areas of the world (Chinapah et al., 2000; Fuller & Magdalena, 1998). Such efforts face tremendous difficulties in building the technical infrastructure needed for the delivery of enhanced educational experiences. Most of the remote locations in developing nations do not have reliable (if any) electricity; communications infrastructures are virtually nonexistent, and its sites are usually quite geographically dispersed (Cogburn & Adeya, 2001; Doutta, Lanvin, & Paua, 2004).

Emerging solutions that rely on low-cost wireless networking technologies and free and open-source software constitute a viable option for addressing some of these challenges. For the project discussed in this section, a complete network solution—one built entirely on alternative technologies—was designed and implemented to satisfy the needs of several schools. This solution used e-learning and video training materials to support local educational processes. The project links together six schools located just north of Johannesburg, South Africa, and in making such connections, the project provides connectivity and Internet access to teachers and students.

The Technology and the Environment

To establish the requisite network connectivity for the project, a local area wireless network was installed in each school, and this local network connected PCs and laptops in the schools to the wider area network. The schools were then interconnected using low-cost, point-to-point wireless links. A major part of the components used in these links was sourced locally. A significant benefit of this approach is the creation of a network flexible enough to enable more schools or other sites to connect to the network in the future.

Once established, the wireless network was used to provide students and teachers in all participating schools with access to e-learning materials and videos. Because of budget constraints, it was not possible to install a content repository in each school; doing so would have incurred significant costs for equipment, maintenance, and staff. Instead, a central server was set up at a central site, and that server supplied the content directly to end-users through the wireless network. This centralization of resources resulted in both appreciable cost savings and less problematic updates and synchronization of content. It also allowed for focusing investments on increasing the capacity of the central server.

The central content repository is built around the Viko system (www.viko.co.za), which consists of an Apple Mac Minicomputer, an external hard disk drive, a wireless networking connection, and a simple ventilation system—all contained in a small, wall-mount case. This system is finely tuned for the delivery of educational content, and it provides several services to clients, including Internet connectivity, e-mail, a media gateway (for video and audio streaming), and a localized television broadcast over the network. The system also includes a Voice over Internet Protocol (VoIP) server that allows connected schools to make free or cheap phone calls with each other.

In order to enhance the network's e-learning capabilities, a customized learning-management system (LMS) was installed and configured on the Viko server that connects the schools. This LMS is based entirely on free and open-source software components, including MySQL for database management, PHP for Web-based scripting, and Apache to serve Web applications. Video on demand is also provided using a complete open-source video-streaming solution. The LMS contains over 5,000 hours of lessons and 150 hours of educational video.

Because the reliability of Internet connectivity in the connected schools is usually a serious concern, the system attempts to address this problem by providing effective caching capabilities to locally store frequently accessed Web pages for offline browsing. A complete mirror of Wikipedia (around 17 gigabytes in size) is also available on the system.

During an initial needs assessment for the project, the system designers found that many schools already have traditional television units installed in classrooms. Therefore a TV broadcasting feature was added to the system, so content can be accessed from any television set in the school. The system can also record and play back TV programs broadcast in the area.

The Outcome

This project provides a colorful illustration of alternative and emerging technologies adapted to suit the local needs of several schools in Southern Africa. It also reveals how such innovation can contribute to the race to bridge the digital divide. Students involved in this project could not only use the educational materials stored in the system, but they could also interact with other students in the same school and in other schools connected to the network. In addition, teachers and students could use this learning platform to create their own content and teaching materials and then share this content with others. This approach offers an excellent solution to the localization problem confronting many development projects working in areas where English is not the primary spoken language. The low cost of the solution lends it to implementation in areas that could never otherwise afford connections or reap the benefits of the emerging e-learning paradigm. (Indeed, in some areas, the network is powered by solar panels because other sources of electricity are unavailable.)

Research is currently underway to evaluate this project's effects and to assess its contribution to educational experiences in participating schools. It is hoped that the findings will confirm what has been hypothesized about the value of information and communication technologies (ICTs)—namely, that they enhance education and produce well-prepared citizens of the global knowledge society.

Conclusion

This chapter demonstrates that emerging technologies, such as wireless networking and free and open-source software, can offer viable options for bridging the global digital divide. The two case studies examined here clearly show the ability of these technologies to satisfy the connectivity requirements of rural and remote communities in developing nations. Though these studies are set in very different contexts and environments, both reveal that local efforts with very few resources—but supported by wireless networking technologies and open-source software—can eventually succeed in building innovative and creative solutions to connect disadvantaged and remote communities to electronic and online resources.

A significant aspect of the solutions presented here is the adaptability of the technologies and a precise understanding of local needs; both cases highlight, too, the need to develop local capacity to maintain and support such projects. These cases also indicate that technology is only part of the solution and that suitability, in turn, is a major issue requiring careful consideration from the outset of any project. Further research is needed in order to develop technology-exploitation models based on these case studies and to explore the feasibility of replicating these models in other contexts. More case studies should be considered, as well, and common success factors should be identified.

References

Annan, K. (2001, April). Message from Kofi A. Annan. Retrieved April 12, 2008, from http://www.itu.int/itunews/issue/2001/04/wtd.html.

Chinapah, V., H'ddigui, E. M., Kanjee, A., Falayajo, W., Fomba, C. O., Hamissou, O., ... Byomugisha, A. (2000). *With Africa for Africa. Towards quality education for all.* Pretoria, South Africa: Human Sciences Research Council.

Cogburn, D. L., & Adeya, C. N. (2001). *Prospects for the digital economy in South Africa: Technology, policy, people, and strategies* (World Institute for Development Economics Research Discussion Paper No. 2001/77). Helsinki, Finland: United Nations University, World Institute for Development Economics Research.

Doutta, S., Lanvin, B., & Paua, F. (Eds.). (2004). *The global information technology report, 2003–2004: Readiness for the networked world.* New York, NY: Oxford University Press.

Fuller, B., & Magdalena, R. (1998). *Nicaragua's experiment to decentralize schools: Views of parents, teachers, and directors.* Washington, DC: World Bank, Development Economics Research Group.

Harmon, A. (1996). Daily life's digital divide. *Los Angeles Times*, p. 3.

Harrison, S., & Sullivan, P. H. (2000). Profiting from intellectual capital: Learning from leading. *Industrial and Commercial Training, 1*(1), 33–46.

Heeks, R. (1999). *Information and communication technologies: Poverty and development.* Manchester, UK: Institute for Development Policy and Management.

Molina, A. (2003). The digital divide: The need for a global e-inclusion movement. *Technology Analysis and Strategic Management, 15*(1), 137–152.

One laptop per child. (n.d.). One Laptop per Child. Retrieved April 12, 2008, from http://www.laptop.org.

Pentland, A., Fletcher, R., & Hasson, A. (2004, January). DakNet: Rethinking connectivity in developing nations. *Computer*, *37*, 4–9.

Small is beautiful. (2008, December 4). *The Economist.* Retrieved August 18, 2009, from http://www.economist.com/sciencetechnology/tq/displayStory.cfm?story_id=12673233.

Subramanian, L., Surana, S., Patra, R., Nedevschi, S., Ho, M., Brewer, E., & Sheth, A. (2006). Rethinking wireless in the developing world. In *Proceedings of the 5th Workshop on Hot Topics in Networks* (pp. x–xx). Irvine, CA: HotNets-V.

United Nations. (2005). *The millennium development goals report.* New York, NY: United Nations.

CHAPTER 5

THE CONTAINER PROJECT IN RURAL JAMAICA

SOCIALIZING TECHNOLOGY AND UNLEASHING CREATIVITY ALONG THE DIGITAL DIVIDE

Francesca da Rimini

Participatory globalization offers a useful conceptual framework for new forms of socially engaged, collective creativity and cooperative labor in a global context. This chapter examines the Container Project, an innovative computing and arts initiative that originated in an extremely deprived Jamaican township. Drawing upon the skills of a global peer network of artists and cultural activists, the Container Project has adapted "street technologies" to suit the needs of marginalized constituencies. The project provides conceptual and digital tools for people to build cultural knowledge using networked communicative platforms. The project also provides a unique example of how participatory globalization can challenge issues of the global digital divide through a transformative method of engagement.

COUNTER-NARRATIVES TO THE DIGITAL DIVIDE

The term *digital divide* connotes various images of the affluent "haves" versus the disadvantaged "have-nots." A superficial examination of the subject will not unearth the limitations of a complex techno-globalism dynamic, therefore this analysis, though limited in scope, begins with the term itself. One obvious linguistic limitation is that *digital divide* emphasizes the digital at the expense of its implicit opposite, the analog. The adjective *digital* can refer to data "in the form of especially binary digits" ("digital," 2010, para. 4), whilst *analog* signifies data "represented by continuously variable physical quantities" ("analog," 2010, para. 2). Thus the digital is limited to binary options: zero/one, on/off, and—by inference—a reductive black-and-white casting of a complex world. In contrast, the analog is almost infinite, with its sequential graduations and incremental transformations.

The word *divide* is also problematic. The Latin *dividere* means to force apart or to share out. This definition conjures up images of the diminishing of a whole into parts. By implication, this perspective of *divide* suggests ever-increasing scarcity on the side of the have-nots. *Divide* also operates as a binary by countering the concept of increasing, as in "to multiply." Contextually, it functions as a kind of barrier in which economically, geographically, and culturally defined groups are cut off from the realm of opportunity. Furthermore, the sentiment of the phrase implies that the power to dismantle this great division rests only with the social elite. Consequently, the notion arises that only in leveraging political will and corporate financing will the majority of the world be able to close the digital gap.

Finally, cultural theorist Armin Medosch has contended that implicit racial undertones are often embedded in the "well intentioned" debate around the digital divide (2005, p. 227). This debate "catalyzed the proliferation of another version of Western hegemonic thinking with its polarized rhetoric of 'access,'" which depicts an "egalitarian, global, democratic, hard to censor" Internet that "'we' have to give 'those people' down in Africa or elsewhere access to" (Medosch, 2005, p. 227). This monochrome conceptualization ignores the continuing evolution of the Internet into "a more diverse cultural space" employing "'mongrelized'" technical protocols (Medosch, 2005, p. 227).

Digital Sociologies: Network Society

When discourses about multiculturalism and the potential for social transformation include information and communication technologies (ICTs), the influential work of social scientist Manuel Castells becomes quite significant. Castells drew upon an enormous interdisciplinary body of empirical research to develop his comprehensive theory of the *network society*, defining it as the "social structure resulting from the interaction between the new technological paradigm and social organization" (2006, p. 3). Many sectors of society have undergone a transformative shift from a dominant hierarchical construct to a networked form of organization in their constitutive processes. Proposing that "globalization is another way to refer to network society," Castells described the "structural transformation" that emerged in the 1970s as a "multidimensional" process (2006, pp. 3–5). The renewal of a very "old form" of social organization—networks—was serendipitously assisted by three emergent phenomena. The first of these took shape in the liberatory social movements that gained renewed traction from the 1960s on; these movements include environmentalism, antiracism, and feminism. Second came the advances in microelectronics that began in the 1970s. Third was the post-1980 collapse of the old industrialism in both Western capitalist systems and Soviet socialist systems.

By contending that the "network society diffuses in the entire world, but does not include all people," Castells avoided framing techno-social inequity as a binary digital divide (2006, p. 5). He instead presented it as something more complex and slippery. Although "all of humankind" is affected by the "logic" of network society, the bulk of the planet's inhabitants are excluded from its potential benefits. Yet societies can empower themselves by recognizing the "contours of our new historical terrain" and then exploring the transformational potential of new technologies. Empirical research can help societies in this regard by identifying emerging terrains and mapping their interconnections. The network society provides a conceptual framework for developing counternarratives to the orthodoxy of the information society and its one-dimensional companion, the global digital divide. This approach invites new configurations of the interrelations among ICTs, knowledge, labor, creativity, and emancipatory social change.

Digital Sociologies: Participatory Globalization

Participatory globalization is one such counternarrative. In reviewing the concept of globalization, George (2004) defined it as "the latest stage of world capitalism and the political framework that helps it thrive" (p. 11). The word is ideological, George argued, because "it conveys the ideas that best serve the interests of people who profit from present economic, social, and political arrangements" (p. 11). Emergent social forms that "contest, interrogate, and reverse" the processes of globalization are discussed by Appadurai (2000, pp. 3–6). These generative structures create "forms of knowledge transfer and social mobilization that proceed independently of the actions of corporate capital and the nation-state system" (Appadurai, 2000, p. 3). The world's poor are producing the visions and strategies for a "grassroots globalization," or "globalization from below" (Appadurai, 2000, p. 3). Imagination in social life is "one positive force that encourages an emancipatory politics of globalization" (Appadurai, 2000, p. 6). The faculty of imagination is unshackled from the Enlightenment myth of individual genius, and it is recast as a "popular, social, collective fact" through which "collective patterns of dissent and new designs for collective life emerge" (Appadurai, 2000, p. 6).

I use the phrase *participatory globalization* to refer to a notional, infinitely scalable, planetary network of human networks that is animated by collective imaginations and cooperative work. This network produces new forms of social agency in opposition to enslavement, impoverishment, and other forms of social, cultural, political, and economic oppression.[1] Such grassroots globalization from below is simultaneously disorganized, semicoordinated, locally anchored, and globally aware. This network of networks is composed of geographically dispersed material, self-managed nodes (i.e., people and projects) that collectively build social visions, communication channels, material and intellectual resources, and electronic and physical environments. Each node has its own set of interdependencies and is plugged into specific discourses and drivers for change. Whereas each node's sociocultural context determines its philosophies, ideologies, and practices, all nodes are energized by a "politics of transformation" (George, 2004, p. x).

A collective radical refusal of a globalization from above generates material examples of counterglobalization's oft-heard declaration, "Other worlds are possible!" Purposeful and creative participation with others is creating effects corporeal, affective, and intellectual. Globalization becomes something that people "do" communally rather than something "done to them." Even some skeptics agree that new paradigms are being constructed from this "biopolitical" labor, which "creates not only material goods but also relationships and ultimately social life itself" (Hardt & Negri, 2004, p. 109). For example, whilst building a case refuting "over-arching claims" that an information revolution has occurred, Christopher May (2002) conceded that "newly emerging political networks and virtual communities outside the core information societies [are] linking Diasporas together and providing new possibilities for social engagement" (p. 13).

Digital Sociologies: The Case of the Container Project

The Container Project is one node within the vast networks of networks sketched earlier. The project is a socially inclusive, digital media and arts center in the impoverished Jamaican rural township of Palmers Cross. Founded by mervin Jarman (*sic*), the Container Project targets the community's most marginalized members.[2] Its pedagogical praxis is based on mutual respect, social cooperation, and skill sharing. Characterized by a communal sharing of everything from food to computer code and ideas, the project manifests a distinctly Jamaican style of participatory globalization. That is, it draws upon specific cultural traditions, social values, and historical movements unique to Jamaica. Since the project's launch in 2003, a profound social healing has transformed lives in this and other deprived locations that have hosted Container Project workshop programs in Jamaica. By tapping into art, education, and media activism networks, the project creates ripples of local change that enter global flows.

The Container Project's inherent participatory, creative processes arise from its philosophical base and from a political conviction that social change needs to come from below and be activated by the many. This largely unfunded project has flourished, and its existence challenges the inevitability of a globalization agenda determined by narrow neoliberal economic imperatives. Attention to the symbolic resonances and material processes generated by what Appadurai referred to as "creative forms of social life" reveals that techno-globalism is more complex than the state of simply being digital—being on the lucky side of a contestable divide—suggests (Appadurai, 2000, p. 6).

THE CONTAINER PROJECT

The Container Project began as an experiment with physical space. That is, the founder of this project began with an actual shipping container (hence the name). He employed this container as a physical location from which he could provide a local community with access to both computing technologies and the necessary training to use them. The shipping container housed computer workstations and portable digital equipment that local individuals could use free of charge. Over time, the notion of the Container Project expanded beyond the initial physical space of the original shipping container; today, the project embodies a sense of philanthropy, involvement, and community spirit focused on exploring new ways that computing technologies can revitalize and heal impoverished communities in other locations. This chapter explores the dynamics of this project—dynamics that involve the use of physical space and community space to empower people through creative computing.

Located in the parish of Clarendon in south central Jamaica, the Palmers Cross community is burdened with its rural township's reputation. A blighted place of crosses and tribulation, it has been considered a town from which nothing good can come: It was "a place disliked and disregarded by the upper class, where unemployment was the order of the day, with no industry, no infrastructure, no wages, no economy, a dead zone" (Jarman, 2004, p. 3). This unlikely locale is the home of the Container Project, a community access point for digital arts and multimedia. The center is a social hive and an open space in which people can realize their personal aspirations. Here, learning occurs along multiple pathways ranging from basic computing skills (e.g., using e-mail and Internet search software) to certified technical courses and training workshops. Digital artist and activist mervin Jarman conceived the initiative as an instrument that could encourage people to look at themselves differently by providing them with possibilities for self-expression.

What distinguishes this intervention from conventional ICT skill-building programs? For a start, the project involves more than uncomplicated technology transfer. Its holistic approach operates on an existential level as well, for Jarman aims to transfer "sophisticated thought, intellectual longing, social action, [and] stability" to marginalized Jamaicans (Jarman & Mills, 2007, pp. 87–88). Because the Container Project's philosophy "is encoded in the Container itself—the way it's built, the way it's run" and in Jarman's "writings and other artistic output," much of it must be "received subliminally" (Jarman & Mills, 2007, pp. 87–88).

Another difference is that this social intervention was built by community members themselves rather than being "flown in from the outside," explained Jamaican-born artist and regular Container collaborator Camille Turner.[3] Jarman spent his young adult years in Palmers Cross, and consequently, Turner explained, he is a "big part of what makes [the project] so different." He is a powerful role model because he shared the "same roots" of poverty, and he was proof to others in the community that they, too, could "aspire to break out of the boundaries of their world."

Mongrel: Creating Socially Engaged Media and Social Software

To some extent, the transformations occurring within the community around the Container mirror the circumstances of its founder, mervin Jarman. His pathway ran from a "hard-core" life on the streets of Jamaica and England to art school, and then on to Arts Technology Center (ARTEC), where he learned the latest multimedia programs. As he browsed the Internet, he discovered that he could not find himself or those like him—with origins on society's margins—represented in cyberculture. This experience of race and class invisibility propelled Jarman's campaign to put the individual and his or her experiences in the public domain for others to see.

Thus began Mongrel, an art collective cofounded by Jarman, Richard Pierre-Davis, Matsuko Yokokoji, and Graham Harwood. Mongrel used the collective "street ingenuity" of its founders to develop multimedia software programs that countered their own experiences of a digital culture "slanted against marginalized people," Jarman recalled. Their imperative was that "no-one got lost, no-one got left behind," said Jarman (personal communication, March 30, 2010). The group ran community-based art workshops around the United Kingdom and Europe and taught people with little or no prior computing experience how to use Mongrel's free software programs to create their own stories. These workshops were "dialogues" that produced "fast artefacts of digital culture with other mongrels," and in so doing they demystified the new digital means of knowledge production (Fuller, 1999c, para. 1).

Despite a popular notion that software is politically and socially neutral and a product of scientific rationality, research suggests otherwise. Software, like any modern technology, carries with it many social histories, economic goals, and political imperatives. Moreover, unlike many other technologies, software can engage people intellectually and affectively, creating a "sensorium: a set of ways of sensing, knowing and doing in the world" (Fuller, 1999c, para. 9). When one is not involved with its design, when one is divorced from its production, one is encumbered with a sensorium that reflects a narrow, and typically conservative, set of concerns.

Mongrel's Linker[4] program was one of the first manifestations of social software. It was built in direct response to user needs and for those people who were excluded from the techno-future, "our own people," as Jarman put it (Fuller, 1999c, para. 3). Mongrel built the Linker software by reverse-engineering and stripping down an expensive industry-standard authoring program, thus melding proprietary code and free software. Linker was "the multimedia equivalent of a throw-away camera" that dissolved technical barriers of clumsy, complicated software interfaces and allowed people to "get on with exploring ideas" (Fuller, 1999c, para. 5). It enabled people to make collaborative multimedia artworks by combining digital images, audio files, video files, and texts into hypertextual maps. Each map could hyperlink to maps made by others, making the exploration of the resultant nonlinear screen-based artworks a rich experience for users and audiences by linking common themes. In an early critique of software as a cultural artifact, Fuller (1999c) signaled that a "structure that in itself is fairly limited, particularly in size, becomes with the possibility of reiteration a far more powerful means of linkage. Collections become collectivities" (para. 7).

Whereas Linker was content neutral in that it was a platform within which user-generated content could be set, other Mongrel-built software art projects (e.g., the Web-based BlackLash game, the Heritage Gold digital color-manipulation software, and the Natural Selection search engine) were overtly confrontational: They used politically charged content such as racialized stereotypes to "attack the 'tolerance' of the middle classes," noted Medosch (2005, pp. 232–233). The National Heritage interactive computer artwork, for instance, required users to virtually click and spit on virtual faces in order to proceed to deeper levels of a multiauthored narrative exploring experiences of racial discrimination. The art group's "aggressive 'mongrelization' of popular software programs and search engines made race an issue at a time when the Internet hype was getting into full swing, and everybody was meant to forget that such problems still existed, or made to believe that the Internet would somehow, magically, make them disappear" (Medosch, 2005, p. 233).

Repatriating Technology

The Container is not only a multimedia center but also a "metaphor," said Jarman: "On its outward journey, it takes ... produce from the Caribbean to the developed world. Now it is being used to 'repatriate' technology into these islands, bridging both the economic and the digital divide" (Jarman, 2004, p. 2). Because the notion of technological repatriation is core to the Container Project's praxis, it is useful to understand the cross-cultural context from which it emerged.

During the 1990s in London, new economic opportunities were emerging as commercial culture was rebranded "creative industries"; ICTs were central to this boom (Medosch, 2003). An emergent "digital economy" within postindustrial societies like Britain was beginning to " 'capture' ... larger pools of social and cultural knowledge" (Terranova, 2004, p. 79). As these processes of the commodification of the common were taking root, alternative systems of production and exchange were flowering, and these alternative systems resisted the easy classification and enclosure common at that time. This brief, vibrant period was "a historical juncture at which several different parts of culture ... had expanded, making certain kinds of thinking, dancing, computing, and communication possible" before being "normalized" (Fuller, 2005, para. 6). A "radical interdisciplinarity" threw out political challenges: "to take that opportunity to invent as much as possible, to create such a sense of expectation and participation that it would be difficult to fit a straight-jacket over reality once that conjunction moved on" (Fuller, 2005, para. 6).

In 1990 the 28-year-old mervin Jarman arrived in London and initially continued the same kind of hard-core street life that he had lived in Jamaica. At some point, however, Jarman experienced an epiphany through which he realized that if he was to avoid ending up imprisoned or dead, he needed to jump off the "perpetual conveyer belt of nothingness" (Jarman, personal communication, March 19, 2007). His realization coincided with the flowering of England's post–punk alternative culture scene. Consequently, Jarman learned film and video production, animation, and multimedia in an extremely stimulating social context. This holistic learning experience inspired him to return to his Jamaican birthplace of Palmers Cross in order to establish an experimental art and technology center.

Jarman believed that digital tools and community-sensitive learning experiences could be pathways to link marginalized communities to their "heritage and cultural backbone" (Jarman, 2003a, para. 4). A *recodalisation* would happen: that is, a recoding of existing negative social relations (Jarman, personal communication, March 19, 2007). Digital technology was the "cutting-edge thing" that he needed to take back home, to share with people "who have a hell of a lot more to contribute to society than the misery that gets strapped to us" (Fuller, 1999a, para. 15). The "repatriation of a tool, which was a technology, back into the streets" would make people "notice those whom they have not paid any attention to over the years" (Jarman, personal communication, March 19, 2007). The driving vision was to create something that would "engage people affected by various divides—be that political or social" (Fuller, 1999b, para. 3). Experiences, equipment, and personal connections acquired during Jarman's time in London would be taken home to Jamaica for the inception of new vistas.

Container: Materiality and Material Space

The Container Project is described as being many things—an art and media lab, an inclusive social hub, a first point of access for digital technology, a space of healing and hope, and a channel for flows. Although they are clearly part of more than a technology center, the digital media tools and creative learning programs of the Container Project act as a lure to stimulate people's curiosity. The interplay of the material architectural space, the networked electronic space, and the relational social space generates hybridized platforms for learning and artistic expression. As community dynamics have shifted, microbusinesses have been established. An innovative portable media lab takes workshop programs to other Jamaican locations, and a new Caribbean Open and Distance Learning platform is in development.

The site for the Container was Jarman's family land, where he envisaged that people could build their dreams "on the graveyards of time"

(Jarman, 2003b, line 2). In April 2003, a shipping container donated by a Jamaican transport company was retrofitted by volunteers working from Jarman's design plans. The converted container was painted an eye-catching yellow and peeled open through the installation of large kiosk-style, breeze-channeling windows on both sides. The rear doors could open up and a temporary stage was attached for performances. This highly localized design countered community fears about foreign or "alien" technology. Jamaica has long been an exporting country—bananas, bauxite, sugar, music, and Rastafari—thus the familiar form of a sea/land transport container was an "unintimidating point of contact for new users"—in contrast, for example, to a high-tech concrete, glass, and steel building that locals would have interpreted as an "exclusion zone" (Jarman, personal communication, March 14, 2007).

The laborers who transformed the structure were some of the Cross's most disenfranchised people, the "average guys on the street" whom some people treated with disdain. Community members undertook "all the work of customizing" the shipping container (Jarman, personal communication, August 6, 2007). The building site became a social space as people came to look, work, or just hang out, and plentiful communal cooking and music kept the energy high. The community's shared labor created a sense of a common ownership and inclusion because it became *their* space, a place community members monitored and cared about. If, however, the Container team had flown in with snazzy computers, the community would not have experienced that sense of "We made this!" In a very poor area riddled with crime, it was a point of pride for the community to declare and maintain the Container as a "safe space."

Rather than building "tight cold cubicles where it's just you, the individual, interacting with your screen and everything else is secret," the Container's design encourages people to "copy take," to look at "what others are doing on their screens, and then make copies of it on your screen" (Jarman, personal communication, March 14, 2007). This method fosters communication between learners. The Container's windows were "deliberately low cut, two feet from the base up" so that people of all ages and heights could "easily look into the Container and see what's taking place" (Jarman, personal communication, March 14, 2007). A long, central desk supports back-to-back monitors that face out to the windows, so that "wherever you are around the Container, the screen is always visible to you" (Jarman, personal communication, March 14, 2007).

Self-Organizing Systems and Entrepreneurial Engines

The Container's media lab functions as a self-organizing system. Annual membership of the Community Computer Club costs JMD $1,000 (USD $15) plus a small charge for hourly access for those who can afford it. This income is used to pay power and phone bills, and it includes people as stakeholders. People borrow portable recording equipment on an honor system. The community's respect for the project is reflected in that, in over seven years, nothing has ever been stolen or lost in this high-crime zone.

In recent years, the Container Project has nurtured the establishment of various community-driven social enterprises and microbusinesses. Some of these entrepreneurial engines, such as printing and other desktop publishing services, are run by the Container itself as part of its sustainable initiative. A bakery and a restaurant offer employment and training for locals, and plans are in place for the establishment of other small businesses, including a flower shop, on the Container's block. These income-generating initiatives not only encourage confidence and self-sufficiency but also address the ongoing issue of people's dropping out of training programs because "they needed to be earning" (Jarman, personal communication, March 29, 2010).

Participants in the Container's local and traveling workshop programs acquire confidence, problem-solving capabilities, technical skills, and generate artistic output; some go on to earn a direct economic benefit for their labor as creative producers and skilled technicians. In 2009, for example, a number of workshop participants were offered either regular salaried work or periodic consultancy employment contracts by local and national businesses. These prospective employers had been impressed by the technical proficiency and creative achievements they witnessed in just one art exhibition. In addition, a Jamaican national bank and the Container Project have started a dialogue about providing small loans for community-driven microbusiness ventures, a partnership that could generate additional sponsors for the Container and related projects.

The iStreet Lab Initiative

In 2008 the Container node launched the iStreet Lab, an initiative to engage at-risk youth between 9 and 25 years of age—people Jarman said are often described as "fit only for dumping" (Jarman, personal communication, March 29, 2010). This socially engineered technology takes the form of a miniaturized multimedia lab located inside a plastic wheelie rubbish bin: a portable infrastructure ready to interface with street culture. The technical core of the iStreet Lab comprises five Apple laptops loaded with user-friendly multimedia software, a terrestrial radio station, an Internet radio station, a low-range television transmission facility that covers a 1-mile radius, a sound-mixing desk, digital video and sound recording devices, a color printer, a sound system, and an LCD monitor attached to the interior bin lid. UNESCO's Kingston Cluster Office for the Caribbean supported the construction of the iStreet Lab prototype, and it might become involved in similar projects as it assists with upgrading the Container Project into a certified regional training center.

The lab is a piece of "social artwork" designed by Jarman to roll into "hostile environments," into the "trenches" in any rural or urban community where those in the "shadows," the "hardest to reach, the ones with a real attitude" are to be found. Functioning as a temporary autonomous zone,[5] this inclusive alternative space invites workshop participants to consider themselves both as "part of the Container … part of the wheelie bin lab" and as part of a global network of creative producers and mentors. Workshops can be adapted and transported at minimal cost "from street to street, from city to city in any crevice and corner" (Murphy, 2007, para. 5). The initiative is a "behavioral change lab," according to Mongrelstreet artist Richard Pierre-Davis (Jarman & Pierre-Davis, 2009, para. 4–5). Rather than attempting "to recycle the planet," the iStreet Lab "focuses on recycling human behavior because you cannot change the world without changing the people" (Jarman & Pierre-Davis, 2009, para. 4–5). The lab embraces "the recycle-to-produce-a-better-environment concept whilst demonstrating that even trash can be morphed into something as gracious as an orchid" (Murphy, 2007, para. 5).

In 2009 the iStreet Lab facilitated workshops focusing on "skills training, literacy, and counseling" in four locations around Jamaica. The participants were young "risk takers" inhabiting the streets. Because each Jamaican street has its own "don" who controls the activities of the area, Jarman first needed to gain each local don's permission to run workshops. The creative multimedia workshops had specific themes, including photojournalism, video production, and sound production. Twice a day, people had to mount and demount the lab and grapple with an array of cables. For the participants, this was an easily acquired skill because that kind of grappling or struggling is "what you do on the twisty, windy way of the streets, you have to know whom to avoid and to whom you should go" (Jarman, personal communication, March 29, 2010). Consequently, the participants' lived experience of the intricacies and nuances of street culture enabled them to negotiate the "street technology" to which the lab exposed them. Feedback from participants was posted on the iStreet Lab's social networking Website and was highly positive (Jarman, 2010). Moreover, a few young people in one host community are now raising funds to build their own iStreet Lab.

The Interactive Teaching and Learning (ITAL) Platform

In Jamaica's Rastafarian dialect, the word *I-tal* (or *ital*) signifies a vital, natural, and healthy state. The word is used most commonly in reference to traditional food and its manner of preparation. Eating wholesome ital foods is one of the ways in which people maintain their "livity," a holistic concept that incorporates how people live on a daily basis in order to ensure their minds, bodies, and spirits are fit (Hill, 2005). This cultural concept has been transposed to the digital realm through the development of ITALEducation.net, a recent initiative pioneered by educational technologist Rohan Webb and mervin Jarman.

ITALEducation.net is a portal that uses the ITAL (Interactive Teaching and Learning) platform, an online teaching and learning system that incorporates rich multimedia as an integral part of its primary pedagogical approach. ITAL uses a multimodal concept to provide a supportive, student-centered learning environment. The goal is for ITAL Education to guide the development of the online content that the Container and iStreet Lab will use on the new ITALEducation.net Website. This initiative aims to capture the extraordinary knowledge base that has developed organically in Jamaica over the past eight years. The electronically available knowledge repository would enable educators, social and media activists, and community-development workers to employ Container workshop methods.

The new site responds to the challenge that cyberculture to date has not inspired many Caribbean schools "to adopt Open and Distance Learning (ODL) on a large scale" (Webb, personal communication, April 7, 2010). This situation ultimately affects students' abilities "to compete effectively in today's economic markets" because they "must not only be familiar with the modern instruments of communication but also master the languages and science" that compose those instruments (Webb, personal communication, April 7, 2010). The platform's design embodies educational research demonstrating that "students learn well through play, … self-discovery [and] by relating new information to existing cognitive paradigms" (Webb, personal communication, April 7, 2010). ITAL is a learning shell into which educators can input specific educational content tailored to their students' needs; it is designed so that local, regional, or national standards can be written into the system.

As of July 2010, Webb was continuing empirical research in order to equip ITALEducation.net with its own unique approach to teaching and learning based on the specific characteristics of the Container Project's pedagogical approach—the way Jarman and the artist teams create and deliver educational content. Webb is also designing a three-month pilot course for primary school teachers in Jamaica. The course will guide instructors in course-material development and will test the feasibility of this innovative Container Project online educational portal. The site is poised to serve educational services throughout the Caribbean region and offer education administrators, school officials, and individual students the opportunity to establish their own online schools and independent-study programs. Various instructors and trainers will be able to set up and teach their own courses using ITALEducation.net or create their own sites using the ITAL platform—and thus help develop "a modern community of learners" across the Caribbean (Webb, personal communication, April 7, 2010).

Through its initiatives, the Container Project aims to deliver outcomes that communities themselves can continue to reproduce. Opening up opportunities for those in one's environment, sharing what one has, and passing on knowledge and skills are practices embedded and valued in many societies. Is there something specifically Jamaican in the way the Container enacts these principles within the context of the global digital divide?

Specificity: Cultural Considerations

In an analysis of the various ways a project is grounded in specific localities, the spatial divisions that project expresses can be understood in the context of globalization. History, culture, language, religion, and values can all be examined as part of this process. My research has identified three historical movements that have influenced, and now contextualize, the philosophy and work of the Container Project. These are (a) the slave resistance movement of the 18th and 19th centuries, (b) the 20th-century pan-African movement, and (c) the religious and social movement called Rastafari. Each of these movements produced charismatic leaders—Sam Sharpe, Queen Nanny, Marcus Garvey, Leonard Howell—who rose above intolerable circumstances to drive social and political change by inspiring others with courage, tenacity, rhetoric, and action. Moreover, the communicative aspects of these grassroots movements and their self-managed cooperative labor prefigure the contemporary phenomenon of participatory globalization. Similarly, the charismatic mervin Jarman has come from the streets, identifies the generic street as the origin of the Container Project's global constituency, and has inspired whole communities to believe that no situation is unchangeable. In what follows, I draw out the connections between Rastafari and the Container Project.

Collective survival skills requiring risk-taking and an inventive approach to everyday problems have always been a part of Jamaica's social fabric. The Container Project harnesses these national attributes and applies them in a globalized digital world, thereby forging new pathways beyond individual survival into community self-sufficiency and social harmony. These developments feed back into new networks of production and exchange. When a social divide is named and subsequently acted upon collectively, a transformative process is set in motion. The Container Project continues the social program of Rastafari but broadens it significantly. First, it includes not only self-identified Rastas but also all those who experience marginalization. Secondly, on a microscale, the Container Project reterritorializes and democratizes the domain of the digital.

Rastafari has been described as an indigenous Jamaican religion, a philosophy, a social movement, and a worldview (Chevannes, 1998; Edmonds, 2003).[6] It emerged in the 1930s from Kingston's ghettos—places densely populated by a dispossessed rural proletariat, the urban poor, and diaspora returnees. A groundswell of activity spontaneously arose from the severe economic and social hardship caused by inequitable government policies, a situation these disenfranchised people could not alter at the ballot box. The emergent movement rejected British economic and cultural imperialism and instead promoted self-sufficiency and a righteous way of living. People manifest Rastafari by coming to consciousness and by participating in a high level of intellectual critique of both self and external oppression. The interrelated moral values, economic systems, and legally sanctioned mechanisms of human exploitation, production, and exchange of tainted commodities—all associated with a transnational class of white oppressors—were conceptualized as Babylon, and Babylon was seen as the root cause of black suffering (Hill, 2005).

The crowning of a black Ethiopian emperor Haile Selassie I—whom some Jamaicans regarded as the promised Messiah—was the primary "catalytic event" that called Rastafari into existence (Edmonds, 2003, p. 32).[7] Some who identify as Rastas, including Jarman (personal communication, March 31, 2010), distance themselves from the phenomenon's theology (e.g., the divinity of Haile Selassie I) and social mores (e.g., the sacramental status of marijuana), and view certain key traditions as politically manipulated and detrimental to the movement's goals. However, it is generally agreed that, although the movement was driven by key figures (e.g., Leonard Howell in the 1930s) and popularized and internationalized by Reggae musicians (e.g., Bob Marley in the 1970s), it remains an acephalous, horizontally organized phenomenon that is now deeply "embedded in the social and cultural fabric of Jamaican society" (Edmonds, 2003, p. 4).

Whereas Rastafari's early phase had emphasized redemption and repatriation (echoing Marcus Garvey's Back to Africa program) and had set up autonomous communities, its second phase (1940s–1970s) became increasingly politicized, including the incorporation of traditional protests and some guerrilla activities. The complex reasons for this politicization are beyond the scope of this chapter, but it should be noted that events within Jamaica and internationally "created a very volatile climate … for people who think and have this imperative to be free" (Webb, personal communication, April 8, 2010). So although the expanded movement now included middle class people of both genders and individuals of mixed-race backgrounds, Rastafari continued to address the yearnings and sufferings of those at the very bottom of Jamaican society.

Over time, urban youth used their indigenous music forms "to express Rastafari ideas, yearning and critique," creating a mass phenomenon as Reggae music became Rastafari's international export vehicle (Chevannes, 1998, p. 14). The "more radical edge" to the Rastafari movement was "evident in these sounds from the 1960s and 1970s" (Webb, personal communication, April 8, 2010). At the same time, Rastafari youths became involved in national politics, and their vote helped Michael Manley's left-wing People's National Party (PNP) win the 1972 general election. Youth engagement, however, was not so much about casting a vote; it was, rather, a means to escape "the reality, the economic and political hegemony that existed" (Webb, personal communication, April 8, 2010). Whereas previously, "Jamaicans had seen the failure of many of their heroes," Manley's election to the post of prime minister ushered in "a new era" in which some Rastas chose to maintain a traditional expression of Rastafarianism, and others chose the path of "nation building" (Webb, personal communication, April 8, 2010). Rastafari's current phase is marked by less ideologically driven youth, greater female participation, and the secularization of certain symbols. The movement "retains great moral authority" in Jamaica because it both continued Garveyism's liberation of cultural identity and placed Jamaican culture on the world stage (Chevannes, 1998, p. 16).

Rastafari, like the grassroots emancipation and pan-African movements, engaged people's imaginations with a vision of a different reality and evolved material forms through which people could begin to transform their situations. For some, this transformation meant exodus to separatist communities; for others, it meant the evolution of a uniquely Jamaican form of cultural expression in the urban ghettos and gullies spawned by Babylon. A new multitude was emerging from below, and cooperative creative labor was again at the heart of this new class formation. Those resistant to capitalism's exploitation and to Babylon took up cultural arms and used the power of the word—especially through music. In Rastafari, more so than in preceding movements, the expressive arts played a fundamental role in transmitting visions of hope, redemption, and transformation.

Despite Jamaica's intertwined histories of resistance, resilience, and regeneration, the contemporary situation remains bleak for the majority of its population. The historical burden of centuries of inequity and disempowerment has been compounded by outside political interference and internal machinations since Jamaica's independence in 1962. The complex causes of these destructive currents are beyond the scope of my discussion, but some of their main consequences bear mentioning here because they encapsulate the social landscape in which the Container is emplaced.

The Container Project, Resistance, Reciprocity, and Rasta Software

Embedded within Jamaica and its diaspora is a culture of resistance and an appreciation of its history and its heroes. The Container asserts commonality with the most disenfranchised and, like earlier grassroots movements, it opens up new horizons that begin with the imagination and are expressed through contemporaneous communicative platforms and channels. Thus the Container Project is "like what the church was to slaves and freed slaves," (Webb, personal communication, April 9, 2010). The church provided "solace" and "redemption," and "when there was not food it provided hope" (Webb, personal communication, April 9, 2010). In a similar fashion, the Container highlights what is possible.

Jarman felt that he was a "Rasta from birth" because he was "born in poverty, grew up in poverty and still exist[s] in poverty" and because he had been persecuted for his race and social standing (personal communication, March 19, 2007). After the abolition of slavery, the lack of clear pathways created a devastated mass of people who began to search out their own sense of purpose. A society with many social divisions evolved—a society in which "everybody a-pull for themselves"—and these divisions included the "little cliques" within the church and state (Jarman, personal communication, March 19, 2007). The Container Project attempts to change that through its all-inclusive character. Jarman thus focused on his interpretation of the Rastafari concept of "I and I"—"whatever is good for me is good for you. So I and I [we] share in all things ... we work together" (Jarman, personal communication, March 19, 2007). Just as Jamaica's problems are complex, the solutions must be holistic, engaging not only the mind, but also the senses and the emotions.

Rastafari was the avenue through which the "African Caribbean working class found a way of fermenting resistance to the continued legacy of colonialism, racism, and capitalist exploitation" (Medosch, 2005, p. 222). Because the movement and philosophy are "eclectic and culturally hybrid," core Rastafari principles and cultural artifacts have been readily adapted by other communities. Rastafari and reggae music have long been exported to, adapted by, and exploited by the global north (Gilroy, 1991, pp. 153–222). Cognizant of this, the Container Project's team aims to redress cultural power imbalance by "fostering the creative abilities of Jamaicans and continuing to distribute our values like we have done in the UK over the last 50 years" (Mute, 2004, para. 1). Practices of reciprocity can help leverage longer-term, broad-based change, as Jarman indicated: "[The] UK and Europe need to feed back their technological skills into Jamaica to help sustain the culture clash that is contemporary mongrel culture" (Mute, 2004, para. 1).

Such reciprocity already occurs on a microlevel within some free-software communities. In a declaration entitled "This Is Rasta Software," activist software programmer Jaromil (n.d.) made a link between the dyne:bolic Linux distribution (packaged with artist-made multimedia tools specifically developed for the global south)[8] and revolutionary social movements:

> Jah Rastafari Livity bless our Freedom! … This software is about Resistance in a Babylon world which tries to control more and more the way we communicate and we share information and knowledge. This software is for all those who cannot afford to have the latest expensive hardware to speak out their words of consciousness and good will … [F]reedom and sharing of knowledge are solid principles for evolution, and that's where this software comes from … The roots of Rasta culture can be found in Resistance to slavery. This software is not a business. This software is free as of speech and is one step in the struggle for Redemption and Freedom. ("This is Rasta Software," n.d., para. 2–5)

The Container's demonstrable achievements indicate its positive impact on residents of Palmers Cross; improved self-esteem, newly acquired skills and aptitudes, increased employability, and reduced participation in harmful or illicit activities can be ascertained by a mixture of subjective (e.g., anecdotal accounts) and objective (e.g., formal IT-skills testing) measures. Likewise, changes in community dynamics can be reflected through residents' perceptions and quantifiable measures of factors such as crime rates. As beneficial changes amass locally, they seed an emancipatory social field that ripples outward. These changes nurture the longer term community politicization. They also strengthen people's resolve to collectively mobilize around pressing issues of poverty, inequity, and prejudice—particularly as they relate to the global digital divide.

Gangs, Political Tribalism, and Local Social Change

Gang rivalries in Palmers Cross have complex poverty-related causes that are exacerbated by party political machinations, and the increased proliferation of gun use aggravates already tense situations (see *Report of the National Committee on Political Tribalism*, 1997; *Report of the National Committee on Crime and Violence*, 2002). The Container Project's pedagogical methods dealt directly with divisive social fragmentation. In so doing, it achieved an unprecedented harmony amongst people who would normally consider themselves enemies because of political and gang affiliations. Jarman was a known supporter of the People's National Party (PNP), but many of the average people on the street were Jamaica Labor Party (JLP) supporters and others who were affiliated with the PNP.

Armed with an understanding of gang dynamics and political tribalism born of his own lived experiences, Jarman divided the technical training within the lab. "I never teach different people the same things; we divide the skills, and then they have to teach each other" (Jarman, personal communication, March 19, 2007). This strategy created independent "experts" in different areas—software programs, hardware maintenance, and recording equipment. Because the Container is a neutral space in which the only rule is to respect others, lab users needed to communicate with each other respectfully in order to learn how to use the tools. The deliberate inversion of conventional hierarchies of knowledge within the spaces of learning and play produced a profound shift in social dynamics both inside and outside the Container. The effectiveness of a simple pedagogical method in healing decades-old wounds caused by political tribalism has impressed other communities, and some are taking initial steps to build their own iStreet Labs and community media centers based on the same approach.

As a result of such projects, a new sense of camaraderie is emerging in Palmers Cross. "What is so charismatic about the case of the

Container, and mervin himself, is that once inside the space—the physical and psychological space, that is—it is possible to feel the potential for change and the power of faith" (Jarman & Mills, 2007, p. 88). This potential is being actuated because the community has created a "safe haven, an oasis where there is a possibility of healing" (Turner, personal communication, August 6, 2007). Community elders value the changes that this community institution has brought, for they have witnessed the previously unimaginable: youth from rival gangs now playing soccer and having fun together. For the first time, something had come to the community that was not exploiting it.

Learning and Literacies

Much of the Container's knowledge work is learner-driven. Peer leadership programs focusing on leadership skills, pedagogical methods, and technical training complement the self-learning opportunities. Peers become the "interface between the technology and the communities" (Turner, personal communication, August 6, 2007). Once a person has learned a skill, he or she is considered an expert and proves it by sharing knowledge. Even those undertaking informal training are taught to be teachers, thus reinforcing their abilities and increasing their self-esteem. When given the chance to lead, sometimes the most unlikely people "step into their own and surprise everyone" (Turner, personal communication, August 6, 2007). Peer training also builds learners' confidence as students see people like themselves in leadership roles.

Both an enhanced sense of social responsibility and fundamental life skills are being acquired through this initiative. Learning is "always easier and more relevant when participants have a reason to apply skills they acquire" because "the more engaged the students are, the more they learn" (Turner, personal communication, August 6, 2007). Much of the learning is also of an incidental nature:

> People are learning to read now, but they never come into the Container to read. People are learning maths, but they didn't come into the Container to be mathematicians.... People are

> learning social skills that they never came to the Container with any intention to learn.... It's a learning, involving environment ... giving people skill sets that they need in their everyday lives. (Jarman, personal communication, March 19, 2007)

The acquisition of basic survival skills and the strategic division of training have affected broader social relationships, said Jarman, pointing out that no Container members "have suffered a burglary or a mugging" (Jarman, personal communication, March 19, 2007). Although it is not possible to prove a causal link between a lowered local crime rate and the Container's influence, the prevailing climate of distrust and enmity in the community has shifted.

The Digital Storytelling program illustrates the interplay between digital and social literacy. As the first artist in residence at the Container's inaugural 2003 Boot-Up workshop, Camille Turner brought her experience as a performance artist, filmmaker, and curator to the video-editing workshop she facilitated. The students were people "who don't normally see themselves in the technological world" (Turner, personal communication, August 6, 2007). Three years later, they participated in follow-up workshops run by Turner and two Canadian colleagues. Stories "bubbled up," and participants then scripted, filmed, edited, and screened them. This "powerful method of community engagement" allows everyone not only "to look at what's under the rug" but also to be witnessed and "counted as part of the society," said Turner.

The learning that occurs through the artist residencies and workshops is not a one-way global north-to-south street: Visiting artists become immersed in the local culture, and although they come "expecting to give," they receive much more (Turner, personal communication, August 6, 2007).

Some learning achievements resulting from these projects have been revealed by standardized testing. For example, 60 trainees between the ages of 9 and 45 participated in a Heart/National Training Authority computer course run at the Container in 2006. They gained exceptional examination results: 53 of the 60 students received full certification, and the remaining 7 students received a lower pass. In another example, a young woman who had trained and taught at the Container went on to become the only corporate IT recruit that an international airline did not need to retrain.

Nevertheless, some locals choose not to participate in Container programs. "Regardless of how much we do here, there will still be those who want no part of it and those who cannot get enough of it," Jarman acknowledged (personal communication, March 19, 2007). Jamaica is a class-based society, and some people self-exclude for reasons related to class concerns. There are those "who think they know everything about the youth in the community and so that familiarity has made them contemptuous of the youngsters" (Jarman, personal communication, March 19, 2007). Moreover, a small minority hang back because "they want to see how much the participants (their friends) will make money-wise because their interest is all into making … fast money."

Nodes and Networks

The concept of participatory globalization begins to take form when one considers the Container as a single node or connection point in an emergent, geographically dispersed network of socially engaged projects. The Container node is culturally specific and yet internationalized. It enfolds its external connections and social capital within localized settings, whether these be Palmers Cross, other Jamaican communities, or abroad. Something of a chameleon on the outside, the Container exhibits core values and principles that embody an inner cohesion and authenticity.

Communication and cooperation are essential within the global field inhabited by the Container and countless other projects. The key drivers are social, cultural, and political rather than purely economic. Hence social relations within the interconnected networks resist commodification. These nodes and networks are strengthened through the exchange of ideas and labor and are not necessarily rewarded with direct financial remuneration. However, in the Container's case, as more workshop participants find employment because of their training, the potential for this expression of participatory globalization to bring direct economic benefits to people is materializing.

One of the closest networks (in geographical terms) with which the Container interfaces is the local education system, including Cross Primary and Junior High Schools and Vere Technical High School. Students from other schools also share unlimited access to the project. The social capital earned by the Container's local successes has extended a regional reach; for instance, a 3-week Community Multimedia Center Management Workshop in March 2006 involved people from around the island. Guest facilitators from the Container Project's international network trained groups in digital storytelling, multimedia production, computer repairs, and the use of sensor technologies.[9] Participants gained skills enabling them to run similar projects in their home communities. In July 2008, the same facilitators returned to Palmers Cross with new digital toolkits. Participants in Ruxton's (2008) workshop built their own cyber Containers within the online multiuser environment of Second Life using virtual land loaned by the Ontario College of Art and Design.

The Container Project's ambitious vision is to cultivate more global ambassadors from the grass roots of Jamaica. If successful, this would facilitate the community's "moving in a direction that was conducive to global trend" (Murphy, 2007, para. 3). Rather than creating a cheap labor pool of info-workers for the North American IT industry, Jarman has emphasized that Jamaicans can produce their own "catalogue of creative contents" feeding into and benefiting from "a multi-billion-dollar industry that requires no external plug-ins" (Murphy, 2007, para. 13). The key is to "step away from the technology consumerist mentality and become producers of our own technology instruments that are sought after globally" (Murphy, 2007, para. 13).

Art, Experimentation, and Hybridity

The Container Project is an "open concept" in which "everyone leaves their trace and changes the space by what they bring to it" (Turner, personal communication, August 6, 2007). The result is a "hybrid space," an "organic, holistic entity bridging many worlds"; this "ever-evolving" space is "created and recreated on the fly and constantly adapted by the unique community in which it functions." It epitomizes network culture in that it is a dynamic place of creative and information flows and is influenced by "people from the outside who come into contact with it" (Turner, personal communication, August 6, 2007).

Jamaican culture is a "mix-mash of everything that is the world today" and "derivative of something from somewhere" (Jarman, personal communication, March 19, 2007). When opportunity arises, people can "mongrelize tools and make them into our own"; the nexus between the arts and technology is an "experimental space … where we can experiment with old *and* new tools." Because the global concept is a "middle class, middle ground thing," it misses the "fringes" and the risk takers. In contrast, cultural activists and "hacktivists" are producing tools for "diverse, much smaller, much more dispersed groups," tools that will enable them to "plug into" the mainstream so that "their voices can be heard, [so] that their expression can be represented, in the global space" (Jarman, personal communication, March 19, 2007). By extension, a critical mass of cultural production emanating from the "margins" is creating an emergent "ourstream," and eventually "ourstream" will become the mainstream (Jarman, personal communication, March 29, 2010).

Commodification, however, is not necessarily a bad thing—especially when independent creative producers guide the circumstances of exchanges. Commercial success in which nodes from the global south set up the terms of exchange with nodes in the north could bring much-needed finances into impoverished communities and benefit many. In 2004 there was "very little creative technology … outside of the corporate landscape in Jamaica," despite it's being "one of the loudest cultural producers of the last 40 years. We want to hot-wire Jamaica into the machine that will make the Upsetters of the future" (Mute, 2004, para. 1). In 2010 fledgling nodes of cultural production, especially in the field of music, were springing up where the Container had planted workshop seeds. The result is that people are making "very innovative beats" where previously they "just listened" (Jarman, personal communication, March 29, 2010). By sharing their music and music video productions on social networking Internet sites, some of these young musicians and mix artists are already tapping into global circuits of exchange.

Future Directions

Long-term sustainability poses a major challenge for the Container Project. Because Jamaica has no dedicated arts-funding agency, core funding from government is not an option. UNESCO has sponsored some specific Container initiatives, but its charter does not permit ongoing funding for any one project. Overcoming institutional prejudices is a significant issue when fund-raising in Jamaica, and the stigma of the Container Project's location in Palmers Cross has forced the community to make extra efforts in order to ensure that the project is taken seriously. The magnetism experienced by the clients of the Container is not in question; the problem is how to sustain it and transfer it in a viable way (Jarman & Mills, 2007, p. 88).

Another challenge is the sustainability of the project's human resources. The community of Palmers Cross is reluctant to let Jarman go, for he has been instrumental to the local social changes that have occurred. Yet as long as community members expect him to shoulder the lion's share of responsibility, the project will not experience the full benefits returned by the network form of self-organization. Although the Container Project's media lab in Palmers Cross is basically self-managed, the responsibility of coordinating workshops, training programs, exchanges, and initiating regional iStreet Labs and residencies still rests with Jarman. Consequently, Jarman can extricate himself only "when everyone sees and understands that they are the ones who have the power" (Turner, personal communication, August 6, 2007).

In essence, the Container is a "social enterprise" in which people can unite "to market their products and services and to find creative ways to sustain their community" (Turner, personal communication, August 6, 2007). In 2010 a "new generation of Container people" was scheduled to come through Palmers Cross and other workshop locations around Jamaica. These young people "have purpose, direction, know what they want to learn, and to do with that learning" (Jarman, personal communication, March 28, 2010). The Container's success has relied heavily on Jarman's active participation, but new initiatives such as the iStreet Lab empower participants to adapt and manage such projects themselves and in their own communities. As the now mostly service-driven Container in Palmers Cross soon could be economically viable, Jarman is guiding new recruits to take increased responsibility as he approaches the exit. The core team is implementing programs to strengthen the operations of the project in the "final chapter in the teaching and learning stage" (Jarman, personal communication, March 20, 2010).

CONCLUSION

The *global digital divide* is a catchy phrase evoking uncomplicated images of class, nationality, and technology. It fails, however, to capture the complexities of techno-social relations in a globalized world. Interchanges typically occur between dominant nodes in networks (financial/human/mechanical configurations of an info-cultural elite who might be in the global north, south, or periphery) and subordinated nodes (configurations of an info-social deprived, through economic or geopolitical circumstances, similarly emplaced anywhere in the world). But, in fact, there is no divide; rather, there are uneven rates, directions, and material consequences of global information flows.

Participatory globalization offers an alternative framework for considering emergent network-based forms of social organization. Interlinking nodes (individuals, groups, and sub- and meta-networks) are actively engaged in creative cooperative labor across a global field. This biopolitical labor is facilitated by the exponential advances in ICTs and increased access for those who can afford to buy into techno-globalism. New kinds of social relations, political agency, and collective imaginaries compose this field of activity.

Distributed forms of collaborative cultural production signal a return to liberatory praxis from earlier periods of social struggle. For example, feminism's construct of "the personal is political" now mutates to "the interpersonal is political" and envelops many areas of contestation. Technologically assisted forms of communication and work shared via networks are generating new political subjectivities and avenues for agency. The mongrelized multitudes—poor-to-poor becoming peer-to-peer—are building new social relations.

The Container Project in Jamaica is a spatial example of participatory globalization. It combines the technological (digital and analog media tools) with the sociopolitical (radical pedagogies and localized social change) and the symbolic (production of imagination via the arts). Embedded in a rural community marked by poverty, deprivation, and hopelessness, the project draws strength from historical Jamaican social movements and taps into global networks for reciprocal exchanges. A process of recodalisation is set in motion as people put themselves—materially and symbolically—into the global flows that animate network society in the postindustrial era.

The Container can be more broadly considered a social-media ecosystem. Examination of its component parts and processes reveals an open and adaptable system. In naming its struggle—against the perpetuation of marginalization, poverty, and inequity—and its visible successes, the project is inspiring other deprived communities to develop their own culturally attuned projects for transformation within the context of globalization. Such projects can operate on the symbolic and speculative planes and become one more seed added to a global seed bank for the production of new social imaginaries. For it is, in essence, on the immaterial level of the individual and collective imagination that the conditions for material emancipatory social change across the world's many divides must first be prepared.

ENDNOTES

1. The ideas of Michael Hardt and Antonio Negri (2004) have shaped my conceptualization of participatory globalization through their identification of a new political subject they term the *multitude*. Likewise, Terranova (2004) and Virno (2004) have illuminated related concepts of immaterial labor, intellectual virtuosity, and "biopolitical production" in the post-Fordist era.
2. The Container Project's founder, mervin Jarman, requests that his name be rendered *mervin*. The small *m* indicates his "commonness" and his refusal to subscribe to the notion he is "somehow special and different from the others—the other good for nothing wasters mostly described as good for nothing" (m. Jarman, personal communication, March 20, 2010).
3. All quotes from Camille Turner in this chapter, unless otherwise stated, are derived from my records of her public talks and workshops as part of the Coding Cultures Project in Australia in March 2007, and from our informal discussions and e-mail interviews in August 2007.
4. Although Linker is now unsupported by Mongrel, and Mongrel itself has disbanded, the software and help manual remain downloadable from http://linker.mongrel.org.uk/Linker/download.html.
5. The Temporary Autonomous Zone (TAZ) is a concept developed in a seminal book by Hakim Bey (1985). The concept has been enacted in diverse material (and electronic) forms by various subcultures, especially those within media arts and activist domains.
6. *Rastafari* refers to the broad phenomenon, whereas *Rastafarianism* refers to the phenomenon's religious expression. The word *Rasta* can signify either someone who identifies with Rastafari or someone who identifies as being a Rastafarian religious follower.
7. Prior to his coronation in November 1930, the emperor had been Prince Ras Tafari. In the Ethiopian Semitic language, Amharic *Ras* means prince, lord, or duke.
8. One distinguishing feature of the Dyne:bolic LiveCD distribution of the GNU/Linux operating system and multimedia and streaming tools is its optimization for very basic or "ancient" hardware systems. Jaromil has consulted with users based in extreme situations in Palestine and Africa, and their feedback has shaped the software's development accordingly. The operating system is "optimized to run on slower computers, turning them into full media stations: the minimum you need is a Pentium1 or

k5 PC 64Mb RAM and IDE CD-ROM, or a modded XBOX game console" (Jaromil, dyne:bolic, retrieved 3 February, 2010, from http://www.dynebolic.org).

9. Digital stories produced are online at LaFontaine & Turner (2006). Container Project stories retrieved Aprill 10, 2010, from http://www.thestoryproject.ca/container_stories/index.html. See also LaFontaine (2006) and Turner (2006).

REFERENCES

Analog. (2010). *Merriam-Webster's online dictionary* (11th ed.). Retrieved April 9, 2010, from http://www.merriam-webster.com/dictionary/analog.

Appadurai, A. (2000). Grassroots globalization and the research imagination. *Public Culture, 12*(1), 1–19.

Bey, H. (1985). T.A.Z.: The temporary autonomous zone, ontological anarchy, poetic terrorism. New York, NY: Autonomedia. Retrieved January 31, 2009, from www.hermetic.com/bey/taz_cont.html.

Castells, M. (2006). The network society: From knowledge to policy. In M. Castells & G. Cardoso (Eds.), *The network society: From knowledge to policy* (pp. 3–21). Washington, DC: Center for Transatlantic Relations.

Chevannes, B. (1998). Introducing the native religions of Jamaica. In B. Chevannes (Ed.), *Rastafari and other African-Caribbean worldviews* (pp. 1–19). New Brunswick, NJ: Rutgers University Press.

Digital. (2010). *Merriam-Webster's online dictionary* (11th ed.). Retrieved April 9, 2010, from http://www.merriam-webster.com/dictionary/digital.

Edmonds, E. B. (2003). Rastafari: From outcasts to culture bearers. Retrieved February 4, 2010, from http://dx.doi.org/10.1093/0195133765.001.0001.

Fuller, M. (1999a, June 22). mervin Jarman—The Container. Retrieved January 7, 2005, from http://www.nettime.org/Lists-Archives/nettime-l-9906/msg00138.html.

Fuller, M. (1999b, Summer). Tun yuh hand and meck fashion. *The Container Project, 2*(8). Retrieved April 2, 2010, from http://www.variant.org.uk/8texts/Container.html.

Fuller, M. (1999c, September 27). *Linker*. Retrieved August 3, 2007, from http://www.nettime.org/Lists Archives/nettime-l-9909/msg00154.html.

Fuller, M. (2005). Matthew Fuller: Interview by Simon Mills. Retrieved August 3, 2007, from http://www.framejournal.net/interview/5/matthew-fuller.

George, S. (2004). *Another world is possible if....* New York, NY: Verso.

Gilroy, P. (1991). *There ain't no black in the Union Jack: The cultural politics of race and nation.* Chicago, IL: University of Chicago Press.

Hardt, M., & Negri, A. (2004). *Multitude: War and democracy in the age of empire.* New York, NY: Penguin Books.

Hill, O. (Writer). (2005). *Coping with Babylon: The proper Rastology* [DVD]. Produced by Sonerito.

Jarman, m. (2003). The Container Project: Repatriating technology. Retrieved July 3, 2010, from http://www.container-project.net/C-Web/project.html.

Jarman, m. (2004). *The Container Project: 2003–2004*. Retrieved January 21, 2010, from http://www.container-project.net/C-Web/publications/booklet-pages.pdf.

Jarman, m. (2010). iStreet Lab: Corners transformation and youth development. Retrieved March 7, 2010, from http://istreetlab.ning.com.

Jarman, m., & Mills, S. (2007). Mongrelstreet: The culture of codes. In F. da Rimini (Ed.), *A handbook for coding cultures* (pp. 87–95). Sydney, Australia: d/Lux Media Arts & Campbelltown City Council.

Jarman, m., & Pierre-Davis, R. (2009). iStreet Lab information pack. Retrieved April 3, 2010, from http://www.mongrelstreet.org/iStreet.html.

Jaromil. (n.d.). This is Rasta software. Retrieved November 13, 2005, from http://dynebolic.org/manual-in-development/dynebolic-x44.en.html.

LaFontaine, J. (2006). The Container Project. Retrieved July 23, 2007, from http://www.cnh.on.ca/spring%202006%20cnh.newsletter.pdf.

LaFontaine, J., & Turner, C. (2006). Container Project stories. Retrieved April 10, 2010, from http://www.thestoryproject.ca/container_stories/index.html.

May, C. (2002). *The information society: A sceptical view.* Cambridge, UK: Polity Press.

Medosch, A. (2003, November 19). London.Zip – Digital media arts in London. Retrieved January 31, 2009, from http://www.nettime.org/Lists-Archives/nettime-l-0311/msg00042.html.

Medosch, A. (2005). Roots culture: Free software vibrations "inna Babylon." In M. Narula, S. Sengupta, J. Bagchi, & G. Lovink (Eds.), *Sarai reader 2005: Bare acts* (pp. 222–239). Delhi, India: Sarai.

Murphy, X. (2007, June 22). *The Container Project Jamaica.* Retrieved August 7, 2007, from http://www.jamaicans.com/articles/primeinterviews/interviewcontainerproject.shtml.

Mute. (2004, January 12). Hot-wire Jamaica. Retrieved August 23, 2007, from http://www.metamute.org/en/Hot-Wire-Jamaica.

Report of the National Committee on Crime and Violence. (2002). Kingston, Jamaica.

Report of the National Committee on Political Tribalism. (1997). Kingston, Jamaica.

Ruxton, J. (2008, July 22, 2008). Second life in Cross. Retrieved July 26, 2011, from http://web.archive.org/web/20090121053826/http://thecontainerproject.ning.com/profiles/blogs/2166702:BlogPost:495.

Terranova, T. (2004). *Network culture: Politics for the information age.* London, UK: Pluto Press.

This is Rasta software. (n.d.). Retrieved October 10, 2010, from http://rastasoft.org/resistance.txt.

Turner, C. (2006). Container Project blog. Retrieved January 8, 2010, from http://www.year01.com/containerproject/blog.html.

United Nations Educational, Scientific, and Cultural Organization [UNESCO]. (2004, June 16). Self-evaluation tool now available for community media projects in the Caribbean. Retrieved January 31, 2009, from http://portal.unesco.org/ci/en/ev.php-URL_ID=16022&URL_DO=DO_PRINTPAGE&URL_SECTION=201.html.

Virno, P. (2004). *A grammar of the multitude: For an analysis of contemporary forms of life*. Los Angeles, CA / New York, NY: Semiotext(e).

Williams, E. (1966). *Capitalism and slavery*. New York, NY: Capricorn Books.

Witness. (n.d.). Retrieved January 10, 2010, from http://witness.org.

CHAPTER 6

THE WEB PRESENCE OF EUROPEAN AND MIDDLE EASTERN COUNTRIES

A DIGITAL DIVIDE

Alireza Noruzi

This chapter investigates the Web presence of European and Middle Eastern countries by focusing on how specific features (e.g., Internet access, language, number of Internet users, and literacy) influence the Web presence of different cultures. The study presented here indicates that European countries, especially the United Kingdom, Germany, and France, have the highest international Web presence, whereas Middle Eastern countries—apart from the exceptions of Israel, Iran, and Saudi Arabia—have the lowest international Web presence. The study also reveals that countries with populations generally literate in information and communication technologies (ICT) and with broadband (high-speed) Internet access (e.g., the United Kingdom, Germany, and France) also have a stronger international Web presence than those that do not.

INTRODUCTION

In the age of global digital information, individuals unable to access the Internet through the application of information and communication technologies (ICTs) are increasingly disadvantaged in their access to information (Cullen, 2001). Yet the Web is an unprecedented medium in which anyone can publish his or her ideas. The Web is also a reflection of human culture: It is a massive sociocultural network of resources authored by millions of people and organizations around the world. Overall, "the Web displays a striking 'rich get richer' behavior, with a relatively small number of countries having a disproportionately large number of websites and pages and share of hyperlink references and traffic" (Pennock, Flake, Lawrence, Glover, & Giles, 2002, p. 5207). Countries with a higher number of Internet users publish more Web pages in general on any given topic than do countries with limited access to the Internet. The results of the research reported here have important implications about who speaks and who is heard—or which cultures speak and which cultures are heard—in this age of the global Internet. These results, moreover, provide an important perspective on the forces and factors contributing to the global digital divide.

ACCESS AND THE GLOBAL DIGITAL DIVIDE

Digital divide is a generic term used to describe the extreme differences in access levels to ICTs (such as computers and the Internet) because of linguistic, sociocultural, political, educational, economic, and geographic factors. From an Internet user's point of view, the digital divide is a gap between those who have ready access to the Internet and make effective use of it as a communications and information medium and those without such access or skills. Such distinctions are important, for a particular concern exists that ICTs could exacerbate existing inequalities. For example, former World Bank president James Wolfensohn (2000) has stressed the need to bridge the technological gap between rich and poor nations. According to Wolfensohn, "the digital divide is one of the greatest impediments to development, and it is growing exponentially" (Norris, 2003, p. 40). From this perspective, the global digital divide becomes a matter of information and access. That is, the global division of the Internet becomes a matter of distinguishing those who have digital information to share globally and those who do not (Gil de Zúñiga, 2006).

Following the enlargement of the European Union (EU) from 15 to 25 member states in 2004, the digital divide in the EU widened substantially; national Internet connectivity across member states varied from less than 10% to more than 90%. This disparity in Internet access across member states should continue to increase as more developing nations of Eastern Europe join the EU. Such a situation will likely bring problems associated with communication, dissemination of information, and the economy (e-commerce) that arise from national and regional disparities in technological infrastructure and from a range of cultural and psychological factors (Hubregtse, 2005). Internet access and use are important information resources, and inequality in Internet access is thus a significant concern for all countries. For geopolitical and economic units such as the EU, consistent and uniform access across all member nations becomes a central consideration in governance. In this case, the key question is whether all member states have easy and ready access to the various online materials essential for a uniform understanding of EU policy and its implementation. It is necessary to examine and answer such questions now in order to prevent a widening of the digital divide within the EU, and timing is of the essence. The more nations merge into political or economic blocs, the more important equal online access will be to the uniform information sharing needed to manage such blocs effectively.

WEB PRESENCE AND WEBOMETRIC STUDIES

Web presence evaluation is an important part of Webometric research, which studies the online presence of different countries. Webometric studies display several similarities to informetric and scientometric studies and use bibliometric methods to gather data (Almind & Ingwersen, 1997). For example, simple counts and content analyses of Web pages are like traditional publication analysis; counts and analyses of outlinks (outgoing links from Web resources) can be seen as references, and inlinks (backlinks pointing to Web resources) can be seen as citation analysis. Webometric studies of the structures, content, and link structures of Websites in various countries are therefore important to an understanding of the international virtual highway and interconnections between countries. Web presence studies, in turn, provide quantitative tools for ranking, evaluating, categorizing, and comparing Websites, top-level domains, and second-level domains. According to this approach, a country with a large number of Internet users and Internet content providers would have a high-level Web presence.

One of the most convenient ways of measuring countries' Web presence is to use the advanced search facilities of large-scale search engines; indeed, studies have been carried out using Yahoo's search facilities (Noruzi, 2006a; Noruzi, 2006b). In this context, Web presence evaluation can be a useful measure of the overall presence of a country on the global Internet. Researchers use the number of Web pages published by the given country to assess that country's online presence. Individuals can then use the results of Web presence studies to determine how much presence a given country has in international cyberspace. By comparing the online presence of different countries, researchers can also determine the relative extent of a global digital divide between rich and poor countries.

The study presented in this chapter examines how such factors help determine which nations and cultures have the greatest Web presence. This study also reveals the ways recent geopolitical developments are affecting national and cultural presence in global online environments. The primary aim of this research is to evaluate the Web presence of different countries at country code top-level domain (ccTLD) levels. More specifically, the objectives of the study are as follows:

- To compare the Web presence of all the European countries
- To compare the Web presence of all the Middle Eastern countries
- To show the number of Web pages from these countries indexed by Google
- To show the relationship between the literacy rate and the number of Internet users
- To measure the scope of the digital divide between Middle Eastern and European countries

This research helps ascertain which nations and cultures seem to have the greatest presence on the Web and thus exert control over the international online environment. The information presented here can shed light on the dynamics of the global digital divide. It should be noted that as a Middle Easterner living in Europe, I was particularly interested in comparing these two regions; this interest prompted me to select the countries in these two regions for this study.

Web-Address Structure

Web addresses are hierarchical in structure. This hierarchy has its origin in the domain name system (DNS) that governs the configuration of the uniform resource locator (URL) used as a location or address for posting online information. The DNS translates the plain English address (e.g., www.ox.ac.uk) into a corresponding numeric IP address (e.g., 129.67.1.190). From left to right, the domain name structure increases in hierarchy from host level (site domain) to second level to top level. The following is the hierarchy for the example ox.ac.uk:

- Top-level domain for the United Kingdom (.uk)
- Second-level domain for academic sites under the U.K. domain (.ac)
- Host-level domain for Oxford University (ox)

The ccTLD allotted for each country in accordance with two-letter codes is based on ISO-3166 (e.g., .uk for United Kingdom, .fr for France, .de for Germany). The ccTLD for each country in this study is outlined in tables 6.1 and 6.2.

METHODOLOGY

Before examining the degree of online presence different nations can have, it is important first to understand how to collect data about the number of Web pages under any given top-level domain. In general, large-scale search engines are used for collecting such data. Most of the well-known search engines offer special commands to search for matches in Web elements such as pages, domains, and links. Google and Yahoo are currently the most widely used search engines.

In this study, Google was used to collect data for comparison at different levels. This study's data-collection method extensively used the special command *site:* to collect the total number of Web pages per ccTLD domain from Google. The search engine reports the number of Web pages retrieved against each search. For example, site:uk/ will find the number of pages under the .uk domain indexed by the Google search engine. Google also provides a quantitative tool for ranking and evaluating top-level and second-level domains. It can compare the Web presence of second-level domains under .uk domain (ac.uk/, org.uk/, co.uk/, net.uk/, gov.uk/, etc.)—for instance, site:ac.uk/.

The number of Web pages under ccTLDs of European and Middle Eastern countries was counted using the Google search engine. Data collection took place on October 25, 2009. All the domain names were searched to ascertain whether Google includes these ccTLDs. A search was then carried out to determine the total number of Web pages in each country's domain.

At this point, it should be noted that a Webometric study, in general, represents a "snapshot" taken at a key point in the history of the Web. This is the reason why a one-day period was used; different time frames might have yielded different results. Although results can vary somewhat on a short-term basis, overall trends or patterns in Web use at one time can generally be effective indicators of trends that persist for longer periods. A one-day snapshot, for example, might note that the number of French Websites online is exponentially larger than the number for Albania. The exact number of Websites for each nation might change on a daily basis, but the more general trend that the number of French Websites available is markedly larger than the number of Albanian Websites will likely not change significantly over longer periods (e.g., weeks, months, or even years).

Findings

Table 6.1 displays Internet-user statistics and population for 53 European countries and regions; table 6.2 shows Middle East Internet usage and population statistics.

Table 6.3 shows that only 28.13% of Middle Eastern users have access to the Internet, compared to 51.47% of European users. It is worth noting that the literacy rates of the European countries studied are 14% higher than those of the Middle Eastern countries studied.

Data Analysis

The data obtained from various search statements according to the methodology already described are displayed in tables 6.1 and 6.2. The Web presence of each country has been shown at ccTLD level, and is determined by considering all the Web pages that originate in each country.

In European countries, Pearson correlation coefficients indicate a significant correlation at the 0.886 level between the number of Internet users and the number of Web pages. Thus the Web presence of each European country is positively related to the number of Internet users and the number of Web pages for that nation. In other words, European countries with a higher number of Internet users tended to enjoy higher visibility on the Web. This research also reveals that there is not a significant correlation between the number of Internet users in a given nation

TABLE 6.1. Web presence of European countries.

Europe	ccTLD	No. of Web Pages*	Population (2009 Est.)†	Internet Users, Latest Data†	% Population (Penetration)†	Literacy‡
Albania	.al	3,040,000	3,639,453	580,000	15.9 %	98.7%
Andorra	.ad	4,100,000	83,888	70,040	83.5 %	100%
Austria	.at	933,000,000	8,210,281	5,601,700	68.2 %	98%
Belarus	.by	112,000,000	9,648,533	2,809,800	29.1 %	99.6%
Belgium	.be	958,000,000	10,414,336	7,006,400	67.3 %	99%
Bosnia-Herzegovina	.ba	32,100,000	4,613,414	1,441,000	31.2 %	96.7%
Bulgaria	.bg	228,000,000	7,204,687	2,368,000	32.9 %	98.2%
Croatia	.hr	174,000,000	4,489,409	2,244,400	50.0 %	98.1%
Cyprus	.cy	5,750,000	1,084,748	324,880	29.9 %	97.6%
Czech Republic	.cz	1,350,000,000	10,211,904	4,991,300	48.9 %	99%
Denmark	.dk	619,000,000	5,500,510	4,629,600	84.2 %	99%
Estonia	.ee	25,000,000	1,299,371	854,600	65.8 %	99.8%
Faroe Islands	.fo	3,430,000	48,856	37,500	76.8 %	99%
Finland	.fi	489,000,000	5,250,275	4,353,142	82.9 %	100%
France	.fr	2,910,000,000	62,150,775	42,050,465	67.7 %	99%
Germany	.de	8,860,000,000	82,329,758	55,221,183	67.1 %	99%
Gibraltar	.gi	840,000	28,796	9,853	34.2 %	80%
Greece	.gr	341,000,000	10,737,428	4,932,495	45.9 %	96%
Guernsey & Alderney	.gg	2,100,000	65,484	36,000	55.0 %	**NA**
Hungary	.hu	966,000,000	9,905,596	5,500,000	55.5 %	99.4%

Iceland	.is	130,000,000	306,694	273,930	89.3 %	99%
Ireland	.ie	265,000,000	4,203,200	2,830,100	67.3 %	99 %
Italy	.it	2,540,000,000	58,126,212	29,140,144	50.1 %	98.4%
Jersey	.je	9,280,000	91,626	28,500	31.1 %	**NA**
Kosovo	NA	NA	1,804,838	377,000	20.9 %	91.9%
Latvia	.lv	332,000,000	2,231,503	1,324,800	59.4 %	99.7%
Liechtenstein	.li	14,200,000	34,761	23,000	66.2 %	100%
Lithuania	.lt	273,000,000	3,555,179	2,103,471	59.2 %	99.6%
Luxembourg	.lu	34,500,000	491,775	363,900	74.0 %	100%
Macedonia	.mk	35,200,000	2,066,718	906,979	43.9 %	96.[illegible]%
Malta	.mt	3,440,000	405,165	200,200	49.4 %	92.8%
Man, Isle of	.im	4,030,000	76,512	**NA**	**NA**	NA
Moldova	.md	39,200,000	4,320,748	700,000	16.2 %	99.1%
Monaco	.mc	1,390,000	32,965	20,000	60.7 %	99%
Montenegro	.me	45,700,000	672,180	280,000	41.7 %	96%
Netherlands	.nl	2,300,000,000	16,715,999	14,272,700	85.4 %	99%
Norway	.no	538,000,000	4,660,539	3,993,400	85.7 %	100%
Poland	.pl	3,860,000,000	38,482,919	20,020,362	52.0 %	99.8%
Portugal	.pt	389,000,000	10,707,924	4,450,800	41.6 %	93.3%
Romania	.ro	882,000,000	22,215,421	7,430,000	33.4 %	97.3%
Russia	.ru	4,110,000,000	140,041,247	38,000,000	27.1 %	99.4%

(*continued on next page*)

TABLE 6.1. *(continued)*

Europe	ccTLD	No. of Web Pages*	Population (2009 Est.)†	Internet Users, Latest Data†	% Population (Penetration)†	Literacy‡
San Marino	.sm	2,960,000	30,167	16,000	53.0 %	96%
Serbia	.rs	57,800,000	7,379,339	2,602,478	35.3 %	96.4%
Slovakia	.sk	473,000,000	5,463,046	3,018,400	55.3 %	99.6%
Slovenia	.si	134,000,000	2,005,692	1,300,000	64.8 %	99.7%
Spain	.es	1,350,000,000	40,525,002	28,628,959	70.6 %	98.7%
Svalbard & Jan Mayen	.sj	0	2,198	**NA**	–	**NA**
Sweden	.se	1,060,000,000	9,059,651	7,295,200	80.5 %	99%
Switzerland	.ch	1,160,000,000	7,604,467	5,762,700	75.8 %	99%
Turkey	**.tr**	284,000,000	76,805,524	26,500,000	34.5 %	87.4%
Ukraine	.ua	740,000,000	45,700,395	6,700,000	14.7 %	99.4%
United Kingdom	.uk	4,330,000,000	61,113,205	48,755,000	79.8 %	99%
Vatican City State	.va	185,000	545	93	17.1 %	100%
TOTAL		**43,414,245,000**	**803,850,858**	**402,380,474**	**51.47 %**	**97.16 %**

* *Source.* Google.com (2009).
† *Source.* Internet World Stats (2009).
‡ *Source.* CIA (2009).

TABLE 6.2. Web presence of Middle Eastern countries.

Middle East	ccTLD	No. of Web Pages*	Population (2009 Est.)†	Internet Users, Latest Data†	% Population (Penetration)†	Literacy‡
Bahrain	.bh	5,700,000	728,709	250,000	34.3 %	86.5%
Iran	.ir	99,200,000	66,429,284	23,000,000	34.6 %	77.4%
Iraq	.iq	99,600	28,945,569	275,000	1.0 %	74.1%
Israel	.il	437,000,000	7,233,701	5,263,146	72.8 %	97.1%
Jordan	.jo	4,110,000	6,269,285	1,500,500	23.9 %	89.9%
Kuwait	.kw	10,900,000	2,692,526	900,000	33.4 %	93.3%
Lebanon	.lb	4,090,000	4,017,095	1,570,000	39.1 %	87.4%
Oman	.om	3,450,000	3,418,085	469,000	13.7 %	81.4%
Palestine	.ps	12,200,000	2,461,267	355,500	14.4 %	89.8%
Qatar	. qa	4,630,000	833,285	436,000	52.3 %	89.0%
Saudi Arabia	.sa	37,000,000	28,686,633	7,200,000	25.1 %	78.8%
Syria	. sy	3,150,000	21,762,978	3,565,000	16.4 %	79.6%
United Arab Emirates	. ae	29,700,000	4,798,491	2,860,000	59.6 %	77.9%
Yemen	.ye	248,000	22,858,238	320,000	1.4 %	50.2%
Gaza Strip	NA	NA	1,551,859	**356,000 ‡**	**NA**	**92.4**
TOTAL		**651,477,600**	**202,687,005**	**47,964,146**	**23.7 %**	**82.99 %**

* *Source*. Google.com (2009).
† *Source*. Internet World Stats (2009).
‡ *Source*. CIA (2009).

and the literacy rate of that nation. Furthermore, there is no evidence for a correlation of the number of Web pages for a nation and the literacy rate for that nation.

In Middle Eastern countries, Pearson correlation coefficients at the 0.314 level point to a weak, not significant positive correlation between the number of Internet users and the number of Web pages. No correlation was observed between the number of Web pages and the literacy rate. In conducting this research, I found no significant correlation (at the 0.314 level) between the number of Internet users and the literacy rate.

RESULTS

Table 6.1 and figure 6.1 show that Germany, the United Kingdom, and France have the highest number of Internet users for European nations, whereas figure 6.2 shows that Germany, the United Kingdom, and Russia have the highest number of Web pages among European countries. Table 6.1 also highlights a fundamental divide between the European countries with the most Web presence and the European countries with the least Web presence.

The divide that occurs among the highly populated countries examined (Germany, the United Kingdom, France, Spain, and Italy), moreover, is significant. These results indicate that a sort of digital divide seems to exist even among European countries. The total number of Web pages in the United Kingdom, for example, is 15.2 times higher than that in Turkey (a nation sometimes viewed as a prospective EU member), 12.7 times higher than that in Greece, 4.6 times higher than that in Austria, 3.2 times higher than that in Spain, 1.7 times higher than that in Italy, and 1.5 times higher than that in France. This situation leads to a key question for future research: Does English-language bias affect the Web presence of countries on Google?

Table 6.2 and figures 6.3 and 6.4 show that Iran, Israel, and Saudi Arabia have the highest number of Internet users and Web pages among the Middle Eastern countries studied. The greater the number of Web

FIGURE 6.1. European countries with the highest number of Internet users.

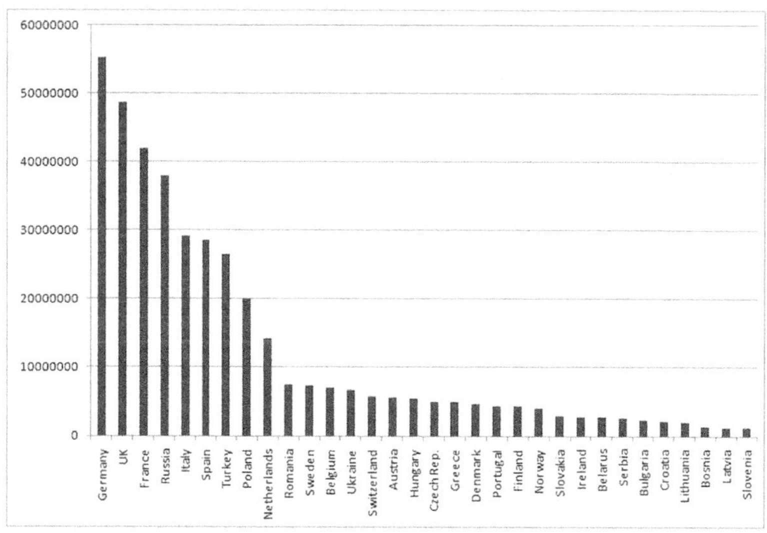

FIGURE 6.2. European countries with the highest number of Web pages.

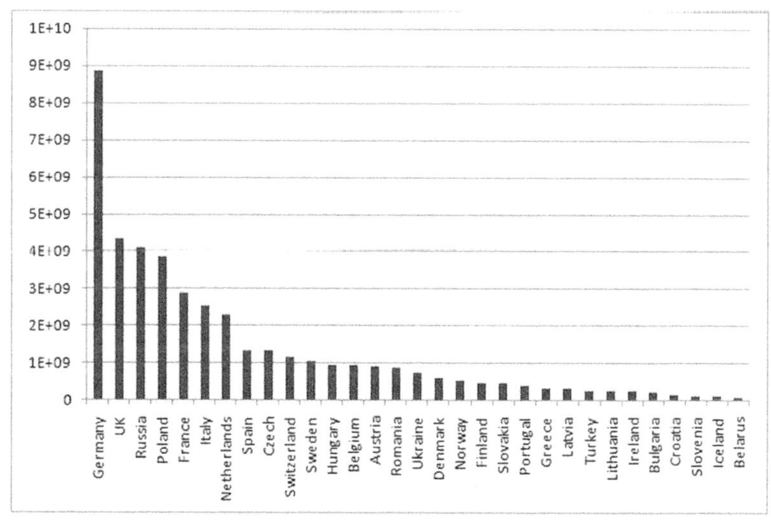

FIGURE 6.3. Middle Eastern countries with the highest number of Internet users.

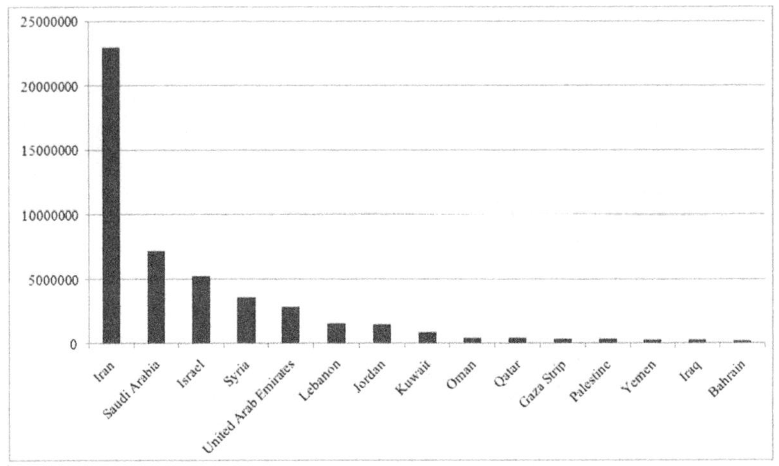

FIGURE 6.4. Middle Eastern countries with the highest number of Web pages.

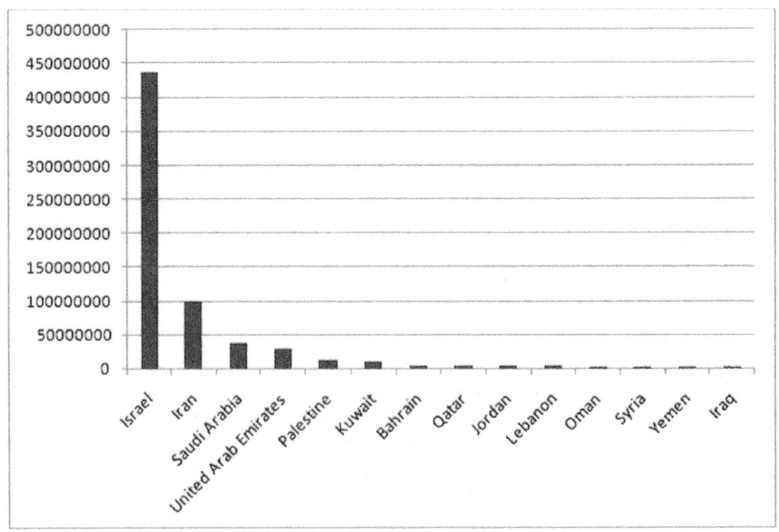

TABLE 6.3. Internet usage statistics in Europe and the Middle East.

Regions	No. of Web Pages	Population (2009 Est.)	Internet Users, Latest Data	% Population (Penetration)	Literacy‡
Europe	43,414,245,000	803,850,858	402,380,474	51.47 %	97.16 %
Middle East	651,477,600	202,687,005	48,320,146	28.13 %	82.99 %

pages associated with a particular nation, the greater the country's Web presence.

Percentages of population penetration (seen in column 6 of table 6.1) show that Iceland (89.3%), Norway (85.7%), and the Netherlands (85.4%) have the highest percentages of Internet users. The population-based penetration rate (column 6 of table 6.2), however, shows that Israel (72.8%), United Arab Emirates (59.6%), and Qatar (52.3%) have the highest percentages of Internet users. In other words, a high number of Internet users does not necessarily translate into a high number of Web pages. Other factors should be taken into account, including the Internet-using culture of a nation, the information and communications infrastructure in a region, ICT literacy, research literacy, and writing culture. Each of these factors would be a legitimate subject for further (and much-needed) research on this topic area and on the global digital divide in general.

Finally, tables 6.1 and 6.2 show that European and Middle Eastern countries with a higher number of Internet users have a higher Web presence. In sum, the more access users from a given country have to the Internet, the greater that country's Web presence will be. In addition, results displayed in table 6.3 suggest that Middle Eastern Internet access and usage is somewhat limited; thus there is a digital divide between Europe and the Middle East.

DISCUSSION

Search engines are the primary data-gathering instruments in Web presence studies. However, they are designed for content retrieval and not the analysis of Web presence. Despite the recognition that Web presence evaluation based on search engines is an imperfect measuring tool, there is no obvious alternative. Thus researchers forced to use search engines for direct Web presence comparison should be open minded, cautious, and aware of the inherent limitations of search engine use.

Moreover, a Web presence study is a "snapshot" of a search engine database at a specific time. Comparisons should be performed with caution and preferably be carried out within the same snapshot, for Web presence varies across different snapshots taken even at closely spaced intervals. A retrospective Web presence study is not reproducible, for it depends on the dynamics (expansion or contraction) of Websites (Noruzi, 2006b), and the Web is a growing organism.

The challenge of the global digital divide as manifest on the Web relates to the core of the Internet's mission to provide equitable access to information for all users regardless of language, ethnic group, religion, social class, sex, age, or any other factor. Every cybercitizen has a right to information (Noruzi, 2004). Previous studies show that geographical, sociocultural, and psychological factors (e.g., race, age, gender, education, ICT literacy, income) play a crucial role in determining a person's degree of Internet access, even if such factors vary depending on the country examined. In fact, in countries where Internet access and use are limited, the digital divide will be fostered and exacerbated, and its progress perhaps accelerated (Gil de Zúñiga, 2006).

CONCLUSION

The study presented here confirms the hypothesis that, in general, countries with a higher number of Internet users publish more Web pages than countries with a limited number of Internet users. The results also show that, generally, Middle Eastern countries have a limited Web presence in comparison to European nations. This comparison raises interesting questions about the place of different countries, cultures, and languages on the Web. In terms of prospective global impact—particularly impact beyond the borders of a particular nation—these Middle Eastern countries are outside the Web's mainstream, which is dominated by the United States, the United Kingdom, Europe, Canada, and Australia. It thus appears that Middle Eastern countries might have a more limited presence on the Web *because* they are outside the current mainstream of the Internet. The current global digital divide is therefore a warning to cybercitizens; it shows that the Internet has not yet provided equal access to information for all cultures, nations, or individuals.

Overall, one can conclude that because of the relatively limited Internet access and resultant limited Web presence of various Middle Eastern and European countries, an international digital divide exists. To address this situation, developing countries and developed countries with limited access to the Internet should facilitate Internet access for their citizens. The ready access to the Internet available in European countries (e.g., the United Kingdom, Norway, the Netherlands, Germany, and France) might be one of the main reasons for the high Web presence of European countries and their cultures on the Internet. Therefore, easier access to ICTs in Middle Eastern countries might help increase their international Web presence.

Further research is needed for a better understanding of the nature of search engines. In-depth studies might also be necessary in order to identify reasons for the limited number of Middle Eastern Web pages—in particular, researchers might consider the factors that play a role in Web access in each country (e.g., language, ICT literacy and facilities, and search engine problems with sites in languages other than English). In addition, investigating the Web presence of Asian and African countries and comparing them both to each other and to European and Middle Eastern nations in terms of global Web presence could prove a fruitful line of inquiry.

REFERENCES

Almind, T. C., & Ingwersen, P. (1997). Informetric analyses on the World Wide Web: Methodological approaches to Webometrics. *Journal of Documentation, 53*(4), 404–426.

Central Intelligence Agency. (2009). *The world factbook.* Retrieved October 1, 2010, from http://www.cia.gov/cia/publications/factbook.

Cullen, R. (2001). Addressing the digital divide. *Online Information Review, 25*(5), 311–320.

Gil de Zúñiga, H. (2006). Reshaping digital inequality in the European Union: How psychological barriers affect Internet adoption rates. *Webology, 3*(4), Article 32. Retrieved October 1, 2010, from http://www.webology.org/2006/v3n4/a32.html.

Hubregtse, S. (2005). The digital divide within the European Union. *New Library World, 106*(3/4), 164–172.

Internet World Stats. (2009, October 25). *Internet world stats: Usage and population statistics.* Retrieved October 1, 2010, from http://www.internetworldstats.com.

Norris, P. (2003). *Digital divide: Civic engagement, information poverty, and the Internet worldwide.* Cambridge, MA: Cambridge University Press.

Noruzi, A. (2004). Application of Ranganathan's laws to the Web. *Webology, 1*(2), Article 8. Retrieved October 1, 2010, from http://www.webology.org/2004/v1n2/a8.html.

Noruzi, A. (2006a). Web presence and impact factors for Middle-Eastern countries. *Online Magazine, 30*(2), 22–28.

Noruzi, A. (2006b). The Web impact factor: A critical review. *The Electronic Library, 24*(4), 490–500.

Pennock, D. M., Flake, G. W., Lawrence, S., Glover, E. J., & Giles, C. L. (2002). Winners don't take all: Characterizing the competition for links on the Web. *Proceedings of the National Academy of Sciences, 99*(8), 5207–5211.

Wolfensohn, J. (2000). Interactive debate. United Nations Conference on Trade and Development. Retrieved October 1, 2010, from http://www.unctad.org/en/docs/ux_tdxm11.en.pdf.

CHAPTER 7

THE DIGITAL DIVIDE IN CHINA

SOCIOECONOMIC AND CULTURAL DIMENSIONS

Yun Xia

This study incorporates both socioeconomic and cultural factors in a framework to examine three digital divides within China: users/nonusers, dropouts/users, and veteran users/current users. Socioeconomic and cultural factors were employed to analyze different Internet users and Internet nonusers in China, and the findings reveal that age, gender, income, education, employment, and marital status on the socioeconomic dimension correlate with the digital divides in China. Collectivism, personal relationships, and high-context communication on the cultural dimension are also significantly correlated with these divides. The cultural meanings of Internet users and nonusers examined in this study point to the significance of cultural sources in the complex ecology that is used in scholarly literature to study the concept of the digital divide.

INTRODUCTION

Since 1997 the China Internet Network Information Center (CINIC), the state network information center of China, has released statistical reports on Internet use in China twice a year. According to the 19th report (CINIC, 2007), the total number of Internet users in China was 137 million as of December 2006; this population trails only the United States in size and makes China the second-largest Internet user population in the world. However, the Internet penetration rate in China accounts for only about 7.9% of the country's overall population of 1.3 billion people, whereas the penetration rate in the United States is over 70% (Madden, 2006).

Internet access in China, moreover, is not uniform across the country. China's Guangdong Province, for example, has about 18 million Internet users (the largest Internet user population in a Chinese province), whereas Tibet has the smallest user population, with about 160,000 users. The highest Internet penetration rate in China is about 30% of the local population in Beijing, and the lowest rate is 3.8%, in Guizhou Province.

The enormous disparity in Internet use within China makes the study and understanding of the digital divide critical for the evaluation of Internet adoption in China. In the context of globalization, China's digital divide has shared features with divides in other countries, yet it also maintains uniqueness in a distinctive cultural tradition. In this study, I used a framework of both socioeconomic and cultural dimensions in order to examine Internet use and nonuse, as well as different kinds of Internet use in China.

SOCIOECONOMIC DIMENSIONS OF THE DIGITAL DIVIDE

In the literature, researchers approach the concept of digital divide from different perspectives. As Brock (2005) summarized, the survey reports about Internet use in the United States from the U.S. National Telecommunications and Information Administration (NTIA) focused on computer ownership initially and then made the shift to Internet access.

Access to information and resources in terms of Internet use, as well as access to other new media technologies, has, in turn, become one of the major perspectives in numerous digital divide studies (Cooper & Kimmelman, 1999; Katz & Rice, 2002; Rice & Katz, 2003).

Moving beyond the access perspective, studies have also discussed the digital divide in terms of the relationship between Internet skills and Internet usage (Hargittai, 2002 & 2005; Lenhart, 2003). In addition, special focus has been placed on literacy and education in the evaluation of technology diffusion (Warschauer, 2002, 2003). As Internet diffusion has increased in countries such as the United States, attention has shifted from the digital divide to digital inequality (DiMaggio, Hargittai, Neuman, & Robinson, 2001; Hargittai, 2002; Robinson, DiMaggio, & Hargittai, 2003).

Whether from a perspective of access, diffusion, or inequality, factors such as age, gender, income, education, and employment are key contributors to the digital divide (Katz & Rice, 2002; Katz, Rice, & Aspden, 2001; Miller, 2001; Rice & Katz, 2003). In the study presented here, all these factors compose the socioeconomic dimension of the digital divide. Moreover, this socioeconomic dimension has previously been noted in different national reports. For example, the analysis report from the U.S. National Telecommunications and Information Administration (NTIA, 2002) concludes that the digital divide was no longer a concern in the United States in 2002, and the survey reports from previous years (NTIA, 1999, 2000) consistently attribute the digital divide to factors such as age, income, gender, education, and employment.

Meanwhile, the socioeconomic dimension of the digital divide digital divide in China has been reported consistently. A survey report from the China Internet Network Information Center (CINIC, 2007) indicates 18 to 24 year-olds make up 35% of Internet users, followed by the group aged 25 to 30 years (20%) and the group under 18 years of age (about 17%). In terms of gender, about 58% of Internet users are male, and 41% are female. This difference constitutes roughly a 17 percentage-point gender gap in Internet use in China.

The report also indicates a divide related to education and one related to income. The largest group of Internet users in China has a high school degree (31%); this cohort is roughly 5% larger than the country's second-largest group, which has bachelor's degrees (CINIC, 2007). In terms of income, individuals who make between RMB 500 and 2,000 (about USD $60 to $280) monthly represent approximately 43% of the Internet users in China. Individuals who have a monthly income of less than RMB 500 (about USD $60) account for just over 25% of China's Internet users (CINIC, 2007). In terms of employment and occupation, the largest group of Chinese Internet users is students (about 32%), followed by individuals working as staff members for various enterprises (close to 30%) (CINIC, 2007). Unemployed individuals, in comparison, account for only about 7% of all Internet users in China. Moreover, the CINIC report also shows a divide related to marital status: Close to 59% of China's Internet users are unmarried, whereas 42% of users are married.

CULTURAL DIMENSIONS OF THE DIGITAL DIVIDE

In the study presented here, the theoretical underpinning for the cultural dimension of the digital divide comes from social constructivism of communication technology. Social constructivism holds that social interaction shapes social behavioral patterns regarding technology use (Fulk, 1993; Fulk & Boyd, 1991; MacKenzie & Wajcman, 1985). Through negotiations and struggles among various groups of people, the meanings in people's use of technologies are not only internally constructed but are also redefined in changing social contexts (Barley, 1990; Leonardi, 2003). In Fulk, Schmitz, and Ryu's (1995) discussion, the underlying theme in social constructivism approaches is social interaction that defines the uses and the effects of communication technology. In addition, individuals' attitudes and behaviors tend to converge with those of others in the same social context because of shared symbolic systems and shared interpretive schemes in the interaction process.

Communication technology, including the Internet, is not objective. Social interaction becomes the key to influencing the use of communication technology within the context of a culture because "by nature it is interactive rather than stand-alone technology" (Fulk, Schmitz, & Ryu, 1995, p. 266). Thus, the use of communication technology is shaped by the social interaction it facilitates.

An expansion of the social constructivism perspective is the need to examine communication technology's cultural fit, especially by situating the exploration of communication technology in the context of users' various cultural practices. Culture—the convergence of social, political, and economic contexts—shapes people's expression and drives their social interactions (Brock, 2005). In the research literature, the analysis of the cultural fit of communication technology includes American Latinos' perception and use of the Internet and of mobile phones (e.g., Leonardi, 2003), the impact of values and communication styles on Chinese adoption of mobile phones (e.g., Xia, 2006) and the unique cultural conditions and social interactions in the diffusion of mobile phones in Korea (e.g., Kim, 2002).

Digital divide studies, too, develop the argument to include a cultural dimension in the research framework used to examine the topic. Selwyn (2003), for example, suggested that information and communication technologies (ICTs) cannot be evaluated simply in terms of use and nonuse. Thus it is misleading to base an evaluation of the digital divide on the assumption that access to and use of ICTs is beneficial to every user. In their study of nonusers, Wyatt, Thomas, and Terranova (2002) found that people might deliberately choose not to use the Internet. After identifying four categories of nonuse, the researchers argued that the choice not to use the Internet might not represent a position of disadvantage. More recently, Wyatt, Henwood, Hart, and Smith (2005) argued that much of the digital divide literature focuses exclusively on the "generic or ideal users without examining the everyday practices of people looking for information, and if and how the Internet is inserted into those practices" (p. 203). These authors thus called for more analysis on the day-to-day experiences of users in order to better understand access and the digital divide.

In essence, experiences with technology are driven and shaped by the cultural context in which technology users communicate with each other on a daily basis. Culture, thus, is not about human nature or individual personality; rather, it is a collective mind that makes one group of people different from another in terms of everyday interactions (Hofstede, 1997). With culture as the interaction-driving force, people in some cultures might choose not to use or not to communicate through the Internet.

Moreover, information and communication technologies are not free from cultural values and behaviors. Brock (2005), for example, argued that in examinations of the digital divide, deficiency models, such as the lower skill levels or the higher illiteracy rates of minorities, do not capture the entire picture. After discussing W. E. B. Du Bois's analysis of black and white culture, Brock formulated a cultural framework to evaluate the content (e.g., images, links, and text) of one mainstream U.S. Website and one African American Website. Brock then contended that the ideological dimension of information, as well as required access and necessary technical skills, can block participation of a certain social group. Brock also argued that mainstream Web content in the United States reproduces existing social norms, rules, values, and power relations, and some of this content might be perceived as antagonistic to African American identity, culture, and information needs. Thus African American culture might not be represented in most of today's U.S. cyber-culture. According to this perspective, the perceived cultural irrelevance of sizable amounts of online content might turn African Americans away from using the Internet. Brock's examination of these topics expanded scholars' understanding of the digital divide to include consideration of unique cultural frameworks.

CHINESE CULTURAL VALUES

In this study, I include both socioeconomic and cultural dimensions as a framework for studying the digital divide in China. In order to understand Chinese cultural practices, values, and communication styles, scholars have long turned to the paradigm *individualism versus collectivism*, a central dimension of cultural variability as identified by intercultural communication theorists (Gudykunst & Ting-Toomey, 1988). Individualism emphasizes independence from the groups or organizations to which one belongs. In individualistic cultures, the goals of the individual, self realization, and self-advancement are generally considered more important than the collective good or the good of the group (Hofstede, 1980). Individualistic cultures, thus, place a high degree of value on individual rights and personal autonomy. Collectivistic cultures, by contrast, emphasize solidarity and integration with others and prioritize the needs of the group over the needs of the individual and the self. Being collectivistic, Chinese culture emphasizes belonging to in-groups, personal interdependence, and social harmony (Lu, 1997; Zhang & Oetzel, 2006). Chinese culture also demands that individuals fit into the group, and it prioritizes the common good over individual wishes (Yang, 1994; Zhang & Oetzel, 2006).

Related to the dimension of collectivism are Chinese values concerning smooth and harmonious personal relationships (Yang, 1994). The concept of personal relationship networks summarizes the reliance on harmonious personal relationships in Chinese culture. These personal relationship networks are often encountered when people seek to establish friendships or business partnerships. Connections and contacts are essential to cultivating and maintaining personal relationship networks, and they generally involve the creation of obligation and indebtedness through the exchange of gifts. In personal relationship networks, people are supposed to give, receive, and repay (Yang, 1994).

Aspects of power and status also become important factors in such relationships. Chinese culture is generally classified as a high power distance culture that accepts superior–subordinate relationships as hierarchical (Hofstede, 1980; Zhang & Oetzel, 2006). The idea behind power distance is that inequality exists in any culture, but the degree to which such inequality is accepted varies from culture to culture (Hofstede, 1980). In a high power distance culture, the less powerful individuals view inequality as normal and accept it in the power relationship. China is a high power distance culture, and traditional Chinese cultural values emphasize submission to authority, obedience to superior power, and fitting into social hierarchy (Zhang & Oetzel, 2006). As with the dimension of collectivism,

Chinese culture values harmony in interpersonal relationships. In order to maintain harmony in terms of power and relationships, individuals are expected to respect authority and to learn to fit into the social hierarchy.

In terms of information sharing and information presentation within relationships, Chinese culture is on the high end of what is often called the continuum of high to low context (Hall, 1976). In a high-context culture, most of the information in communication is implicit (Hall, 1976). Meanings are to be inferred from the context in which individuals interact or internalized in the communicators themselves. Low-context cultures, by contrast, use explicit information in the transmission of verbal messages. Because theirs is a high-context culture, the Chinese normally engage in indirect modes of communication and infer unstated meanings from contextual cues.

RESEARCH QUESTIONS

From the intersection of reviewed bodies of literature comes the following research question about the digital divide in China: How do socioeconomic and cultural factors relate to the digital divide in China? To address this question, this study examines the relationship between socioeconomic and cultural factors with respect to the digital divide.

In addition to examining the digital divide, the current study furthers the exploration of how socioeconomic and cultural factors affect Internet use in China. As a part of the World Internet Project started at the University of California at Los Angeles (UCLA), the Research Center for Social Development in the Chinese Academy of Social Sciences (CASS) under the direction of Liang Guo has released survey reports of Internet use in different Chinese cities in 2000, 2003, and 2005. Following the CASS Internet survey report in 2005 (CASS, 2005), the current study includes the 10 most popular Internet activities in China: (a) reading news, (b) general browsing, (c) gaming, (d) downloading music, (e) accessing entertainment information, (f) downloading tools, (g) using search engines, (h) e-mailing, (i) instant messaging (QQ[1]/ICQ), and (j) using chat rooms (IRC/IM).

These patterns of Internet use form the foundation of a second research question about the digital divide in China. How do socioeconomic and cultural factors affect different Internet uses in China? In order to facilitate a better understanding of the digital divide, this study also explores the relationship between socioeconomic and cultural factors and Internet nonuse. The survey reports from CINIC (2005a, 2005b, 2006a, 2006b, 2007) consistently show that the top reasons for not using the Internet in China include (a) lack of necessary skills, (b) lack of facilities or Internet connections, (c) lack of time, (d) lack of demand or belief that Internet is useless, and (e) lack of interest. The top reason for Internet nonuse in China is lack of skills (CINIC, 2007), in contrast to the top reason for Internet nonuse in the United States, lack of need or interest (NTIA, 2004). Following CINIC's 2007 survey report, this study uses skills, access, time, usefulness, and interest to explore Internet nonuse in China through a third research question: How do socioeconomic and cultural factors affect Internet nonuse in China?

METHOD

Sampling

The data presented here are from a large-scale survey in Chengdu, one of the major provincial capital cities in the western region of China. In Chengdu, there are about 6.9 million Internet users, who account for 5% of the total Chinese Internet population (CINIC, 2007). The Internet penetration rate in Chengdu is about 8% of the local population, and this percentage is roughly parallel with the national Internet penetration rate across China.

With the assistance of a friend who works as a sales manager at China Telecom, one of the largest state-run phone service providers in China, I mailed 2,000 surveys and customer evaluation forms to randomly selected China Telecom subscribers (both mobile and land line) in Chengdu during the summer of 2006. Altogether, a total of 1,162 subscribers responded and returned the surveys by postal mail. Of the returned surveys, 184 were not included in the analysis because of apparent mistakes in survey responses. Thus the survey yielded 978 valid responses. As a follow-up, 90 respondents were randomly selected for telephone interviews about their Internet use or nonuse.

Instrumentation

Digital Divides

In comparing Internet and mobile phone usage, Rice and Katz (2003) identified and evaluated three kinds of digital divides: usage, adoption, and dropouts. Rice and Katz contended that there is no simple or singular digital divide: "The simple distinction of the digital divide as consisting of one between usage and non-usage is just that—only the simplest of several relevant distinctions" (p. 601). Using Cooper's report from the Consumer Federation of America, Rice and Katz called attention to differences across four levels of Internet connectedness: fully connected, partially connected, potentially connected, and disconnected. Income, education, race, age, and household size all significantly predict differences among the four divides. Rice and Katz also emphasized the differences between nonusers and dropouts. As former users of the Internet, dropouts have significantly different reasons for nonuse than those given by nonusers who have never connected at all. Based on these findings, Rice and Katz formulated three different kinds of digital divides—users/nonusers, dropouts/current users, and veteran users/recent users—which this study incorporates in its analysis of Internet use in China.

Internet Use and Nonuse

The current study includes 10 Internet uses: reading news, general browsing, gaming, downloading music, accessing entertainment information, downloading tools, using search engines, e-mailing, instant messaging (QQ/ICQ), and using chat rooms (IRC/IM). In addition, five reasons for Internet nonuse are covered in the analysis: lack of skills, lack of access, lack of time, belief that the Internet is useless, and lack of interest. A 5-point Likert-type scale with response options ranging from *strongly disagree* to *strongly agree* was used for measurement.

Socioeconomic Dimensions

Age, income, gender, education, and employment were used as factors to examine the socioeconomic dimension associated with Internet use in China. Age and income were used as continuous variables, and gender and employment were treated as dichotomous variables. Education was an ordinal variable that included the following levels: below high school, high school, college diploma, bachelor's degree, master's degree, and doctoral degree. Following the survey reports of CINIC (2005a, 2005b, 2006a, 2006b, 2007), the current study also included marital status as a dichotomous variable of the socioeconomic dimension.

Cultural Dimensions

Chinese cultural values and communication styles were used as the cultural dimension to analyze the digital divide in China. This measurement has 22 items that evaluate four dimensions of Chinese cultural values and communication styles: collectivism, personal relationships, high power distance, and high-context communication styles. The scale was created and used to study the effect of Chinese cultural values and communication styles on Chinese adoption of the mobile phone (Xia, 2006). After a factor analysis for principal components with varimax rotation, the scale was found to have Cronbach's alpha of .89.

For the items on the scale, subjects were asked to respond using a 5-point Likert-type scale with response options ranging from *strongly disagree* to *strongly agree*. In the dimension of collectivism, six items measured people's interdependence in groups and their prioritizing needs of the whole over individuals, such as "I love to go to my friends' gatherings in my spare time" and "I always ask my friends when I can't make up my mind." In the dimension of personal relationships, six items indicated people's value of harmonious personal relationships, both in personal friendships and business partnerships. Such a value placed on relationships can be seen in comments such as "Good personal relationships are an inseparable part of my life" and "When I get to know a person, I always keep a record of his or her name, contact information, and his or her background information for the future use."

In the dimension of high power distance, five items illustrated Chinese values about submission to authority, obedience to superior power, and fitting into social hierarchy, such as "I normally accept my boss's ideas even if I have different ones at the beginning" and "When I was in school, I never challenged my teachers in classrooms." In the dimension of high-context communication styles, five items represented Chinese indirect communication styles and emphasis on inferring meanings from contextual cues. Such connections can be seen in comments like "I don't like to talk to people who are really straightforward" and "I try very hard to get the meanings between [the] lines when I talk to others."

Analysis

Because Internet usage as the dependent variable is dichotomous, logistic regression was used to evaluate the relationship between socioeconomic and cultural factors and the digital divide in China. To further the exploration of Internet use and nonuse, a series of multiple regressions was conducted with the factors on socioeconomic and cultural dimension as the predicting variables.

RESULTS

Of the 978 respondents, 251 were current Internet users (25.7%), and 651 had never used the Internet (66.6%). In addition, 76 people (7.8%) had stopped using the Internet. Of the Internet users, about 68% were recent users (had only recently begun to use the Internet), and 32% were veteran users with at least three years of Internet experience.

Research Question 1

How do socioeconomic and cultural factors relate to the digital divide in China?

In order to answer this research question, logistic regressions were conducted to evaluate the relationship between socioeconomic and cultural factors and Internet usage. Table 7.1 summarizes the regression results.

Table 7.1. Beta coefficients from logistic regressions predicting Internet usage.

Independent Variables	Users/ Nonusers	Dropouts/ Users	Veteran/ Recent
Socioeconomic Dimension			
Age	-0.56**	0.12	0.09
Gender	0.45	-0.31*	0.47*
Education	0.64**	0.03	0.12
Income	0.05	-0.44**	0.07
Employment	0.24	0.01	0.58**
Marital Status	-0.75**	0.69**	-1.47**
Cultural Dimension			
Collectivism	0.18	0.14	0.06
Personal relationships	-1.98**	0.66**	-0.58**
High power distance	0.05	0.04	0.10
High-context communication	-0.78**	0.12	0.08
χ^2	**124.40****	**56.82****	**38.10**
Nagelkerke R^2	**0.18**	**0.14**	**0.48**
Correctly Predicted	**75.4%**	**62.8%**	**64.0%**

Note. $*p < 0.05$, $**p < 0.01$ (statistically significant).

The divide between Internet use and nonuse can be predicted by age, gender, education, and marital status on the socioeconomic dimension and by personal relationships and high-context communication on the cultural dimension. According to these factors, the typical Internet user is a young, unmarried, well-educated male who does not value personal relationships or high-context communication as much as the average person in China.

Gender, income, and marital status on the socioeconomic dimension and personal relationships on the cultural dimension predict the divide between dropouts and current users. The results of this study indicate that a dropout is usually a married female who has a low income and who is likely to value personal relationships.

Gender, employment, and marital status on the socioeconomic dimension and personal relationships on the cultural dimension predict the divide between veteran and recent users. A typical veteran user is an unmarried, fully employed male who is not likely to value personal relationships much.

Across different Internet divides, gender, marital status, and personal relationships are significant predicting variables.

Research Question 2

How do socioeconomic and cultural factors affect different Internet uses in China?

In order to understand why and how people use the Internet in China, a series of multiple regressions was conducted to explore the relationship between the socioeconomic and cultural factors and differing uses of the Internet. Tables 7.2 and 7.3 present the summary of these regression analyses.

Age, gender, and education predict the use of Internet news sources. Those individuals who use the Internet to get their news are most likely to be older women who have at least a college degree. Marital status and personal relationships predict the use of general browsing. An unmarried person who values personal relationships less tends to browse generally on the Internet. Age, gender, and personal relationships predict game playing on the Internet, and a gamer on the Internet is usually a young male who values good personal relationships.

Age and gender also predict downloading entertainment information and music on the Internet; usually young males engage in these Internet activities. Age, education, and employment predict the use of search engines; older, well-educated people with full-time employment tend to be more likely to use search engines. Age, education, personal relationships, and high-context communication predict the use of e-mail. That is, a young, well-educated person who values personal relationships less and does not like high-context communication usually uses e-mail. Age, collectivism, personal relationships, and high-context communication predict the use of instant messaging programs such as QQ and ICA; young

TABLE 7.2. Beta weights and T values for regressing socioeconomic and cultural factors on Internet uses.

Independent Variables	News	General Browsing	Games	Entertainment	Downloading Music					
		T		*t*		*t*		*T*		*t*
Socioeconomic Dimension										
Age	0.08	2.32**	0.02	0.32	–0.14	–1.32**	–0.06	–1.78**	–0.13	–1.24*
Gender	–0.06	–1.76*	0.16	0.54	0.28	2.44**	0.42	2.22**	0.12	1.22*
Education	0.04	3.12**	0.38	1.42	0.00	0.32	0.02	0.12	0.02	0.13
Income	–0.20	–0.12	–0.68	–0.32	–0.02	–0.84	–0.04	–0.86	0.12	0.32
Employment	0.14	1.42	0.04	1.02	0.04	0.22	0.00	0.10	0.14	0.44
Marital Status	–0.06	–0.32	–0.68	–2.72**	0.12	1.02	–0.10	–0.64	0.08	0.88
Cultural Dimension										
Collectivism	0.25	0.02	0.00	0.25	0.21	1.20	0.25	0.02	0.00	0.32
Personal Relationships	0.26	0.12	–0.36	–2.27**	0.24	2.48**	–0.23	–0.24	-0.06	–0.64
High Power Distance	0.25	0.20	0.00	0.68	0.04	1.12	0.25	0.20	0.04	0.32
High-Context Communication	0.46	0.12	0.12	0.42	0.28	1.28	0.12	0.78	0.16	0.55
Linear Combination	*R* = 0.28	*F* = 2.21*	*R* = 0.16	*F* = 2.44*	*R* = 0.22	*F* = 2.84*	*R* = 0.24	*F* = 3.28*	*R* = 0.16	*F* = 2.71*

Note. $^{*}p < 0.05$. $^{**}p < 0.01$ (statistically significant).

TABLE 7.3. Beta weights and T values for regressing socioeconomic and cultural factors on Internet uses.

Independent Variables	Downloading Tools	Search Engines	E-mail	QQ/ICQ	IRC/IM					
		T		*t*		*t*		*T*		*t*
Socioeconomic Dimension										
Age	0.04	0.44	0.22	2.42*	–0.22	–3.04**	–0.16	–2.16**	–0.14	–1.89*
Gender	0.02	0.34	0.08	1.02	0.02	0.68	0.04	0.48	0.02	0.24
Education	0.00	0.14	0.66	3.04**	0.14	3.86**	0.02	0.22	–0.12	–1.38*
Income	–0.42	–0.34	–0.03	–0.62	0.00	0.56	0.00	0.14	0.04	0.32
Employment	0.14	0.68	0.26	2.68*	0.01	0.44	0.01	0.18	0.06	0.48
Marital Status	–0.16	–0.88	–0.10	–1.02	0.05	0.80	0.08	0.68	0.08	0.68
Cultural Dimension										
Collectivism	0.08	0.68	0.22	1.88	0.02	1.08	0.22	2.84**	0.05	0.38
Personal Relationships	–0.12	–0.58	0.06	0.78	–0.08	–2.04*	0.14	2.08**	0.07	0.64
High Power Distance	0.00	0.12	0.02	0.42	0.04	0.68	0.06	1.56	0.03	0.32
High-Context Communication	0.06	0.54	0.00	0.14	–0.08	–2.32**	0.12	1.98**	0.02	0.26
Linear Combination	$R = 0.03$	$F = 1.04$	$R = 0.16$	$F = 2.44$*	$R = 0.38$	$F = 4.21$**	$R = 0.44$	$F = 4.01$**	$R = 0.12$	$F = 2.04$*

Note. *$p < 0.05$. **$p < 0.01$ (statistically significant).

people who value collectivism, personal relationships, and high-context communication are more likely to use instant communication. Finally, age and education predict the use of chat rooms, such as IRC and IM. Accordingly, a young person with a poor education is more likely to use IRC and IM.

Research Question 3

How do socioeconomic and cultural factors affect Internet non-use in China?

This research question evaluates various kinds of Internet nonuse from socioeconomic and cultural factors. A series of multiple regressions was conducted to answer this research question, and table 7.4 summarizes the regression analysis. Age, gender, and education predict a lack of Internet skills as the reason for Internet nonuse, and an older female with poor education is least likely to have the necessary Internet skills. Age, education, and income predict lack of access as the reason for Internet nonuse. An older person with less education and low income tends to have problems with Internet access. Age, gender, education, collectivism, and personal relationships predict the perception of the Internet's usefulness and interest in the Internet. Accordingly, an older female with less education who values collectivism and personal relationships is likely to think that the Internet is useless and likely to have no interest in it.

Discussion

Indicators of Use

On the socioeconomic dimension, gender and education positively predict Internet use. Marital status and age, however, are negatively related to Internet use. These findings match those of other studies and reports (CASS, 2005; CINIC, 2007) that have characterized a typical Chinese Internet user as young, well-educated, and male. The current study reveals marital status, too, as one significant factor contributing to the divide between Internet use and nonuse. According to the CINIC reports (2006a, 2006b, 2007), there are 10% more unmarried users than married users in China.

TABLE 7.4. Beta weights and T values for regressing socioeconomic and cultural factors on Internet nonuse.

Independent Variables	No skills	No Access	No Time	Not Useful	No Interest					
		T		*t*		*t*		*T*		*t*
Socioeconomic Dimension										
Age	0.36	2.02**	0.16	3.02*	0.04	0.32	0.12	2.20**	0.16	2.02*
Gender	−0.28	−1.86**	0.02	0.02	0.18	1.04	−0.08	−1.58*	−0.42	−3.62**
Education	−0.48	−3.24**	−0.38	−1.88*	0.00	0.02	−0.16	−1.68*	−0.34	−2.86**
Income	0.02	0.12	−0.68	−4.42**	−0.02	−0.42	0.00	0.56	0.04	0.26
Employment	0.14	0.78	0.04	1.02	0.14	0.82	0.01	0.44	0.02	0.14
Marital Status	0.00	0.12	−0.28	−1.42	0.12	1.02	0.04	0.80	−0.08	−0.56
Cultural Dimension										
Collectivism	0.15	1.06	0.00	0.25	0.05	0.46	0.24	2.62**	0.14	1.86*
Personal Relationships	0.16	1.24	−0.06	−0.08	0.10	0.88	0.42	3.84**	0.12	1.64*
High Power Distance	0.05	0.20	0.00	0.22	0.02	0.34	0.02	0.48	0.00	0.04
High-Context Communication	0.06	0.94	0.04	0.32	0.22	1.23	−0.06	−0.88	0.06	0.48
Linear Combination	$R = 0.18$	$F = 2.02$*	$R = 0.16$	$F = 2.42$*	$R = 0.08$	$F = 1.08$	$R = 0.28$	$F = 3.42$**	$R = 0.29$	$F = 3.24$**

Note. *$p < 0.05$. **$p < 0.01$ (statistically significant).

Marriage seems to turn people away from using the Internet. In the interviews conducted as a part of this project, people explained that the Internet, as a new medium, is a "gadget" thought to be appropriate for use by young people, such as students who are not yet considered mature adults. After marriage, a person is more likely to have a family and start a serious career—factors that symbolize maturity in Chinese culture. Family and career do not go hand-in-hand with youngsters' activities, which are seen as including "hanging around" on the Internet. This perceived association of the Internet with youth culture is tied to the most important reason for going online in China: entertainment (CASS, 2005). The most popular online activity, reading entertainment news—along with playing games online—is seen as conflicting with the responsibilities of serious married life.

On the cultural dimension, personal relationships and high-context communication negatively predict Internet use. People who value personal relationships more tend not to use the Internet. In the interviews, people indicated that they viewed the Internet as a barrier to their face-to-face personal relationships, although communication through the Internet was seen as helping interactions among friends. In the research literature on the topic, studies have revealed that use of computers and of the Internet does not seem to help family relationships in certain cultures (e.g., Leonardi, 2003).

In this context, Bockover (2003) described the Internet as "a potentially harmful foreign product" that can lead to conflict with Confucian values related to the Chinese way of life (p. 159). The Internet—driven by the ideas of free expression, equal opportunity, free trade, and individualism—is also often seen as contradicting the Chinese values of harmonious personal relationships and the fulfillment of self in a social role through interaction with others in a collectivistic society (Bockover, 2003). Moreover, without the social contextual cues common in face-to-face communication, communication through the Internet tends to be task-oriented, characterized by a direct expression of messages (Kiesler & Sproull, 1992; Walther & Parks, 2002). This feature is at odds with the high-context communication dominant in Chinese culture. In fact, some studies have shown possible conflicts between communication on the Internet and Chinese high-context communication preferences (Chen, 1998; Chung, 1992; Gunawardena et al., 2001; Simons, 1998).

Dropout and Current Users

The divide between dropouts and current users can be explained by gender, income, and marital status on the socioeconomic dimension. In China a female who has a low income tends to stop using the Internet after marriage. Income as a factor for affordability is one of the major reasons for Internet dropouts across different cultures (NTIA, 2004). After marriage, women in China often find little time for Internet interactions because double duties inside and outside the home (especially if there are children to care for) greatly reduce the time for such activities. (This perspective was supported by data collected from interviewees.)

On the cultural dimension, people stopped using the Internet or used the Internet progressively less after realizing that going online can possibly isolate one from his or her family, friends, and colleagues. As Bockover (2003) argued, the main moral goal in China has always been a form of harmonious interdependence, a perspective that is different from the U.S. tendency toward autonomous independence, a value that the Internet embodies. Bockover concluded that the autonomy afforded by the Internet can present a threat to cultural identity and relationship stability in collectivist China. As Katz and Rice (2002) contended, "dropping out" or discontinuing use of a new medium (such as the Internet) has been rarely studied. The divide between dropouts and current users can, however, be significant to both the policy community and service providers because, across various countries, millions of people stop using the Internet each year (Rice & Katz, 2003). In China the dropouts' reasons for their choice indicate some significant cultural factor underlying such decisions.

Veteran and Recent Users

Gender, employment, and marital status predict the divide between veteran and recent Internet users, and an unmarried male with full-time employment is likely to have more years of Internet experience.

According to the CASS (2005) report, Chinese Internet users usually have less experience; only 35.5% of the Internet users have more than five years of experience interacting online. Once again, personal relationships on the cultural dimension are significantly related to one's status as a veteran or a recent user. It is unclear whether people who value face-to-face personal relationships less tend to use the Internet more or whether people who use the Internet more turn away from their actual personal relationships in offline interactions. The causality between personal relationships and length of Internet use needs further exploration.

Types of Use

The CINIC reports (2005a, 2005b, 2006a, 2006b, 2007) and the CASS report (2005) about Internet usage and influence offer detailed descriptive statistics about different Internet uses in China. This study fills in the gap about how and why people use the Internet in China. Age, gender, and education predict news reading on the Internet; an older female with a good education is likely to read news on the Internet. In China the most-read online content is entertainment news (CASS, 2005), and women are the largest group reading entertainment and domestic news on the Internet. According to the current study, only marital status and personal relationships are negatively related to general browsing online; an unmarried person who values personal relationships less is likely to browse on the Internet.

Once again, general browsing on the Internet can have the effect of replacing people's face-to-face socialization in China. Among the interviewed Internet users, about 36% regarded general browsing online as an "escape." After news reading and general browsing, three entertainment activities rank—gaming, downloading entertainment information, and downloading music—and all three have the same predicting factors. A young male plays games, downloads music, and seeks entertainment information on the Internet. Personal relationships are also a significant predicting factor for gaming because in China playing online games has become a way of socializing. Not surprisingly, people who value personal relationships more play games as a part of their social lives.

In addition, age, education, and employment predict the use of search engines, and a young, well-educated person with full-time employment is likely to use search engines.

Internet use solely for communication ranks at the bottom of the most popular online activities in China. According to the CASS report (2005), one third of Internet users in China do not use e-mail at all, and more than half of Chinese Internet users use e-mail only occasionally. More than one third of Chinese users check e-mail only once a week or less. Compared with other countries, China also has fewer e-mail users. For example, the e-mail users in the United States accounted for over 80% of the Internet-using population in 2003 (NTIA, 2004). In the evaluation of Chinese people's perceptions and attitudes toward the Internet, a surprisingly low number of users (less than 10%) envision the Internet as a post office (CASS, 2005). Instead, the Chinese seem to prefer instant communication, such as instant messaging, to asynchronous e-mail. On the socioeconomic dimension, age and education are closely related to e-mail use: A young, well-educated person is most likely to use e-mail.

In the CASS report (2005), employment is also a factor contributing to the use of e-mail because people in the workplace are sometimes required to use e-mail in order to complete tasks at work. In the current study, students are classified as unemployed—but students are the largest group of Internet users in China. Thus the "student effect" confounds the employment effect for e-mail use. It is worth noting that personal relationships and high-context communication are negatively related to e-mail use. Some studies (e.g., Xia, 2007) position e-mail as the core of Internet communication that might be the barrier to the development of personal relationships in China. Face-to-face communication is the best mechanism for maintaining relationships in China, and the cultural value of direct honesty in relationship negotiation cannot be communicated through asynchronous e-mail. The emotional tones and indirect messages inherent to high-context communication are similarly made impossible in emotionally detached and task-oriented e-mail interactions (Chen, 1998; Chung, 1992).

Instant messaging systems, in contrast, such as QQ and ICQ, are welcomed by Chinese Internet users, who view them as tools for the development of personal relationships. Age is the only socioeconomic factor relating significantly to the use of QQ and ICQ; younger people tend to use instant messaging systems more. As studies and reports (CINIC, 2005a, 2005b, 2006a, 2006b) show, younger Chinese (individuals under 34 years of age) like to use instant messaging and chat rooms, whereas older Chinese (individuals over 34 years of age) like to use online bulletin board systems (BBSs) and blogs.

Collectivism, personal relationships, and high-context communication on the cultural dimension are all positively related to the use of instant messaging. The synchronicity and immediate interaction in instant messaging not only help personal relationships but also enable fast, convenient coordination of activities among friends, colleagues, and fellow students. Age and education factor into the use of chat rooms. A young person with a poor education (under high school) tends to spend time in chat rooms on the Internet.

Indicators of Nonuse

In the current study, the top reason for Internet nonuse is the lack of necessary skills (about 26%). This factor matches CINIC survey results (2005a, 2005b, 2006a, 2006b), which state that more than one third of nonusers indicated their lack of skills as the major barrier to Internet use. Age, gender, and education are significantly related to a lack of skills. For example, an older female who has a poor education is unlikely to possess the skills needed to use the Internet. Surprisingly, employment does not predict the lack of skills. In the literature, studies show that full-time employment helps people acquire different levels of skills (Katz & Rice, 2002). However, in the current study, students—that is, individuals classified as unemployed—are the largest group of Internet users. The identification of students as "unemployed" might make the employment factor insignificant in predicting the lack of skills.

In terms of access, about 22% of nonusers in the sample rated lack of access as the reason for Internet nonuse. Age, education, and income seem to predict Internet access, for an older person who is poorly educated and has a low income is less likely to have access to the Internet. Education, however, positively predicts access, as evidenced by the largest group of Internet users: students who have better education and who can access the Internet through schools, homes, and Internet cafés (CINIC, 2007). Yet education might overlap with income in terms of its effect on access. In the sample used for this study, 8% of nonusers rated lack of time as the reason for Internet nonuse. None of the socioeconomic and cultural factors predict lack of time.

In Dutton's (2004) reconfiguration of the access perspective of ICT, access is not an independent force but "an intermediate outcome" (p. 34). Digital choices about whether and how to design and use a technology as reshaping access do not take place in isolation but, rather, in the midst of a complex mix of social factors. People might decide not to use the Internet because of their negative perceptions and attitudes toward the Internet's functionality (CASS, 2005). In the current study, an individual's perception about Internet usefulness and his or her interest significantly affect Internet nonuse. Age, gender, and education (socioeconomic factors) and collectivism and personal relationships (cultural factors) all predict the perception of Internet usefulness and interest. For example, an older female who is poorly educated and who values collectivism and personal relationships more is likely to think that the Internet is not useful and thus will likely have no interest in using it.

A negative perception of the Internet, moreover, seems to obtain in China generally. In the CASS report (2005), only one third of Chinese Internet nonusers and half of Chinese Internet users believed that the Internet would make the world better place. This negative perception comes partially from traditional media's reports on the aspects of the Internet that conflict with social harmony and stability. In terms of collectivistic values, a person, as an essential part of a larger social group, is defined by his or her harmony with other people in a greater network of relationships. This harmonious interdependence is always in conflict with the autonomous independence that information and communication on the Internet present (Bockover, 2003). Only one third of Chinese nonusers regard the Internet as a meeting place, and only 6% of them think of the Internet as a post office. According to Chinese values, personal relationships are best maintained by face-to-face negotiation and renegotiation without in-between mediations, and communication through the Internet does not allow much interaction in personal relationships.

Implications for Digital Divide Research

These findings about the socioeconomic and cultural dimensions effects on the digital divide in China expand the research framework of that divide. More and more scholars now realize that access to technology is intertwined with a complex array of factors, including economic, technical, human, institutional, and social resources. After criticizing the view of access to a technology as an independent force leading to patterns of use and predicted effects, Dutton (2004) reconfigured ideas of access to address a number of perspectives. These include the ecology of economic resources and constraints, ICT paradigms and practices, conceptions and responses of users, geography of space and place, institutional arrangements and public policies, and strategies of others. Katz and Rice (2002) contended that the digital divide is more social and cultural than technical, and they summarized three different perspectives that help explain communication technology use: (a) gender, racial, and ethnic differences in usage patterns of interpersonal communication technologies (built-in bias); (b) sex and race differences in Internet usage (uses, needs, and gratifications); and (c) class differences in communication technology (resource availability). Warschauer (2003) rejected the very concept that the digital divide is overwhelmingly tied to the physical availability of computer and connectivity. He instead proposed the idea of social inclusion that redirects attention from the concept of a divide to one of social context, social purpose, and social organization that continuously co-construct technology.

The study described in this chapter points to cultural significance as a part of the complex ecology in the discussion and the understanding of the digital divide. Chinese society, with its unique cultural values, forms a distinctive ecology that is co-constructing communication technologies, such as the Internet. As a critical cultural value, the maintenance of harmonious personal relationships is related to all three divides between users and nonusers, dropouts and current users, and veteran users and recent users. The traditional value of the face-to-face cultivation of relationships contradicts the mediated communication of the Internet. That most people in China do not view the Internet as a meeting place or post office supports the divide between personal relationships and Internet use. Gender and marital status on the socioeconomic dimension are also significantly related to the three digital divides as well as to different forms of use and nonuse.

A cultural explanation of gender and marriage in China can also lead to a better understanding of digital divide. In Chinese culture, computer use in general, as well as spending time online, is symbolically masculine. First, online games, as one of the most popular Internet activities in China, feature gun combat, martial arts, and car racing—all of which construct masculinity in different Internet uses. Second, Internet cafés, popular places to congregate, play a significant role in Internet diffusion in China (CASS, 2005). Most customers in Internet cafés are males because the noisy and sweaty café is usually considered men's territory in Chinese culture (Guo & Wang, 2004). In the Chinese language, the literal translation of Internet café is *net bar*, and as a kind of bar, Internet cafés attract mainly male customers seeking entertainment online.

Marriage in China redefines the roles of man and woman for the context of a household. After marriage, both men and women are said to achieve the status of maturity and independence. Having a family and starting a professional career are the two major goals in a married person's life. The perception of the Internet in China as primarily a means of entertainment thus does not match these serious life goals; not surprisingly, then, marriage seems negatively related to Internet use.

In his comprehensive study of the Internet in China, Tai (2006) added regional and rural–urban differences as unique factors affecting the digital divide in China. The current study goes further and argues that in the ecology framework—in which behavior emerges out of the surrounding context or environment—for the digital divide, not all sources have the same weight in explaining the digital divide. Across different cultures, some sources (e.g., cultural factors) are more significant than others. Income and affordability are the major reasons for Internet nonuse in the United States (NTIA, 2004); in China, by contrast, a lack of necessary skills as related to low levels of education is the top reason for Internet nonuse. Thus researchers exploring the digital divide need to adopt the complex array of social factors from an ecological perspective. They should also pay attention to the evaluation of each source in the framework when discussing the digital divide in a particular cultural context in which the Internet (as well as other communication technologies) is used.

Future Research

The research presented in this chapter used a convenience sample; the generalization of the findings might be improved upon in future research with a probability sample. A quantitative method was used here to evaluate the relationship between socioeconomic and cultural factors and the digital divide. In future research, qualitative methods could be used to explore Chinese use of the Internet and the meaning of the digital divide from the Chinese perceptive. The current study also used four dimensions as Chinese cultural values and communication styles. Because China has experienced major social, economic, and cultural changes under the influence of Western culture, Chinese cultural values and communication styles should include more dimensions.

A digital divide also exists in different geographic regions of China. The northern coastal area, the East China coastal area, and the South China coastal area all have levels of Internet resources that are proportionally higher than the population percentage (Giese, 2003; Tai, 2006). Because the majority of China's people live in rural areas, there is a rural–urban digital divide. For these reasons, future research on Internet use in China should consider both internal (intranational) and external (global) divides in examining socioeconomic and cultural factors of the digital divide.

CONCLUSION

In this study, both socioeconomic and cultural dimensions were used to evaluate the different digital divides: user/nonuser, dropouts/users, and veteran users/current users. In order to understand use and nonuse better, factors reflecting socioeconomic and cultural dimensions were used to explore different kinds of Internet use and reasons for Internet nonuse. Both socioeconomic factors (age, gender, education, income, and marital status) and cultural factors (personal relationships, collectivism, and high-context communication) significantly correlate to explain digital divides in China. Gender, marital status, and personal relationships are related to all three divides. Indeed, in the complex array of ecological factors, cultural values can uniquely contribute to the digital divide.

Endnote

1. QQ, the most popular free instant messaging program in China, was created and is currently maintained by a Chinese company.

REFERENCES

Barley, S. R. (1990). The alignment of technology and structure through roles and networks. *Administrative Science Quarterly, 35*(1), 61–103.

Bockover, M. (2003). Confucian values and the Internet: A potential conflict. *Journal of Chinese Philosophy, 30*(2), 159–175.

Brock, A. (2005). "A belief in humanity is a belief in colored men": Using culture to span the digital divide. *Journal of Computer-Mediated Communication, 11*(1), 17. Retrieved October 1, 2010, from http://jcmc.indiana.edu/vol11/issue1/brock.html.

Chen, G. M. (1998). Intercultural communication via e-mail debate. *The Edge: The E-Journal of Intercultural Relations, 1*(4). Retrieved March 10,2006,fromhttp://www.interculturalrelations.com/v1i4Fall1998/f98 chen.htm.

China Internet Network Information Center [CINIC]. (2005a, January). *15th statistical survey report on the Internet development in China.* Retrieved April 13, 2009, from http://www.cnnic.net.cn/download/2005/2005012701.pdf.

China Internet Network Information Center [CINIC]. (2005b, July). *16th statistical survey report on the Internet development in China.* Retrieved April 13, 2009, from http://www.cnnic.net.cn/download/2005/2005072601.pdf.

China Internet Network Information Center [CINIC]. (2006a, January). *17th statistical survey report on the Internet development in China.* Retrieved April 13, 2009, from http://www.cnnic.net.cn/download/2006/17threport-en.pdf.

China Internet Network Information Center [CINIC]. (2006b, July). *18th statistical survey report on the Internet development in China.* Retrieved April 13, 2009, from http://www.cnnic.net.cn/download/2006/18threport-en.pdf.

China Internet Network Information Center [CINIC]. (2007, January). *19th statistical survey report on the Internet development in China.* Retrieved April 13, 2009, from http://www.cnnic.net.cn/download/2007/cnnic19threport.pdf.

Chinese Academy of Social Sciences [CASS]. (2005, November). *Surveying Internet usage and impact in five Chinese cities.* Retrieved April 13, 2009, from http://www.markle.org/downloadable_assests/china_final_11_2005.pdf.

Chung, J. (1992, November). *Electronic mail usage in low-context and high-context cultures.* Paper presented at the annual meeting of the Speech Communication Association, Chicago, IL.

Cooper, M., & Kimmelman, G. (1999). *The digital divide confronts the Telecommunications Act of 1996: Economic reality versus public policy.* Washington, DC: Consumer Union.

DiMaggio, P., Hargittai, E., Neuman, W. R., & Robinson, J. P. (2001). The social implications of the Internet. *Annual Review of Sociology, 27*, 307–336.

Dutton, W. (2004). *Social transformation in an information society: Rethinking access to you and the world.* Paris, France: United Nations Educational, Scientific, and Cultural Organization.

Fulk, J. (1993). Social construction of communication technology. *Academy of Management Journal, 36*(5), 921–950.

Fulk, J., & Boyd, B. (1991). Emerging theories of communication in organizations. *Journal of Management, 17*(2), 407–447.

Fulk, J., Schmitz, J., & Ryu, D. (1995). Cognitive elements in the social construction of technology. *Management Communication Quarterly, 8*(3), 259–288.

Giese, K. (2003). Internet growth and the digital divide: Implications for spatial development. In C. Hughes (Ed.), *China and the Internet: Politics of the digital leap forward* (pp. 30–58). New York, NY: Routledge.

Gudykunst, W. B., & Ting-Toomey, S. (1988). Culture and affective communication. *American Behavioral Scientist, 31*(3), 384–399.

Gunawardena, C. N., Nolla, A. C., Wilson, P. L., Lopez-Islas, J. R., Ramirez-Angel, N., & Megchun-Alpizar, R. M. (2001). A cross-cultural study of group process and development in online conferences. *Distance Education, 22*(1), 85–121.

Guo, L., & Wang, N. (2004). Internet adoption in China's smaller cities. *IT & Society, 1*(6), 36–43.

Hall, E. T. (1976). *Beyond culture.* Garden City, NY: Anchor/Doubleday.

Hargittai, E. (2002). Second-level digital divide: Differences in people's online skills. *First Monday, 7*(4). Retrieved October 7, 2005, from http://firstmonday.org/htbin/cgiwrap/bin/ojs/index.php/fm/article/view/942/864.

Hargittai, E. (2005). Survey measures of Web-oriented digital literacy. *Social Science Computer Review, 23*(3), 371–379.

Hofstede, G. (1980). *Culture's consequences: International differences in work-related values.* Beverly Hills, CA: Sage.

Hofstede, G. (1997). *Cultures and organizations: Software of the mind.* New York, NY: McGraw-Hill.

Katz, J. E., & Rice, R. E. (2002). *Social consequences of Internet use: Access, involvement, and interaction.* Cambridge, MA: MIT Press.

Katz, J. E., Rice, R. E., & Aspden, P. (2001). The Internet, 1995–2000: Access, civic involvement, and social interaction. *American Behavioral Scientist, 45*(3), 404–419.

Kiesler, S., & Sproull, L. S. (1992). Group decision making and communication technology. *Organizational Behavior and Human Decision Processes, 52*(1), 96–123.

Kim, S. D. (2002). Korea: Personal meanings. In J. Katz & M. Aakhus (Eds.), *Perpetual contact: Mobile communication, private talk, public performance* (pp. 63–79). Cambridge, UK: Cambridge University Press.

Lenhart, A. (2003). *The ever-shifting Internet population: A new look at Internet access and the digital divide.* Retrieved May 7, 2004, from http://www.pewInternet.org/~/media//Files/Reports/2003/PIP_Shifting_Net_Pop_Report.pdf.pdf.

Leonardi, P. M. (2003). Problematizing "new media": Culturally based perceptions of cell phones, computers, and the Internet among United Sates Latinos. *Critical Studies in Media Communication, 20*(2), 160–179.

Lu, S. (1997). Culture and compliance gaining in the classroom: A preliminary investigation of Chinese college teachers' use of behavior alteration techniques. *Communication Education, 46*(1), 10–28.

MacKenzie, D., & Wajcman, J. (Eds.). (1985). *The social shaping of technology: How the refrigerator got its hum.* Milton Keynes, UK: Open University Press.

Madden, M. (2006). *Internet penetration and impact.* Pew Internet and American Life Project, April 26, 2006. Retrieved August 10, 2009 from http://www.pewInternet.org/Reports/2006/Internet-Penetration-and-Impact.aspx.

Miller, J. D. (2001). Who is using the Web for science and health information? *Science Communication, 22*(3), 256–273.

National Telecommunications and Information Agency [NTIA]. (1999). *Falling through the net: Defining the digital divide.* Retrieved October 7, 2005, from http://www.ntia.doc.gov/ntiahome/fttn99/FTTN.pdf.

National Telecommunications and Information Agency [NTIA]. (2000). *Falling through the net: Towards digital inclusion.* Retrieved October 27, 2005, from http://www.ntia.doc.gov/ntiahome/fttn00/contents00.html.

National Telecommunications and Information Agency [NTIA]. (2002). *A nation online: How Americans are expanding their use of the Internet.* Retrieved October 7, 2005, from http://www.ntia.doc.gov/ntiahome/dn/anationonline2.pdf.

National Telecommunications and Information Agency [NTIA]. (2004). *A nation online: Entering the broadband age*. Retrieved October 7, 2005, from http://www.ntia.doc.gov/reports/anol/index.html.

Rice, R. E., & Katz, J. E. (2003). Comparing Internet and mobile phone usage: Digital divides of usage, adoption, and dropouts. *Telecommunications Policy, 27*(8/9), 597–623.

Robinson, J., DiMaggio, P., & Hargittai, E. (2003). New social survey perspectives on the digital divide. *IT and Society, 1*(5), 1–22.

Selwyn, N. (2003). Apart from technology: Understanding people's non-use of information and communication technologies in everyday life. *Technology in Society, 25*(1), 99–116.

Simons, G. (1998). Meeting the intercultural challenges of virtual work. *Language and Intercultural Learning, 16*(1), 13–15.

Tai, Z. (2006). *The Internet in China: Cyberspace and civil society.* New York, NY: Routledge.

Walther, J. B., & Parks, M. R. (2002). Cues filtered out, cues filtered in: Computer-mediated communication and relationships. In M. L. Knapp & J. A. Daly (Eds.), *Handbook of Interpersonal Communication* (pp. 529–563). Thousand Oaks, CA: Sage.

Warschauer, M. (2002). Reconceptualizing the digital divide. *First Monday, 7*(7). Retrieved October 7, 2005, from http://firstmonday.org/htbin/cgiwrap/bin/ojs/index.php/fm/article/view/967/888.

Warschauer, M. (2003). *Technology and social inclusion: Rethinking the digital divide.* Cambridge, MA: MIT Press.

Wyatt, S., Henwood, F., Hart, A., & Smith, J. (2005). The digital divide, health information, and everyday life. *New Media & Society,* 7, 2, 199–218.

Wyatt, S., Thomas, G., & Terranova, T. (2002). They came, they surfed, they went back to the beach: Conceptualizing use and non-use of the

Internet. In S. Woolgar (Ed.), *Virtual society?: Technology, cyberbole, reality* (pp. 23–40). Oxford, UK: Oxford University Press.

Xia, Y. (2006). Cultural values, communication styles, and use of mobile communication in China. *China Media Research, 2*(1), 24–38.

Xia, Y. (2007). Intercultural computer-mediated communication between Chinese and US college students. In K. St. Amant (Ed.), *Linguistic and Cultural Online Communication Issues in the Global Age* (pp. 63–77). Hershey, PA: Idea Group.

Yang, M. M. (1994). *Gifts, favors, and banquets: The art of social relationships in China.* Ithaca, NY: Cornell University Press.

Zhang, Q., & Oetzel, J. G. (2006). Constructing and validating a teacher immediacy scale: A Chinese perspective. *Communication Education, 55*(2), 218–241.

CHAPTER 8

GLOBALIZATION, EPIDEMICS, AND POLITICS

COMMUNICATING RISK IN THE DIGITAL AGE

Yasmin Ibrahim

The dialectical discourses about keeping borders open and shut often securitize and amplify diseases as new types of risk in the global age. In such cases, new viruses force nation-states to consider different ways and means of protecting their borders while simultaneously keeping them open for economic benefits. The risks related to such situations create a pervasive narrative of the postmodern condition. This is because human beings now live in a media-saturated and mediated world where information and communication technologies (ICTs) create new connections and visibilities in mapping risk (such as disease). This chapter analyses the politicization of risk in a globalized world by examining the SARS epidemic of 2003. The chapter argues that whilst ICTs create new ways of sharing and coordinating health information, these technologies can also present challenges whereby the politicization of risk can reiterate geopolitics and amplify socioeconomic imbalances.

INTRODUCTION

With the advent of globalization, the world has opened up not only to electronic communication but also to the communication and transmission of bacteria and viruses. During recent epidemics of swine flu, bird flu, and SARS, the communication of information about new viruses and diseases was facilitated by information and communication technologies (ICTs). As Grein et al. (2000) explained, "reports of disease outbreaks are more widely disseminated and more easily accessible than before" (p. 97). The role of technologies in informing the public and in raising awareness has nevertheless been a double-edged sword in terms of risk communication. In many instances, the flood of information disseminated via the Internet and unofficial sources has led to increased local and global misinformation and paranoia about infectious diseases. Through the case study of the SARS epidemic, this chapter examines how information ICTs are increasingly playing a role in the communication of risk in global contexts. I explore the ways access to and use of ICTs to disseminate information related to health epidemics affect local reactions to such events. The results point to a new, international situation for public health in the context of the global digital divide.

ICTs AND COMMUNICATING RISK

The interconnection of the world through communication technology and transportation infrastructure has provided new ways to conjoin and imagine a globalized world. However, the increased sharing of information through global electronic platforms does not ensure that information is a global resource or a global public good. Similarly, such developments cannot effectively deliver health policy campaigns or raise health awareness uniformly across the globe. The communication of risk via

ICTs, especially during epidemics, is very dependent on a high level of technological penetration, media literacy, and the embedding of these technologies into people's everyday lives. It can equally be molded by how a society engages with information and by that society's approach to making information available to the public via these media. Conversely, communicating risk on the Internet can create unintended consequences whereby both information and misinformation can mediate the efforts of authorities to foster a coherent narrative. This occurred in the United Kingdom where, despite a nationwide imperative to make available information on swine flu, massive panic ensued. In this case, the official Website designed to disseminate information to the public crashed minutes after it was launched by the government in July of 2009 (Meikle, Bowcott, & Carrell, 2009).

From a normative perspective, technology and health care are often viewed from a utopian perspective and without an attendant understanding of how they can create new forms of inequality. Despite the wiring of the world, the uneven spread of access to online information and online communication technologies is not often fully addressed when conceiving global health imperatives. There is, however, an expectation that improved information and communication technologies can better manage diseases and create new forms of health economy (see Altensetter & Bjorkman, 1997; Cartwright, 2000; Leyshon, 1995). Lisa Cartwright (2000), for example, noted that this optimism of the early 1990s was somewhat tempered by big business's discovery of the Internet. Cartwright's point is that telecommunications and new technologies re-mediate geography. In so doing, they create new communities and reach remote spaces. Yet Cartwright contended that the "dynamics introduced in telemedicine are hardly neutral, universal or equivalent among subjects" (Cartwright, 2000, p. 351).

Cartwright's perspective requires individuals to reconsider initial conceptions of the digital divide as related strictly to information access and to infrastructure. Such a divide is often a multifaceted phenomenon that mirrors the dominant power structures in a global society. The incorporation of health communication into the global ICT infrastructure then creates a double-bind situation in which ICTs and their use for global communication during epidemics could exacerbate existing imbalances and inequalities. The situation requires that individuals reframe ideas of distance, geography, and spatial politics through an analysis and construction of risk as it relates to the modern nation-state.

Through a case study of the SARS epidemic, this chapter focuses on health and risk communication in the global digital age, providing insights on how the modern interconnected digital world can present new forms of vulnerability and new digital divides. The digital world is one in which the imperatives are driven less by the management of health and more by economic goals and the desire to keep borders closed to invading pathogens and entities. I argue that despite the normative idea of linking the world through digital and new information technology, health communication becomes a tool enabling nation-states to guard their individual national agendas rather than a means to address wider humanitarian goals.

THE ORIGIN AND THE SPREAD OF SARS

According to Heymann and Rodier (2004b, p. 1), the emergence of Severe Acute Respiratory Syndrome (SARS) was the second major 21st-century event to change perceptions of the infectious disease threat—the first being the anthrax scare that followed the events of September 11, 2001. (In addition to SARS, avian flu—the H5N1 influenza virus—has also become a threat worldwide.) The SARS epidemic of 2003 is often interpreted as imparting important lessons about the tensions among security, health, and risk communication on the global stage. Despite its low level of mortality and threat, SARS generated unprecedented international cooperation amongst 192 members of the World Health Assembly in Geneva (Brundtland, 2003, pp. 417–419).

The concerns related to SARS were connected to the speed with which the disease spread globally. It has been documented that in early 2003, SARS spread within weeks from Guangdong province in China and infected individuals in some 37 countries around the world (Wang & Jolly, 2004). The first case of SARS was reported on February 26, 2003. By May 31, the number of probable cases had reached 8,359, and the mortality rate outside China had climbed to around 14% ("Pandemics and Transparency," 2006; R. Smith, 2006, p. 3113). In the past, diseases required weeks or months to spread; SARS, by contrast, had spread globally within a matter of days, setting a record for the speed of continent-to-continent disease transmission (Menon, 2006, p. 362). SARS was also seemingly democratic, for it affected young, old, poor, and rich alike while crossing borders with impunity.

The disease is thought to have first moved out of southern China on February 21, 2003, when a Guangdong medical doctor who had treated patients suffering from respiratory symptoms spent a single night in a Hong Kong hotel (Heymann & Rodier, 2004b, p. 188). This doctor transmitted the disease to 16 other guests and visitors, all linked to the same hotel floor. The infected individuals then carried the virus with them as they travelled to Toronto, Vietnam, and Singapore. The ease with which the virus crossed continents highlights the way air travel and transport links between countries can present new health and economic problems for nation-states (see Harris & Keil, 2006). This transportation factor prompted the World Health Organization (WHO) to issue a global alert for SARS on March 12, 2003.

The association of SARS with air travel and its rapid spread to various countries in Asia and to Canada illuminate the vulnerabilities of an interlinked world in the 21st century. The outbreak reignited post–September 11 anxieties regarding the permeability of borders and the possibility of unforeseen chaos and disruption in secure and highly governed urban spaces. The very infrastructures (i.e., transport and communication) that had facilitated the process of globalization presented new risks and opportunities for the transgression of boundaries, regarded as sacrosanct for nation-states. The nonstop representation of global risks through ICTs, moreover, can give rise to a global imagination and consciousness in which these connections and visibilities create new forms of tangible and intangible risks. Global interdependencies and infrastructures inevitably create liquid borders, but they do so without obliterating the role of nations-states (Bauman, 2006).

The emergence of SARS in this "climate of fear" captured contemporary society's tendency to extrapolate disparate risks and to weave them into a singular metanarrative of a pervasive risk society (Beck, 2002). In theorizing the consequences of modernity, Anthony Giddens (1990) stressed the intersection of estrangement and familiarity with changing notions of distance and proximity, notions created through ICTs. Giddens articulated globalization as a phenomenon that dislodges human interaction from local contexts and reconfigures it across time and space. Thus the elimination of distance created by ICTs has consequences for both risk communication and risk perception in the global community. SARS created a worldwide response in excess of that generated by more serious infectious-disease threats of recent years, and Richard Smith (2006, p. 3119) contended that much of this disparity in the responses can be attributed to the role of ICTs.

In his book *The Politics of Fear* (2005), Frank Furedi described a society consumed by free-floating anxieties sustained and exacerbated by dramatic events, such as September 11, natural disasters, and epidemics. In this society, fears are less tangible but more diffuse and pervasive. The distinct feature of our time, Furedi asserted, is the cultivation not of fear but of vulnerability:

> In the five years since 9/11, what were previously seen as fairly normal hazards have been turned into exceptional threats by their association with the action of terrorists. So we no longer worry about the apparently everyday hazard posed by a nuclear power station; we also fear that it may be used as a weapon of mass destruction against us by terrorists.... The very fact that risk is used to link together a variety of otherwise unconnected experiences highlights today's mood of uncertainty. (Furedi, 2007, p. 6)

The representation and narration of risks by interlinking various "media events" (Dayan & Katz, 1992), such as the September 11 attacks or the

Bali bombings, mark a moment when globalization and the proliferation of ICTs sustain new anxieties through images and sound bites. These audiovisual media exacerbate, amplify, and politicize risk by reiterating the vulnerabilities of an interconnected world.

Globalization and Risk

At its core, globalization can be defined as a process of changes affecting the nature of human interaction as boundaries become eroded across a range of spheres and along spatial, temporal, and cognitive dimensions (cf. Owen & Roberts, 2005). *Globalization*, as a term in our sociological imagination and in the trajectory of the knowledge economy, occupies tenuous terrain. Often, it is used to convey a host of processes that are shrinking the globe and amplifying people's sense of consciousness about international issues. Such enhanced awareness of global issues can also heighten sensitivities to how events happening in distant parts of the world can indirectly affect and destabilize another country's security. Industrialization and modernization weave patterns of interdependency between nation-states, and in this context, natural disasters or accidents in one part of the world can have repercussions in other countries and places.

ICTs invariably play a vital role in our perception of risks as these technologies occupy the global stage, and they do so while mediating our consciousness. Mattelart (1994) contended that modern media are among the principal means by which a certain type of order has been introduced in large territories. The speed of communication has accelerated social interaction as well as the exchange of knowledge, ideas, beliefs, values, cultural identities, and other thought processes (Lee & Dodgson, 2000). The politicization of risk through the media is also an inevitable part of the postmodern construction and imagination. Muzatti (2005; cf. R. Smith, 2006) posited that the media manufacture threats to public health and that such threats equally draw upon past and present cultural myths of dangerous "others" and lead to unwarranted public fear, intolerance, and distrust.

Because risk is a pervasive part of postmodern consciousness (Beck, 1999; Giddens, 1990; Harvey, 1989), it is constantly politicized and often enmeshed and mediated by our political, cultural, and economic environment. According to Beck (1999), the risks of reflexive modernity are invisible, uninsurable, systematic, generic, and democratic (cf. Turner, 2001, p. 12). The politicization of risks and fears through the pathos of human experience and belief systems continues to shape perceptions of new and emerging risks. Although globalization portends a world with eroding boundaries and seamless human activity, the perceptions of risk as distant, immediate, or contemporaneous are shaped by the mediated reality of ICTs as well as by the local context and its relationship with the rest of the world.

The localization of global risks in terms of perception and response reinforces boundaries in a borderless world. In so doing, the localization of global risks reiterates the role of nation-states in the politicization of risk and the management of health despite attempts to perceive health as a global good in the 21st century. The contextualization of risks within nation-states, however, does not negate the incestuous connections between politics and health, nor does it negate the increasing prominence of health in foreign policy. This notion is particularly salient in the post–September 11 context (Cooper, 2006; Owen & Roberts, 2005, p. 1). Owen and Roberts (2005), for example, cite the HIV/AIDS pandemic, SARS, preparedness for bioterrorism, and the Framework Convention on Tobacco Control as recent examples of the intersection of health and politics. They also stress that since September 11, health and development agendas have been linked with the foreign policy priorities of improving health security and preventing state failure. In addition, risks in the postmodern consciousness are contextualized through the political climate of the post–September 11 context.

According to John Urry (2000; cited in Turner, 2001), globalization often involves the creation of new kinds of social order involving complex and fluid networks through which information moves. These flows of information create a liquid threat for many nation-states, and this threat can be manifested in myriad forms and ideologies (Bauman, 2006).

As Daniel Hamilton (2003) postulates, the greatest security threats to the United States and Europe today stem from problems that defy borders: terrorism and the proliferation of weapons of mass destruction, pandemics, and environmental scarcities. The association of SARS with air travel narrated the epidemic as a disease that is an inevitable by-product of trade and travel. With over two million people crossing international borders every day (about one tenth of humanity each year) and more than one million traveling from developing to industrialized countries each week (Brundtland, 2003, p. 420), worldwide migration and other interconnected transborder processes can mix people and microorganisms on an unprecedented scale.

Globalization, then, entails the inclusion of policy issues beyond national borders and creates an increasing interdependence among people and places. Globalization has also increasingly blurred the boundaries between the domestic and foreign spheres and has raised new challenges for the global community in minimizing the harm and risks and in upholding issues of human rights and equity in an unequal world. Whereas states have sought to retain sovereignty over health issues, the linkages between economics and health have made such control more difficult to contain within national geopolitical boundaries. The Asian financial crisis, the attacks of September 11, and the SARS epidemic highlighted the interconnectedness of the world. These events also reconfigured the notions of proximity and distance whilst amplifying the risk through nonstop coverage, facilitated through ICTs.

Epidemics as an Economic Threat

The attention and focus given to SARS beyond the paradigm of health issues was directly connected to the potential economic destruction that the virus could incur globally. According to Christopher Coker (2004, p. 4), the secondary consequence of lethal diseases is the potential to produce a global system crash. In the case of SARS, the immediate impact on economics was visible. Unlike other endemic threats, such as HIV/AIDS or tobacco addiction, the threat SARS posed to global capitalism stimulated major worldwide cooperation. It is worth noting that the SARS contamination was limited and produced a low death rate of around 5–15%; however, the politicization of SARS as an economic risk and its association with air travel and the hospitality industry ensured that it received immediate attention from the world. Richard Smith (2006, p. 3114) argues that the disproportionate economic impact of SARS needs to be considered, for although it affected some 10,000 individuals (killing around 1,000), it did not lead to the devastating health catastrophe many had feared, as had the 1918 influenza pandemic, for instance, which claimed around 40 million lives. Economically, SARS cost an estimated 2% of the gross domestic product across the Far East, totaling a global bill of between USD $30 and $100 billion (Taylor, 2006).

Security, health, and economics have had an intrinsic connection throughout human history, and in a globalized world, these linkages can have both positive and negative consequences. Brundtland (2003) pointed out that more lives have been lost to the diseases malaria, measles, mumps, smallpox, and typhoid than were lost to bullets in the American Civil War. Likewise, mysterious and fatal diseases have stalled projects such as the construction of the Panama Canal. Thus the interconnected world presents both opportunities and risks. For instance, the Y2K computer bug generated USD $100 billion for the global economy (George, Marley, & Hawaleshka, 2005) despite its ability to destabilize various economic sectors in different parts of the world.

According to Tan and Enderwick (2006, pp. 518–519), during the period from the 1970s through the 1990s, economic risk in a global world was articulated through three forms of discourse: (a) the financial exchange rate, (b) inflationary rate risks, and (c) political risks that provoked host countries' hostility toward foreign investment. Tan and Enderwick asserted that political risks were country-specific. Such risks could also entail a multinational corporation's being constrained in its foreign operations by a host government's policies—measures such as forced divestment, stringent or unfavorable regulation, and interference with operations. In today's context, however, incidents such as global terrorism, SARS, financial crises, and computer viruses have the potential to affect the health of the global economy. Sudden, unexpected, and unpredicted threats—such as SARS—have the ability to spread quickly by means of global processes and forces (Enderwick, 2004).

The SARS epidemic had a direct impact on certain sectors that involve regular human contact, such as tourism and transport. The hotel business in Asia declined by 25% between February and March of 2003; Singapore and Hong Kong were most affected (Lemonick & Park, 2003; cited in Tan & Enderwick, 2006). SARS had a secondary effect on other sectors, such as the food and manufacturing industries. The outbreak also led to a fall in investments and a rise in unemployment, especially in tourism-related sectors in the affected countries. The enmeshing of health with bioterrorism and security issues during the SARS crisis underscored the need for policy makers to consider global issues when making domestic health decisions. The need also arose to acknowledge that globalization had intensified the dialectics of risk and regulation, for few governments can successfully regulate their economies independently in a context of global competition (Turner, 2001, p. 17).

The threat to the economic stability of nation-states nevertheless revitalized the need to protect boundaries during the crisis, simultaneously emphasizing the need for global and regional cooperation in curbing the disease. The issue of borders became a salient concept with the SARS outbreak because many governments imposed stricter border controls and implemented measures for detailed health and contact information. Taiwan, for instance, banned individuals who had travelled to SARS-affected regions (Kaufman & Chen, 2003). This response reiterated the role of the nation-state as governments took on major roles in crisis management. With the rise of globalization and instant dissemination of images and threats—particularly via online media—the local cultural context has become crucial in shaping and politicizing risk in the globalized world.

Infectious disease outbreaks often lead to spatial discourses in which the globe is mapped through the disease. During the SARS outbreak, as people cancelled flights to SARS-affected regions, they treated all of Asia as one place—a perspective that resulted in cancelled flights even to unaffected areas, including South Korea (Hamilton, 2003). In addition, the coincidental preference of SARS for cities like Toronto, Hong Kong, and Singapore gave it an urban veneer, reigniting new forms of risks within metropolitan cityscapes unparalleled since September 11, 2001.

Nevertheless, globalization does not eradicate the stigmatization that diseases can inflict on spaces and people. According to Peter Washer's (2004) study of media coverage of the SARS virus in the United Kingdom, the British media portrayed the virus as a serious threat to the country but also suggested that the disease was not as likely to affect the British as it had the Chinese because the Chinese are different from the British. This stigmatization and discrimination—or "othering"—is a resonant feature of infectious disease discourse throughout human history (Crawford, 1994; Joffe & Haarhoff, 2002; R. Smith, 2006).

SECURITIZATION OF RISK

According to Caballero-Anthony (2006, p. 105), a host of nontraditional security issues—such as environmental degradation, economic security, transnational crimes, ethnic conflicts, and infectious diseases—do not fall under the conventional notion of deliberate military threats. Often, the response has been to securitize these issues so that immediate attention and resources might be commanded to deal with them. The Copenhagen School, comprising a group of scholars from the Copenhagen Research Institute, has propounded the *securitization of risk theory*, in which the notion of security is socially shaped. Consequently, health and security are no longer compartmentalized and confined to the scientific and medical communities alone; they now encompass dialogue among the health, scientific, and foreign policy communities (Caballero-Anthony, 2006).

In tandem with this securitization of health issues, infectious diseases are often framed in the language of security threats in order to persuade audiences of their immediate danger. Because security is socially constructed, an uneven securitization of diseases has taken place; consider, for example, HIV/AIDS, which might not affect economic security or commercial endeavors quite so immediately or directly as SARS did in 2003. Since September 11, 2001, there has been substantial focus on terrorism-related policies, including spending, legislation, and public health measures relating to bioterrorism (Thomson & Wilson, 2005). Fred L. Smith (1995), moreover, contended that the human tendency is to rate a sensational risk affecting humans more highly than a prosaic risk that affects society. Consequently, the SARS virus, which was initially framed as a mysterious illness because of a lack of epidemiology, was seen as a disease that could not be controlled. This perceived lack of control and the apparent vulnerability created by the disease raised concerns about human and border security in many affected countries.

Comparing mortality rates from terrorism and tobacco, George Thompson and Nick Wilson (2005) revealed that the mortality burden from tobacco use is vastly higher than that from international terrorism in the selected countries they studied. In analyzing why tobacco mortality did not receive a proportionate response, they concluded that there may be a misplacement between "normal" and "catastrophic" deaths. The Thompson and Wilson study recognizes the subjectivity of risk perception and the tendencies of populations to overestimate risks that stem from visible, well-publicized violence where there is little apparent control by the individual—compared to risks from causes that appear to be voluntarily undertaken by the individual. In a similar vein, Coker (2004, p. 4) pointed out that the number of people who die from HIV/AIDS every day is twice the number of individuals who died in the World Trade Center attack.

In China the economic devastation caused by SARS alerted the government to the need to attach the same importance to public health as it had to national defense. Because economic success overrode all other priorities, public health organizations failed to predict and react to new types and variants of infectious diseases. The SARS epidemic killed 348 people on the Chinese mainland and cost the country USD $11.3 billion in 2003 (Lei, 2005; "Pandemics and transparency," 2006). The outbreak illuminated the lack of policy integration between health and security not only at a global level but also at national levels. Again, despite global perceptions of risk, the local context plays a significant role in managing health-related issues.

According to Emma Rothschild (1995; cited in Caballero-Anthony, 2006), despite historical linkages between health and security, these two areas developed their distinctive technical aspects, political constituencies, and institutional networks separate from each other. Although health issues might become increasingly securitized in the 21st century, this does not necessarily translate into integrated policy actions between the two discrete fields. Thus, global governance in the 21st century is affected not only by political will and resources but also by the lack of precedent in integrating policy issues. The need to integrate security and health will call for the involvement of a range of new actors in the international arena. The need for integration will also render concerted action more complex and clumsy and require concerted effort and planning at the state, national, regional, and local levels.

Health and Global Governance

Though globalization is often articulated in economic terms, it is inevitably a more expansive phenomenon mediated by a multitude of factors and events that are reshaping modern society rapidly (Huynen, Martens, & Hilderink, 2005, p. 1). People on the move can introduce new or previously eradicated diseases to a region of destination, or they can contract diseases unknown to the migrants' region of origin. Recent examples include the SARS outbreak, the spread of polio from northern Nigeria to Indonesia, the threat of an avian flu epidemic, and swine flu (the H1N1 virus), which is documented to have originated in Mexico.

In today's interconnected world, where bacteria and viruses transgress boundaries effortlessly, globalization is seen as increasing the risk that an infectious disease appearing in one country will spread rapidly to another (Brundtland, 2003; R. Smith, 2006). Lee and Dodgson (2000), who analyzed cholera as a case study of the links between globalization and health, argued that globalization has influenced the pattern of the disease, the vulnerability of certain populations, and the ability of public health systems to respond effectively. Although there are links between health and globalization, there is often a tendency to fuse the risk society and the theory of globalization into a singular view that considers only the dominantly negative consequences of technological change, thus conflating risk with hazards (Turner, 2001).

Conversely, Brundtland (2003) argued that health issues could become a bridge of peace for humanity. Such was the case of polio's eradication, which brought together 16 different countries across West Africa and prompted warring factions to lay down their weapons in order to protect some 60 million children against polio in the space of less than one week. Similarly, Brundtland contended that the Framework Convention on Tobacco Control assembled 192 countries under the banner of health to endorse a treaty to curb tobacco consumption, advertising, and smuggling and to encourage the creation of smoke-free places. Unification for health occurred yet again in 2003, when member states of the World Health Organization adopted a resolution that would revise and strengthen international health regulation by implementing a system to survey, report, and curb infectious diseases (Brundtland, 2003).

The most important organizations in health governance are the World Health Organization (WHO) and the World Bank (WB), but Rennen and Martens (2003) contended that the intensification of cross-national—indeed, global—cultural, economic, political, social, and technological interactions will lead to the establishment of other transnational structures. The SARS epidemic underscored the necessity for global coordination to control communicable diseases and the need to approach health as a global public good. The global risk report by the World Economic Forum (2006) ranked pandemics and natural disasters high on the list of risks currently confronting the international community and clearly acknowledged the varying responses and different assessment of threats globally.

Global governance for health continues to evolve and become more complex and challenging, involving a range of actors and changing ideas of sovereignty in a global market place (Owen & Roberts, 2005, p. 4).

The WHO played a vital role in containing the SARS epidemic, coordinating efforts and sharing information. Since the establishment of the Global Outbreak Alert and Response Network (GOARN) in 2000, the WHO can rely on more than 120 partner institutions worldwide (Heymann & Rodier, 2004a). Since 2000 this mechanism has mobilized international responses to 32 outbreak events in 28 countries, and the SARS crisis provided an opportunity to test the existing framework (R. Smith, 2006); for the first time in a decade, a global alert was issued by the WHO, along with travel advisories. The WHO also established a network of scientists from 11 countries to identify the causal agent and to develop a diagnostic test for SARS (R. Smith, 2006; Stohr, 2003; Zambon, 2003).

According to Heymann and Rodier (2004b, pp. 187–188), the international response to SARS came from a series of mechanisms put in place by the WHO in 1997. These mechanisms were designed to detect worldwide outbreaks of resurgent infectious diseases and to limit the magnitude of their impact. With the return of the cholera epidemic to Latin America in 1991, the economic losses caused by the media coverage of pneumonic plague in Surat, India, and the outbreak of Ebola hemorrhagic fever in Kikwit, Congo, in 1995, a need arose for broad-based international regulations and electronic information systems within the WHO. In 1997 the WHO established an innovative mechanism called the *outbreak verification* that signaled a new approach to global disease surveillance. The objective of this mechanism was to improve epidemic disease control by informing key public health professionals in the international domain about confirmed and unconfirmed outbreaks (Grein et al., 2000, p. 97). The foremost principle of the mechanism was the provision of data derived from an extensive network of information sources.

The reemergence of infectious diseases and mutated viruses since the 1990s has revitalized the dialogue on sustained international global governance. The renewed efforts to tackle the AIDS pandemic also saw the issue of global governance revived and revitalized (Thomas & Weber, 2004). Health issues are thus debated beyond the domestic realm in today's interlinked world. Nevertheless, countries exhibit considerable differences in attitudes toward the relationship between health and foreign policy (Owen & Roberts, 2005, p. 2). In comparing the differing approaches between Canada and the United States, for example, Owen and Roberts pointed out that Canada prioritizes health care not only as a domestic policy issue but also as a key objective for foreign policy. In contrast, U.S. foreign policy is influenced by the domestic policy agenda. Owen and Roberts contended that this approach, which focuses on such domestic agendas, can jeopardize or limit global health solutions, ultimately undermining progress toward global health equity.

The SARS outbreak demonstrated that although a problem may be global and international, solutions must be local and contextual. For example, there were different reactions to the travel advisory warnings issued by the WHO during the SARS crisis. Canada appeared to view its role as that of a national cheerleader rather than as a responsible partner in the global effort to contain the disease. Ontario reacted negatively by attacking the WHO for its travel advisory warning on Toronto (Menon, 2006). Conversely, despite their initial lack of openness dealing with avian flu in China and Thailand, Chinese authorities did eventually work with the WHO in order to share data and to initiate an inoculation program for poultry.

According to the WHO report *Global Public Goods for Health* (2002), markets tend to undersupply public goods because market-based incentives are inadequate (p. 11). The report notes that national governments acting individually lack the incentive to make provisions for such public goods at an adequate level. The WHO recognized that these goods must be provided by an international effort (specifically, public–private partnerships) in order to target areas characterized by an underinvestment in gathering knowledge, product development or operational issues.

In the *global public goods* (GPG) approach, the control of infectious disease is seen as vital for global health and thus requires policy intervention; it also requires more inclusive participation from a wide range of actors (Caballero-Anthony, 2006; Dodgson, Lee, & Drager, 2002). This approach involves both state and nonstate players. It also stresses the notion of shared responsibility, transparent governments, an active and engaged civil society, and socially concerned businesses. Whereas the notion of global governance and the GPG approach, to some measure, expect governments to work in a concerted manner, they do not eradicate the growing disparities between the wealthy and the poor. This disparity frequently offsets the measurable advances in global health care, such as a general rise in life expectancy from 48 years in 1955 to 66 years in 1998 (Thomas & Weber, 2004).

Thomas and Weber (2004) discerned that the history of global health governance has evolved in two phases. The first phase occurred in the 1970s when the United Nations (UN) became the forum for global governance with the 1978 Alma Ata Declaration, which marked a milestone in health-care discourse. This declaration enshrined health as a fundamental human right and was adopted by the WHO's World Health Assembly (WHA) in 1981. The WHA's adoption of the declaration's goal of providing egalitarian health care on a global scale in accordance with a needs-based approach offers an important insight. In particular, it highlights the way in which UN governance at that historical juncture moved closer than ever to bridging the gap between declarative or global politics, on the one hand, and substantive policy development, on the other (Thomas & Weber, 2004, p. 190). This shift made health care a universal human entitlement to which access should not be conditioned upon or determined by particular economic contexts. In 1981 the WHA endorsed the goal of "health for all by the year 2000," which sought to translate the Alma Ata Declaration into reality.

Thomas and Weber (2004) identified the second phase of global health governance as the period from the late 1970s onward. It was during this time that the institutional development of global governance occurred more noticeably through global economic organizations, such as the International Monetary Fund (IMF), the World Bank (WB), and the World Trade Organization (WTO). The late 1990s saw the increasing involvement of a wide range of stakeholders that leveraged the role of private–public partnerships and benefactors in order to tackle specific health problems, including malaria and access to drugs for the treatment of HIV/AIDS.

The Okinawa Convention of 2000 sought to legitimize the increasing role of the private sector as well as public–private partnerships. Thomas and Weber (2004, pp. 195–196) stress that this, in many ways, is a regression for the global governance of health. The resulting new rhetoric emphasizes the potential of medicine to remedy health problems and (indirectly) poverty and does not focus on issues of equity and social transformation. Economic considerations and, inevitably, the forces of capitalism have influenced the form and substance of global governance despite idealistic aspirations.

Global governance is evolving and becoming increasingly complex. Now, making policy decisions about global health issues involves the integration of a diverse range of stakeholders beyond the involvement and participation of nation-states. Therefore solutions to policies will be governed through the politics and resources of a range of actors rather than by the ideals that shaped the Alma Ata Declaration. Although diseases and the threat of bioterrorism will prompt diverse actors and nation-states to cooperate, endemic issues such as HIV/AIDS will be influenced by disparities in local health systems and policies (Coovadia & Hadingham, 2005). Even during the SARS epidemic, these disparities created tensions between local and global agendas. According to Dr. Shigeru Omi, WHO regional director for the Western Pacific, "many health systems were under-manned and under-resourced when SARS struck, and the result was great human suffering, enormous fear, and staggering economic loses" ("NZ urged," 2006, para. 4).

Technology, Disease, and Openness

Despite efforts by the WHO to coordinate global information and initiatives, the local response to the SARS crisis was mediated by both cultural norms and the ability of governments and health authorities to respond to the crisis in terms of policies and health-care provisions. Whereas some governments, such as that of Singapore, created new information platforms like television stations and Websites to disseminate information, Chinese authorities denied the existence of the virus for five months. China's initial understatement of the number of cases, its refusal to give daily reports, and its blocking WHO specialists from visiting Guangdong (where SARS originated) allowed SARS to spread rapidly (see Tan & Endwick, 2006; deLisle, 2003). Vietnam, in contrast, was prompt and open in responding to the virus. Its early request for WHO assistance, rapid case detection, isolation, infection control, and vigorous contact tracing helped bring the disease under control (Tan & Enderwick, 2006). In Taiwan, however, cover-ups of a second wave of SARS cases took place in May 2003 (Menon, 2006).

To some measure, officials and policy makers saw the spread of the disease as a form of failure in health governance and surveillance of the disease. The inconsistencies among nation-states and their political approaches to the control of information had implications for both the management and the communication of the disease. These differences indicate the emergence of a new kind of global digital divide associated with how various national governments choose to use ICTs to share public health information related to outbreaks with citizens and with how governments use ICTs to present such topics to their citizens.

At the same time, such technologies can be used to close divides of physical distance in order to share public health information more quickly around the world—thus shrinking the traditional global divides created by physical distance. Global shrinking through technology, transportation, and communication led to improved coordination efforts during the SARS epidemic. To identify the SARS coronavirus, the WHO reportedly used daily teleconferences and a virtual network of leading research laboratories connected by a shared Website (Menon, 2006, p. 363). During the SARS outbreak, the WHO also began using the Global Health Public Intelligence Network (GHPIN), a computer application designed to improve the speed of outbreak detection. This Web-crawling system searches over 950 news sources and electronic discussion boards worldwide in several languages for key words that could suggest an outbreak (Heymann & Rodier, 2004b, p. 188). In addition, the SARS epidemic prompted various agencies to establish a large number of Websites designed to disseminate information widely and quickly and to share information in real time (Larkin, 2003; R. Smith, 2006).

New forms of technologies were deployed during the SARS crisis to boost public morale and reinforce the notion that borders were monitored and protected. Singapore, for example, installed thermal scanners at airports to detect increased body temperatures. Other technological devices deployed by the Singapore authorities included diagnostic kits, surveillance instruments to monitor quarantined people in households, Web portals, and databases for mass contact tracing (Menon, 2006). The issue of global infectious-disease surveillance inevitably prompted discourse about the use of new and emerging infrastructure for surveillance of other activities, such as cross-border crimes and, in particular, bioterrorism. As mentioned earlier, global governance will require the integration of security and health concerns in the coming years. In order to meet this requirement, organizations will need to address the needs and problems of the globe and resist the dominant policy agendas of powerful nation-states and economic blocs.

China's lack of openness and outright denial in the initial months of the SARS epidemic highlight the discrepancies that arise in global health issues. The country's actions also illustrate a case in which the local political context and national pride mediated the handling of an infectious disease. Before Chinese authorities began controlling the information about the spread of the virus, news was spread through various means, including word of mouth, e-mail, and mobile telephony involving short messaging service (SMS). This "rumor period" (Qiang, 2003) during the initial phase of the disease represented a moment when there was no access to official information, and it created public panic. Subsequent media coverage prompted the Chinese government to crack down on the media in order to maintain an official flow of information from the authorities. In this way, a global digital divide was created in terms of what information was available via ICTs, to whom, and where. These initial government reports, moreover, denied the scale and serious nature of the epidemic.

Nevertheless, that these new forms of media allowed for the dissemination of information in advance of official government reports on the crisis presented a major challenge for governments. In China after the government's takeover and centralization of communications regarding SARS, vigilant censoring of information occurred on Websites, on bulletin boards, and in chat rooms (Qiang, 2003). Xiao Qiang (2003) pointed out that, in contrast, when the disease spread to Hong Kong, many individuals freely posted information on Websites and bulletin boards. All these activities created an information divide between areas of high ICT literacy and those of low literacy and between areas where information was controlled by the authorities and areas where it was not. In this way, global digital divides can become a matter of varying levels of access to online information *between* nations, and not just a matter of access to the ICTs used to disseminate information *within* a nation.

The actions of governments can play a central role in creating such digital divides involving access to information. For example, when Dr. Jiang Yanyong sounded the alarm on the lethal virus in China in April 2003, he was detained by Chinese authorities and labeled a dissident instead of a patriot who was working to save many lives (deLisle, 2003, pp. 597–598). Since Jiang's release and the publication of his SARS revelations, he has been under constant military surveillance. Likewise, in July 2006, the Chinese government halted the work of a Shantou laboratory that had published a paper linking the spread of avian flu from poultry in southern China to migratory birds in the western province of Qinghai (Greenfeld, 2006). In addition, at least six journalists who sought to cover the Qinghai outbreak were detained and forbidden to continue their reporting. China's response to SARS and avian flu is thus indicative of its authoritarian one-party political ideology and its approach to human rights (Jakes, 2004). Despite global governance and a consensus on health imperatives on an international level, the local context and cultural disparities continue to shape global health in an interconnected world. Through its locally focused and culturally distinct actions the Chinese government could easily create a problematic global digital divide by limiting the kind of public health information its citizens can access.

In August 2006, Indonesia's health minister, Siti Fadilah Supari, announced that Indonesia would allow open access to genomic data on avian flu, and that the government was taking this action in the name of addressing essential human interests ("Pandemics and Transparency," 2006). Before this declaration, online access to the information had been blocked, indicating that often the fear of disclosure is linked to concerns about economic impact, national pride, and the desire to find solutions indigenously without the intrusion of the outside world. Although information about SARS and avian flu has been shared through the networks of the WHO and the Food and Agriculture Organization (FAO), there is disappointment that open-source public access networks still remain a dream in an interconnected world ("Pandemics and Transparency," 2006).

Issues of transparency and openness during the 2003 crisis highlighted the differences in the cultural and ethical perspectives of various governments and countries and their use of ICTs to share health-related information with citizens. The virus also drew attention to the need to review animal husbandry practices in Asia in order to reduce the chances of both cross-infection and the emergence of new and dangerous pathogens ("WHO Tells World," 2006). The importance of open and transparent reporting was formally acknowledged in May 2003, when delegates to the World Health Assembly adopted a resolution on SARS. The resolution gives the WHO authority to take on a stronger role in coordinating the response to any infectious disease that is a threat to international public health (Heymann & Rodier, 2004b, p. 195). Culture and ideology, in addition to other factors such as media literacy and access, have mediated the ways new media technologies have been used for health communication. They also create new contexts for considering the nature and the origins of the modern global digital divide. This situation thus reiterates Cartwright's point that technology has been neither neutral nor democratizing and that in an epidemic situation, it can appropriate the ideological agendas of the nation-state.

Conclusion

The global mobility of capital, goods, and labor during an epidemic is an important context in which to study risk discourses and risk management.

The context of global mobility is a particularly interesting one for examining a postmodern world in which proximity and distance can be mediated through technologies that can track and monitor diseases but that can equally amplify risk. With the outbreak of the SARS epidemic in 2003, governments and international organizations faced the dual challenge of managing the spread of the disease and controlling the perceptions of risk within societies and communities. The pervasive use of ICTs in response to these challenges revealed new ways of sharing information and coordinating health agendas; it also reiterated geopolitical divides and inherent socioeconomic imbalances.

The lessons learned from the SARS epidemic are contrasting in nature. The global health crisis prompted global actors to come together (and they proved their ability to do so), but it also highlighted the differences and disparities between nation-states. In an increasingly interlinked world, divergent risks play out on the global stage and are narrated by ICTs as interlinked events. The mediated global stage as a place of narration for various risks creates a postmodern consciousness in which risks, fears, and uncertainties become fluid and permeable in a borderless world. The SARS epidemic's immediate association with air travel and its ability to disproportionately affect certain sectors of the global economy constructed the virus as a borderless security and economic threat that warranted immediate action from the global community and affected countries. The response to the SARS epidemic became an opportunity to scrutinize various issues raised by the virus on the global platform—ranging from the state of global health governance to the incestuous links among economic, security, and health concerns, links that politicize and prioritize risk on national and global levels. Moreover, the response highlighted the divergent cultural norms that will continue to pose a threat to the effective implementation of global policy agendas at the local level. These factors create new contexts for considering the global digital divide and require new perspectives and approaches for addressing global health crises effectively.

References

Altensetter, C., & Bjorkman, J. W. (1997). *Health and reform policy: National variations and globalizations*. London, UK: Macmillan.

Bauman, Z. (2006). *Liquid fear.* Cambridge, UK: Polity.

Beck, U. (1999). *World risk society.* Oxford, UK: Wiley-Blackwell.

Beck, U. (2002). *Risk society: Towards a new modernity.* London, UK: Sage.

Brundtland, G. H. (2003). Global health and international security. *Global Governance, 9*(4), 417–423.

Caballero-Anthony, M. (2006). Combating infectious diseases in East Asia: Securitization and global public goods for health and human security. *Journal of International Affairs, 59*(2), 105–127.

Cartwright, L. (2000). Reach out and heal someone: Telemedicine and the globalization of health care. *Health, 4*(3), 347–377.

Coker, D. (2004). War and disease. Paper presented at 21st Century Trust Conference: Disease and Security. Villa Monastero, Lake Como, Italy. Retrieved March 1, 2007, from http://www.21stcenturytrust.org/coker2.html.

Cooper, S. (2006). Special report: Preparing for a pandemic. *Harvard Business Review, 84*(5), 8–9.

Coovadia, H. M., & Hadingham, J. (2005). HIV/AIDS: Global trends, global funds, and delivery bottlenecks. *Globalization and Health, 1*(13). Retrieved March 26, 2007, from http://www.globalizationand-health.com/content/1/1/13.

Crawford, R. (1994). The boundaries of the self and the unhealthy other: Reflections on health, culture and AIDS. *Social Science and Medicine, 38*(1), 1347–1365.

Dayan, D., & Katz, E. (1992). *Media events: The live broadcasting of history.* Cambridge, MA: Harvard University Press.

deLisle, J. (2003). SARS, Greater China, and the pathologies of globalization and transition. *Orbis, 47*(4), 587–604. Retrieved July 7, 2009, from http://www.fpri.org/orbis/4704/delisle.sarschinaglobalization.pdf.

Dodgson, R., Lee, K., & Drager, N. (2002). *Global health governance: A conceptual review.* London, UK: Centre on Global Change and Health, London School of Hygiene and Tropical Medicine.

Economist Intelligence Unit. (2006). Country profile: China. *The Economist Intelligence Unit Limited*, pp. 6–8.

Enderwick, P. (2004). Responding to new environmental uncertainties: Terrorism and SARS in the global business environment. *Strategy Magazine, 2*, 14–16.

Furedi, F. (2005). *The politics of fear.* London, UK: Continuum.

Furedi, F. (2007, April 4). We have nothing to fear but the "culture of fear" itself. *Spiked.* Retrieved May 12, 2008, from http://www.frankfuredi.com/pdf/fearessay-20070404.pdf.

George, L., Marley, K., & Hawaleshka, D. (2005). Forget SARS, West Nile, Ebola, and avian flu: The real epidemic is fear. *Maclean's, 118*(40), 46–52.

Giddens, A. (1990). *The consequences of modernity.* Stanford, CA: Stanford University Press.

Greenfeld, K. T. (2006, March/April). What's next in the Sino-viral war? *Foreign Policy* (153), 46–47.

Grein, T. W., Kamara, K.-B. O., Rodier, G., Plant, A. J., Bovier, P., Ryan, M. J. … & Heymann, D. L. (2000, April). Rumors of disease in the global village: Outbreak verification. *Emerging Infectious Diseases, 16*(20), 97–102.

Hamilton, D. (2003). Three strategic challenges for a global transatlantic partnership. *European Foreign Affairs Review, 8*(4), 543–555.

Harris, S., & Keil, R. (2006). Global cities and the spread of infectious disease: The case of severe acute respiratory syndrome (SARS) in Toronto, Canada. *Urban Studies, 49*(3), 491–509.

Harvey, D. (1989). *Conditions of postmodernity.* Oxford, UK: Wiley-Blackwell.

Heymann, D. L., & Rodier, G. (2004a). Global surveillance, national surveillance, and SARS. *Emerging Infectious Diseases, 10*(2), 173–175.

Heymann, D. L., & Rodier, G. (2004b). SARS: A global response to an international threat. *Brown Journal of International Affairs, 10*(2), 185–197.

Huynen, M. M., Martens, P., & Hilderink, H. B. (2005). The health impacts of globalisation: A conceptual framework. *Globalization and Health, 1*(14). Retrieved March 26, 2007, from http://www.globalizationandhealth.com/content/1/1/14.

Jakes, S. (2004). A doctor famed for blowing the whistle on China's SARS cover-up learns the limits of Beijing's intolerance. *Time Australia, 28*, 47.

Joffe, H., & Haarhoff, G. (2002). Representations of far-flung illnesses: The case of Ebola in Britain. *Medicine, 54*, 944–969.

Kaufman, J., & Chen, K. (2003, April 28). Beijing imposes new SARS curbs: City's theaters and cafés are shut down as China lists another 161 cases. *The Wall Street Journal*, p. A8.

Larkin, M. (2003).Technology confronts SARS. *Lancet Infectious Diseases, 3*, 435.

Lee, K., & Dodgson, R. (2000). Globalization and cholera: Implications for global governance. *Global Governance, 6*(20), 213–237.

Lei, X. (2005, January 25). How SARS could save a nation. *New Statesman*, p. 25.

Lemonick, M. D. & Park, A. (2003, May 5). The truth about SARS. *Time, 161*, 48–53.

Leyshon, A. (1995). Annihilating space? The speed-up of communications. In J. Allen & C. Hammnett (Eds.), *A shrinking world? Global unevenness and inequality*. Oxford, UK: Oxford University Press/The Open University.

Mattelart, A. (1994). *The invention of communication.* Minneapolis, MN: University of Minnesota Press.

Meikle, J., Bowcott, O., & Carrell, S. (2009, July 23). Swine flu website crashes on launch. *The Guardian*. Retrieved July 27, 2009, from http://www.guardian.co.uk/world/2009/jul/23/swine-flu-figures-helpline.

Menon, K. U. (2006). SARS revisited: Managing outbreaks with communications. *ANNALS Academy of Medicine, 35*(5), 361–367.

Muzatti, S. L. (2005). Bits of falling sky and global pandemics: Moral panics and severe acute respiratory syndrome (SARS). *Illness, Crisis and Loss, 13*(2), 117–128.

NZ urged to "prepare for worst" over pandemic. (2006). *nzherald.co.nz*. Retrieved September 1, 2010, from http://www.nzherald.co.nz/world-health-organisation/news/article.cfm?o_id=422&objectid=10402088.

Owen, J. W., & Roberts, O. (2005). Globalisation, health, and foreign policy: Emerging linkages and interests. *Globalization and Health, 1*(12). Retrieved March 16, 2007, from http://www.globalizationandhealth.com/content/1/1/12.

Pandemics and transparency. (2006, August 12). *The Economist, 8490*, 65–66.

Qiang, X. (2003, June 5). SARS impact on media control and governance. *Testimony before US-China Economic and Security Review Commission.* Retrieved July 7, 2007, from http://www.uscc.gov/hearings/2003hearings/written_testimonies/03_06_05/qiates.htm.

Rennen, W., & Martens, P. (2003). The globalisation timeline. *Integrated Assessment, 4*(3), 137–144.

Rothschild, E. (1995). What is security? *Daedalus, 124*(3), 53–98.

Smith, F. L. (1995). Assessing the political approach to risk management. *Economic Affairs, 16*(1), 11–12.

Smith, R. D. (2006). Responding to global infectious disease outbreaks: Lessons from SARS on the role of risk perception communication and management. *Social Science and Medicine, 63*(12), 3113–3123.

Stohr, K. (2003, May 17). A multicentre collaboration to investigate the cause of severe respiratory syndrome. *The Lancet, 361*(9370), 1730–1733.

Tan, W., & Enderwick, P. (2006). Managing threat in the global era. *Thunderbird International Business Review, 48*(4), 515–536.

Taylor, I. (2006, March 17). Painful lessons from SARS. *Travel Weekly*, p. 5.

Thomas, C., & Weber, M. (2004). The politics of global health governance: Whatever happened to "health for all by the year 2000"? *Global Governance, 10*(2), 187–205.

Thomson, G., & Wilson, N. (2005). Policy research from comparing mortality from two global forces: International terrorism and tobacco. *Globalization and Health, 1*(8). Retrieved March 26, 2007, from http://www.globalizationandhealth.com/content/1/1/18.

Turner, B. S. (2001). Risks, rights, and regulation: An overview. *Health, Risk, and Society, 3*(1), 9–18.

Urry, J. (2000). Mobile sociology, *British Journal of Sociology, 51*(1), 185–201.

Wang, M. D., & Jolly, A. M. (2004). Changing virulence of the SARS virus: The epidemiological evidence. *Bulletin of the World Health Organization, 82*(7), 547–548.

Washer, P. (2004). Representations of SARS in the British newspapers. *Social Science and Medicine, 59*(12), 2561–2571.

WHO tells world to prepare: Risk factors of severe acute respiratory syndrome. (2006, May 22). *Feedstuffs, 78*(21), 34.

World Economic Forum. (2006). *Global Risks* [Report]. Switzerland. Retrieved July 7, 2009 from http://www.weforum.org/pdf/CSI/Global_Risk_Report.pdf.

World Health Organization [WHO]. (2002). *Global Public Goods for Health*. Retrieved February 6, 2011, from whqlibdoc.who.int/publications/9241590106.pdf.

Zambon, M. (2003, April 19). Severe acute respiratory syndrome revisited: Coronavirus may be responsible, but new information arrives every day. *British Medical Journal, 326*(7394), 831–832.

CHAPTER 9

THE COMMERCIALIZATION OF HIGHER EDUCATION AND KNOWLEDGE AS A GLOBAL TREND

IMPLICATIONS FOR THE DIGITAL DIVIDE IN DEVELOPING COUNTRIES

Tatjana Takševa

Recently, the United Nations Educational, Scientific, and Cultural Organization (UNESCO) stated that no one should be excluded from situations "where knowledge is a public good" (2005, p. 18). Connections between digital technologies and higher education in global contexts can, however, jeopardize knowledge as a public good and can actually widen the global digital divide. This chapter examines how the commercialization of higher education is turning knowledge into a commodity—or a kind of property—in many developing nations. The chapter presents an overview of issues that contribute to the global digital divide and suggests potential solutions to this situation.

INTRODUCTION

UNESCO (2005) recently stated that no person should be excluded from the new "knowledge societies where knowledge is a public good" (p. 18). The growing links, however, between digital technologies and higher education—coupled with globalizing trends that push education toward increasing commercialization—can jeopardize the idea of knowledge as a public good. Such trends can also widen the global digital divide and the existing international knowledge gap. This chapter examines the effects globalization is having on higher education, focusing in particular on the consequences of the commercialization of higher education and knowledge for developing countries. First, I review recent global trends concerning higher education, revealing the implications these trends have for the digital divide in developing countries—nations where higher education is a central instrument of development. I conclude by offering solutions to this problematic situation in global higher education. This chapter identifies both the tensions between global and local forces and the interdependence among IT and social, ethical, and political issues in global contexts.

DISPARITY AND THE DIGITAL DIVIDE

In 2005 UNESCO released a *World Report* that assessed the issues involved in the global transition of societies to a technology-driven, knowledge-based global economy. The report acknowledges that the knowledge society is becoming inseparable from what has become known as the information society. The report also defines knowledge as a concept based on information—particularly, information involving a wide range of issues including social, ethical, and political factors. The report emphasizes the importance of education as a public service that can build "real" knowledge societies from which "nobody should be excluded" and "where knowledge is a public good, available to each and every individual" (pp. 17–18, 20).

Because today's knowledge system is increasingly Internet based, the Internet as a public network "seems to be carving out fresh opportunities to widen the public knowledge forum" and thus seems to be narrowing the digital divide (Altbach, 2002, p. 9). At the same time, the UNESCO report notes that "vast swathes of the global population" still lack opportunities for equal access to both technology and education (UNESCO, 2005, p. 17). The report also warns that "today, as in the past, the control of knowledge can go hand in hand with serious inequality" (UNESCO, 2005, p. 19).

Recent research on the global digital divide shows that in this case, "classical sociological concepts of inequality" in terms of "possession" and "relationship[s] to power" could serve as a background for understanding the divide (UNESCO, 2005; van Dijk, 2006, p. 223). These findings indicate that although globalization might not necessarily be the only cause of inequalities among countries, it does "make poor countries poorer" by concentrating wealth, knowledge, and power in the hands of the people who already possess those elements (Altbach & Knight, 2006, p. 2; Thurow, 2005, p. 22). The increasing connections among information and communication technologies (ICTs), higher education, and the global market economy thus have serious consequence for developing countries and for their chances to become full participants in the knowledge societies of the future.

Three Functions of Information

In a society where information can be transformed into economically valuable knowledge, the ability to evaluate information and implement its potential uses has three functions: as a primary good, as a positional good, and as a source of skills (van Dijk, 2006, p. 231). Information is a primary good because it is essential for the development of self-respect and for survival in contemporary global society. As the "digital media are gradually replacing and surpassing analogue print media, traditional illiterates are joined by a new category, 'the digital illiterates'" (van Dijk, 2006, p. 231). Consequently, the issue of who has information and who does not takes on increasing importance in global society. In sum, those individuals who either lack access to essential information or lack the skills needed to use it effectively are increasingly and severely disadvantaged.

As a positional good, information is, by definition, unequal in its distribution, and its uses range in that "some positions in society create better opportunities than others in gathering, processing and using valuable information" (van Dijk, 2006, p. 231). These opportunities, in turn, determine the position individuals have in the media network created by this dynamic. In addition, "the successful appropriation of ICTs creates a so-called skills premium," the attainment of which (or one's inability to attain it) is one of the main causes of increasing income inequality in many countries (van Dijk, 2006, p. 231). The three functions of information in the global world are thus integrally interrelated. Moreover, they establish the potential of individuals or of nations to compete in the global knowledge market.

THE DIGITAL DIVIDE AND HIGHER EDUCATION

A "tiered" understanding of the global digital divide shows that the reasons for the divide's widening include a lack of access to both ICTs and the infrastructure needed for using them (Altbach, 2001, 2002, 2004; Gebremichael & Jackson, 2006; Stromquist, 2007; van Dijk, 2006). In addition, the difference in the rate of technological progress and its use to benefit individuals, nations, and the globalized world is widening existing disparities between the most developed countries in the world and the developing nations. In this context, the United States, Canada, Japan, and the nations of western and northern Europe are usually cited as being among the most developed nations. Conversely, the nations of Latin America, Africa, and Southeast Asia are often referred to as developing countries.

It should, however, be noted that there might be significant differences in rates of development with regard to ICTs among developing nations.

Brazil, for example, was recently ranked as the top Latin American country in terms of Internet readiness, and it was followed closely by Chile. Peru, Ecuador, Paraguay, Bolivia, and Argentina, in contrast, appeared closer to the bottom of this ranking (Oxford Analytica, 2003). Some of the smaller nations of the Caribbean (e.g., Costa Rica, the Dominican Republic, and Trinidad and Tobago) are being acknowledged for their important efforts to improve both their ICT readiness and the effective use of these technologies (deGannes Scott, 2006; Oxford Analytica, 2003). Yet in all national and international contexts, access to ICTs and the effective use of these technologies is becoming increasingly intertwined with access to the skills needed to create, manage, and promote knowledge in the current information economy. Thus even if individuals have access to information, they often still lack the skills needed to turn that information into a primary and a positional good and display their marketable skills. Education can help bridge this divide.

In today's knowledge economy, higher education is increasing in importance because of its role in educating people for the new information economy. In fact, globalization increases the demand for higher education, for the two main bases of globalization are information and innovation—both of which are knowledge intensive (Carnoy, 2005, p. 3). Because knowledge-intensive ICTs are gradually acquiring a prominent place in this context, the global digital divide is also becoming an international knowledge gap, or a global knowledge divide (van Dijk, 2006, p. 221; Young Kim, 2008). Education, however, is a central factor among the constellation of factors that determine whether individuals are able to gain ICT-related benefits; these factors include industrialization, resources (e.g., income), the quality of equipment, and the skill of the user (Crenshaw & Robinson, 2006; cf. Nephew Hassani, 2006, p. 253; Zhao, Kim, Suh, & Du, 2007). Accordingly, institutions of higher education, which serve as centers of knowledge creation and dissemination, have an important role to play in narrowing the digital divide, correcting patterns of digital inequality, and contributing to equitable and sustainable knowledge societies.

However, global trends affecting higher education (e.g., the increasing accountability of academic institutions to industry and the private sector) might eventually compromise higher education's capacity to help individuals realize their potential. And the forces affecting higher education around the world are strikingly consistent. They include less public funding (per student), more private investment, and increasing interest in the implementation of international treaties that govern education policies or regulate educational activities (Carnoy, 2005; Mohamedbhai, 2002; Washburn, 2005). Unprecedented investments of global capital into higher education are turning colleges and universities into centers of the growing knowledge industry, and many societies increasingly depend on knowledge products and highly educated personnel for economic growth (Altbach & Knight, 2006). Thus, globalization cannot be avoided, and colleges and universities should not be cut off from major economic and social trends. Yet the changes and the benefits of globalization bring with them risks that need to be carefully evaluated in terms of their effects on both the global digital divide and the widening knowledge gap between developed and developing nations.

The Commercialization of Higher Education

The rapid expansion of international trade in education services generally presents higher education as a commercial commodity—as something to be traded freely as one of many private services—rather than as a public responsibility. There has always been an international aspect to education in that both students and academics have engaged in educational pursuits across borders. What is different now, however, is not only the volume of such activities driven by ICTs but also the "increasingly market-oriented delivery of higher education and the prominent role played by for-profit providers offering services directly across borders" (Robinson, 2006, p. 1).

The World Trade Organization (WTO), as a leader in this process, has adopted a framework of rules governing free international trade in education services. In so doing, the WTO treats education just like any other commodity (European Students' Union, 2005; Mohamedbhai, 2002; cf. Robinson, 2006). The purpose of the WTO perspective, as presented in the General Agreement on Trade in Services (GATS), is to progressively liberalize trade in education services. The WTO does so through (a) facilitating successive rounds of negotiations with local governments on enabling cross-border supply though distance learning, (b) encouraging the consumption of education services abroad, (c) establishing commercial presence abroad though university branches or partnerships, and (d) importing actual individuals (known as "natural persons"), such as teachers and professors, from other nations. The changes created by the GATS policies have prompted many universities in industrialized countries to set up satellite campuses overseas. These changes have also led to the creation of for-profit educational institutions that function to "sell" education, mainly to developing countries. What is important about these agreements is that they have been created to protect the sellers and the providers, not the buyers and users. As a result, GATS-related policies have negative implications for developing nations (Mohamedbhai, 2002; Raikhy, 2002). Indeed, in many countries, the government agencies most involved with these agreements do not include ministries of education but instead involve departments concerned with trade and export promotion (Altbach, 2004, p. 17).

Under the pressures of globalization, developing countries are increasingly adopting measures similar to those of highly industrialized countries, measures including "greater corporate autonomy for their higher education institutions" as a way to encourage commercialization and "private income generation" (King, 2003b, p. 22). Between 1990 and 1999, for example, the number of private educational institutions in many sub-Saharan African countries "grew from an estimated 30 to more than 85," whereas public funding for education in those nations dropped by 25.8% (King, 2003b, p. 22). Most of these institutions are located in large urban areas, yet 35% of the African population resides in rural and remote areas, lacks basic literacy skills, and is unfamiliar with many of today's ICTs (Gebremichael & Jackson, 2006, p. 274; cf. Gurstein, 2003; Marine & Blanchard, 2004, p. 4).

Moreover, educational partnerships involving universities and colleges from the industrialized North and West and institutions in developing nations tend to be unequal and often of little or no benefit to the host country (Brown & Lauder, 2006; Nephew Hassani, 2006). At the same time, the academic centers located in the United States, the United Kingdom, Canada, Australia, and the larger countries of the EU grow stronger and more dominant. As they do, the peripheries (i.e., the institutions in developing nations) become increasingly marginalized, resulting in ever-increasing inequalities in the world of global higher education (Altbach, 2004; Brown & Lauder, 2006; Young Kim, 2008).

Even though variations exist within the academic systems of developing countries, a number of trends in global education have serious implications for the digital and knowledge divides in developing countries. I see four major issues contributing to the digital and knowledge gap in countries with emerging economies: (a) international treaties governing trade in educational services, (b) decreased public funding for higher education and the consequent increase in student fees, (c) marginalization of the professoriate in developing countries as a consequence of the global digital divide, and (d) devaluation of local knowledge in favor of more profitable kinds of information.

Issues of Globalization and Education

Though some research notes the potentially harmful effects the globalization of higher education has for developing countries (Altbach, 2001, 2002, 2004; Carnoy, 2005; Giroux, 2004; Mohamedbhai, 2002; Smith, 2002; UNESCO, 2005), relatively little research has been conducted on the commercialization of higher education as related to the international digital divide and the growing global knowledge gap (King, 2003b; Mohamedbhai, 2002). In addition, quantitative approaches—rather than interdisciplinary and qualitative approaches—have characterized research on communication and education practices associated with the digital divide (van Dijk, 2006, p. 232). The remaining sections of this chapter present a preliminary inquiry into such approaches. The purpose of this focus is to draw attention to the issues that play a central role in creating the global digital divide in education.

Issue 1: The Influence of International Treaties Governing Trade in Educational Services on the Knowledge Gap in Developing Countries

Globalized higher education is increasingly characterized by new international agreements and arrangements made to manage global interactions relating to educational services. The WTO provided a regulatory framework designed to allow and encourage trade in education and service-related industries as part of the GATS. The free-trade educational services context would facilitate academic mobility in terms of the cross-border supply of educational services. It would also include ICT-facilitated education, the franchising of courses and degrees, and an increased commercial presence as service providers establish facilities (e.g., branch campuses and joint ventures) in other countries.

Although these developments might present opportunities for both sides involved, along with these opportunities come significant risks for developing countries. The European Students' Union (ESU), the Association of African Universities, the Centre for Higher Education Policy Studies at the University of Twente, the International Association of Universities, the European Universities Association, the American Council of Education, and the Association of Universities and Colleges of Canada are among those entities that are concerned about public education and that have spoken out against GATS. Individuals who favor GATS, in turn, come primarily from multinational corporations and areas of government relating to exports (Organization for Economic Cooperation and Development, 2002). It is noteworthy that agreements like GATS permit and facilitate the proliferation of for-profit, private colleges and universities; the key objective of such institutions is financial gain. Some financially strapped nonprofit universities are proponents of GATS as well (Altbach & Knight, 2006, p. 2). Thus commercial and profit-driven forces are in the process of acquiring a legitimate or even a dominant place in global higher education. This dominance allows commercial forces to define knowledge and education increasingly in terms of privately owned goods regulated by international agreements.

The process of liberalizing trade in educational services has some potentially positive effects, including increased access to higher education for many students, greater collaboration between students and faculty in different countries, and improved pedagogy and research (Atkinson, 2001; Liu, Rhoads & Wang, 2007; Mohamedbhai, 2002). Yet in many developing countries, the establishment of for-profit subsidiaries is seen as having a harmful influence on the domestic education system. There have already been indications that subsidiaries of universities from industrialized nations have not focused on local needs in developing countries (Mohamedbhai, 2002; Newman, Couturier, & Scurry, 2004). Recent practice in South Africa, for example, shows that partnerships involving local institutions and foreign universities appear to be "simply profitable marriages of convenience, enabling the foreign partner to enter the South African market with little or no contribution to the development of the teaching and research capacity of the local partner" (King, 2003a, p. 3). In addition, because the primary motivation for the cross-border supply of educational services is profit, the quality of courses and programs offered by foreign providers is often substandard, reinforcing the view that such programs operate as "diploma mills." This situation undermines one of the main functions of universities in developing countries—to participate in the host country's economic, social, and cultural development (Mohamedbhai, 2002, pp. 4, 5).

National governments currently still exert a great degree of regulatory power over the university systems within their borders. Such power can determine the fees full-time students are charged for attending universities in those nations. Governments can also seek wider social access and the promotion of particular areas of research. But the pressures of globalization and the power of large international financial investors force experts to admit that local governments are gradually losing the power to influence or control educational developments in their own countries (King, 2003b).

Increasingly, institutions of higher education are being viewed as instruments for building and maintaining national, international, and global development. However, developing countries' "greatest need [is] for academic institutions that can contribute to national development," for such institutions produce knowledge relevant to local needs and thus strengthen civil society in those areas (Altbach, 2001, p. 4; cf. King, 2003b, p. 22). The function and responsibility of the university to serve the common good of the nation is therefore especially relevant in developing countries. Universities in developing nations cannot successfully transition to the international scene as equal participants until they have established a strong and sustainable national base that would allow them to compete in the knowledge-based global society. In this sense, partnerships with foreign institutions, though they provide some short-term financial benefits, might in fact have adverse long-term effects on publicly oriented social agendas. Given the unequal relationship likely to result from these partnerships, the effects such arrangements have on the global digital divide and the international knowledge gap will almost certainly be negative.

International treaties governing the trade in educational will have many negative effects on developing countries and could widen international digital and knowledge gaps. The gradual liberation of trade in higher education services is set to significantly affect local institutions' ability to respond to the needs of their local communities and adapt teaching and research to local needs (Newman, Couturier, & Scurry, 2004; World Trade Organization, 2001). These GATS-related agreements will increasingly limit national control over decisions concerning education and the assessment of local needs. Because of the growing links between education and industry, moreover, private donors interested in profits will be able to influence the nature and the direction of research conducted at educational institutions. These factors could result in a decrease in incentives and opportunities for investment in certain (i.e., nonprofitable) educational projects; they might also affect funding allocated to locations of great local value but of much less value on the global market or that are not directly profit-oriented. Such decreases in funding could seriously limit opportunities for growth and contribute to the widening of the digital divide in many poor and remote regions.

Finally, a significant feature of international agreements on the privatization of knowledge is the tightening of copyright and intellectual property laws. The idea is to further protect the creators and owners of knowledge, but these modifications do not make adequate provisions for fair use in developing countries. The tightening of copyright and intellectual property laws in academia is implicated negatively in the control and ownership of information and thus also in the control and ownership of information and knowledge, which has traditionally belonged to the wealthy and the powerful. Control of information rewards owners and rights holders, most of whom are in the industrialized countries, at the expense of public dissemination and access to knowledge under the provision of fair use. Limiting access to and dissemination of information and knowledge in an increasingly Internet-based age, thus, has negative effects on developing countries. This will be especially true for nations that are already disadvantaged in terms of access and that often serve as the consumers of knowledge produced by others. In fact, Richard Stallman (2003), the founder of the Free Software Foundation (FSF), has characterized the digital divide as only a symptom of a larger social problem—namely, proprietary software (copyrighting and patenting)—which creates barriers to sharing ideas and information.

Instead of balancing private interests and public needs, colleges and universities are increasingly subject to trends that can become "anti-social instruments of intimidation and control" (Bollier, 2006, p. 2). These trends work against the humanitarian and democratizing potential of digital media in the service of the public, tending instead to reinforce existing inequalities. In terms of developing countries, these trends are counterproductive to efforts to maximize opportunities for Internet access and the online dissemination of information—factors that would enable less developed nations to participate more effectively in a global knowledge-based society.

Issue 2: Decreased Public Funding for Higher Education and Increased Cost-Sharing

Decreased public funding for education has placed institutions on the losing side of the battle for funding, the acquisition of equipment, and the hiring of experts. This trend affects developing countries the most because many of these nations have been highly dependent on outside donors. The digital divide in many developing nations is, in fact, increasing because of a lack of the internal and external revenue needed to establish and maintain access to ICTs and to enable their efficient use. Few individuals in developing nations have seen their teaching affected by IT and "even fewer have been able to use IT to enhance classroom-based teaching as they lack necessary facilities, equipment, knowledge and funds" (Altbach, 2002, p. 9). For example, even though universities in Albania recently received some support in the form of equipment, this support has enabled the establishment of only a basic inventory of hardware. There were no national policies for e-learning, no networks of "universities online," and no online resources for Albanian university students in Albania (Ndroqi, 2002, p. 3).

Nigeria provides another example of such problems. In this case, the major obstacles to the use of ICTs in education include the "high-cost of computer hardware and software; weak infrastructure; lack of human skills and knowledge in ICT; lack of relevant software appropriate and culturally suitable to Nigeria" (Aduwa-Ogiegbaen, 2005, p. 104; Bagayoko, Muller, & Geissbuhler, 2006). Although it is clear that ICTs, in connection with higher education, are a prerequisite for participating fully in the knowledge societies of the 21st century, little is being done to address these issues in a comprehensive, systematic way.

The growing links between the corporate sector and higher education will only compound existing problems. In terms of academic centers and peripheries, the price of entry into the international academic market has risen. Now, colleges and universities require vast resources to remain "fully networked for the Internet and information technology," maintaining, among other things, "access to relevant databases" (Altbach, 2004, p. 5). At the same time, the growing ties between institutions of higher learning and private, corporate donors increasingly shape student-recruitment policies in ways that might have a negative impact on the knowledge gap in the long term. As a result, targeting "preferred student markets" (i.e., those individuals who can pay tuition fees in full), is becoming an important way of generating needed revenue for universities in developing nations (Slaughter, 2001; Stromquist, 2007). The risk here is that the services of the knowledge industry will gradually become geared toward those who can afford them rather than toward those who need them. The potential result could be social conditions that contribute to the widening of the international digital divide and the global knowledge divide.

Exclusionary tendencies will also become more pronounced as growing numbers of profit-centered corporate universities are established in developing countries. Such would be the case for institutions in Egypt, Vietnam, India, Mauritius, Mozambique, Uganda, and Zimbabwe (Altbach & Knight, 2006, pp. 4–7; Banya, 2001; Huang, 2002; Woodhall, 2001). Questions are already arising whether private universities are the solution to the global crisis in higher education (Banya, 2001). And cost-sharing without measures tailored to the specific needs of each country will result in more restricted access to limited resources (Woodhall, 2001). Thus, individuals in developing nations will be increasingly prevented from acquiring skills and accessing resources and information (Huang, 2002) as primary and positional goods in a knowledge-based society.

Given the increasingly corporate orientation of higher education, it is likely that educational-corporate ventures will expand to regions where they are most able to profit from the collaboration. In general, such a choice would generally be implemented at the expense of other regions, where such cooperative ventures could provide great benefit for most of the population they are supposed to serve (cf. Bagayoko, Muller, & Geissbuhler, 2006). Because the new higher education institutions tend to focus on middle-class markets and money, the rural-urban digital divide in many developing regions continues to widen

(Gebremichael & Jackson, 2006, p. 272; Jaeger, Bertot, McClure, & Langa, 2006). This development also reflects what was said recently about the corporate ownership of ICTs: "It seems that it has been primarily the corporate sector and even only certain elements within the corporate sector who have truly taken advantage of the revolutionary potential offered by ICTs" (Gurstein, 2003, p. 2).

Smaller enterprises, such as those with lower access to investment funds, those in developing counties, and "whole strata of those who are not direct financial beneficiaries of the corporate sector—not for profits, the local public sector, those outside the market and beyond the technology enabled networks—are clearly falling ever further behind" (Gurstein, 2003, p. 2). The major risk is treating knowledge as an industry and a private good that benefits individuals rather than society and the public good. This interpretation of knowledge creates a situation in which the needs of those who are most vulnerable and who could most benefit from knowledge as common good and a public responsibility might be overlooked. The result is a widening of the current knowledge gap.

Issue 3: The Global Digital Divide and the Professoriate in Developing Countries

The international digital divide increasingly includes the professoriate. In some cases, this situation results from the growing dominance of the powerful academic centers from the North and West. In other instances, it stems from existing inequalities in terms of available infrastructure, high cost of access to online resources, and inconsistent use of even the most basic equipment available to academics in many developing countries. Thus even though IT has provided many academics in developing countries with unprecedented access to current knowledge, in most academic contexts in developing countries, access and efficient use remain relevant issues. In Africa, for example, many academic staff members do not have their own computers; instead they share with others. In these instances, personal e-mail accounts are far from universal, and connectivity is sporadic and often slow because of inadequate and poorly maintained analogue connections. Slow and sporadic access limits the usefulness of electronic resources because under these circumstances "most sophisticated databases will not run well" (Altbach, 2002, p. 9).

Such limitations prevent the professoriate in certain regions from developing and perfecting the skills valued in an increasingly information-based knowledge economy. These factors also impede the professoriate's consistent access to resources that shape the dominant global academic trends (Brown & Lauder, 2006; Longley, Ashby, Webber, & Li, 2006). Even when individuals do have access to the Internet, it often allows them simply to consume and receive information and knowledge rather than create and distribute it—a distinction relevant to the growing digital divide (Gurstein, 2003). Academics are thus effectively deprived of opportunities for discovery and innovation in the new knowledge-based global economy (UNESCO, 2005, p. 95).

In addition to physical and financial aspects of the digital divide, many of the IT products used in distance education originate in industrialized countries. Because these products have been designed for different social and cultural contexts, they might be irrelevant and largely inapplicable to curricula in developing countries. The recently established African Virtual University, for example, has had "trouble finding content relevant for African countries." This situation reinforces existing patterns of inequality because academics in developing countries are "still peripheral in many ways to the Internet-based knowledge system" (Altbach, 2002, p. 10). These individuals become part of the digital divide in terms of access and efficient use.

The globalization of higher education further exacerbates these patterns of inequality. Research universities in industrialized countries set the patterns, produce the research, control key international journals (many of which are online), and control other means of research-related ICTs. In addition, academic decision-making structures are often based in developed countries and reflect the topics, approaches, and concerns of the academic communities in those nations. Therefore, not much value is accorded to locally oriented research relevant to developing countries (Altbach, 2003, 2004). As a result, knowledge creation in the Internet-based information economy happens increasingly in academic centers in industrialized nations, placing academics from developing countries in a position of dependency with respect to their counterparts in industrialized nations.

There are also linguistic factors to consider. As the language most represented in international ICT use, English is also becoming the language of academic centers. This factor, however, affects education policy and the work of individual students and scholars around the world. It also gives a key advantage to academics in the United Kingdom, the United States, and other wealthy English-speaking countries. Within academic circles, the peer-review system is dominated by those accustomed to both the language and the methodology of the academic centers where English is the language of scholarly discourse. As a result, international and regional scholarly meetings are increasingly conducted in English, academic journals and books in English dominate the international academic market, and English-language journal databases are the most widely used internationally. Access to these resources, moreover, is generally priced according to European or North American markets. As a result, essential academic materials are often extraordinarily expensive for universities in developing countries.

These cost and linguistic factors place academics in developing nations at a disadvantage. They often have to teach and research in a language foreign to them and conform to the unfamiliar norms that dominate the research and publishing processes of different cultures. Academics in developing nations are frequently prevented from gaining access to many digital resources because of either language or cost. Thus "while academe worldwide is affected by the power and influence of the largest academic systems, and especially those that use English, the developing countries are at the bottom in a world system of unequal academic relationships" (Altbach, 2004, p. 8). As a result, these academics and the students and communities they serve increasingly become *consumers* of knowledge that is produced in industrialized countries.

Another consequence of the privatization of higher education is that foreign, for-profit education providers often draw most of their faculty from the host country. They offer attractive salaries in order to lure well-qualified local faculty away from underpaid publicly funded positions at local universities, diminishing the teaching and research capacities of local universities. The outsourcing of local faculty on a part-time basis is a related problem. Overworked and overburdened with teaching responsibilities, local faculty are less able and less willing to undertake research in their fields of expertise or to participate in the production and dissemination of knowledge that would make them equal players in the knowledge-driven economy (Mohamedbhai, 2002).

Issue 4: The Devaluation of Alternative and Local Knowledge Widens the Global Knowledge Gap

The commercialization of education is not only an economic process related to the governance and structure of colleges and universities; it also bears symbolic aspects that, moreover, might negatively affect developing countries' efforts to become equal participants in the global knowledge economy.

Essentially, in a system of globalized education, a number of factors will gradually replace the values traditionally associated with education and knowledge as a public good. These factors include the growing links between the private or for-profit sectors and educational institutions, the values of the marketplace (associated with the idea of private, for-profit ownership), and benefits for those who study or do research in certain nations (Altbach, 2002, 2004). In fact, the principle of correspondence holds that "the strong links between business firms and educational institutions produce a tendency for the latter to imitate the former" (Stromquist, 2007, p. 84). This development leads educational institutions, like businesses, to develop a primary interest in research that is most likely to serve the interests of industry. In this way, industry can exert greater influence over what is labeled valuable knowledge and what is to be produced by a university.

Research indicates that "specialization in fields that ensure a solid return on investment are allowed to grow; in contrast, other specializations that suffer from a lack of external funding … are closed down gradually by non-replacement of faculty or by simply declaring them unproductive" even when they serve to address important social issues (Stromquist, 2007, p. 84). Moreover, concurrent tendencies indicate that faculty participation in major decision making is decreasing whereas the administration's participation is growing considerably (Stromquist, 2007, pp. 88, 92). Because of this shift, academic considerations involving the promotion of knowledge as a public service may be considered less relevant than managerial or profit-seeking ones. Such situations could also result in the abandonment of some subject areas in local universities because those subjects are deemed unprofitable and or because market demand for these studies is poor. And although it is true that "industrial sponsors cannot tell universities what to study," those financially powerful entities can exert a great deal of influence by sponsoring only the programs that best align with their particular interests (Mohamedbhai, 2002; Stromquist, 2007, p. 96).

As certain preferred models of knowledge embedded in this outlook become more dominant, the value of alternative, local forms of knowledge decreases (UNESCO, 2005). Such local knowledge is often rendered irrelevant and replaced by the dominant models, even when these are not appropriate or relevant to local conditions. A significant aspect of this process is the rise of English as a global language. Of course, a single international and global language can facilitate communication among diverse societies and across linguistic barriers; this is potentially beneficial. However, the rise of English as the lingua franca of higher education, in combination with the increasing links between the for-profit sector and higher education, might create social and cultural conditions resembling those of neocolonialism. Language as a cultural and social tool is never value neutral; as a result, the dominance of English in ICTs and higher education might lead to the increasing dominance of values and assumptions typical of powerful, highly industrialized nations in which English is the primary—or a major—language.

Accordingly, if English gradually replaces local, indigenous languages, the ideas of English-speaking cultures might also gradually replace the values transmitted through those indigenous languages. Thus a widening knowledge gap would obtain between individuals who have and control the kinds of knowledge preferred on the global market and those who live on the peripheries of globalized society and who possess the kinds of knowledge that have no value in the global economy. The study, creation, and transmission of many forms of local knowledge (such as local histories) and the preservation of local languages and systems of religious beliefs take place beyond the market imperative and are not profit oriented. But because the power on which ICT-driven knowledge societies are based comes from a nation's culture and political values (Devlin, 2005; UNESCO, 2005), the globalization process can be especially detrimental to developing countries.

SOLUTIONS

In the global knowledge economy of the future, the demand for learning and education will increase (UNESCO, 2005, p. 59). As the main centers for knowledge creation and transmission and one of the main providers of ICTs, institutions of higher learning need to be committed to the promotion of knowledge as a public good that is truly and easily accessible to as many people as possible. Commitment to the public interest on the part of local governments would facilitate the creation and the transmission of knowledge through low-cost, high-speed Internet connections. Although globalization might be unalterable, the internationalization and commercialization of higher education still involve many choices (Altbach & Knight, 2006, p. 2). Increasing access to technology in schools, developing a culture of teacher learning to support use of the Internet in the classroom, and increasing community access to ICTs might help decrease the global digital divide. Such steps, however, are not sufficient, for access is only a precondition to effective use (Fisher & Bendas-Jacob, 2006, p. 4; Gurstein, 2003).

The multidimensional nature of the global digital divide is complicated by the increasing commercialization of higher education. Yet transnational education is now a reality that must be accepted and that can potentially benefit developing countries. At the same time, commitment to public interest need not be an unattainable utopian ideal; it requires that policy actors and decision makers properly understand the importance of balancing private interest and public needs. Building a global and equitable knowledge society entails student career training and workforce development; however, it also entails students' education not only as workers but also as critical citizens who are capable of contributing to their local and global communities economically, socially, culturally, and politically.

Turning higher education into an appendage of corporate values and power can seriously obscure, if not eradicate, the vital relationship between education and democracy. It can also affect universities' traditional function of educating citizens in critical thought and in applying their education to the shaping of a healthy civic culture (Giroux, 2004). What is essential in the current situation is that all nations—especially local governments in developing countries—ensure and agree that the contributions of foreign education providers is sufficiently controlled and limited.

Two prerequisite conditions must be in place to ensure that the solutions presented in the following paragraphs will be effective:

1. More effective communication and cooperation is needed among governments on all levels: academic institutions, nongovernmental organizations (NGOs), and the private sector—including the WTO and the World Bank Group.[1]
2. Ministries of education and educators must be involved in all processes affecting education, and they must be empowered to make decisions in consultation with other involved parties.

The solutions presented in this section address issues of access to ICTs and their efficient use in the context of higher education in national and global terms.

Solution 1: Increase National GDP for Education Spending and Raise the ODA

The primary goal for each country should be to earmark more of its gross domestic product (GDP) for education spending. Doing so puts into practice a government's commitment to education as a key instrument of national development. In order to ensure that this goal is achieved, donor countries should significantly raise the percentage of official development assistance (ODA) designated for education, and they should do so "in partnerships with the beneficiary countries, mak[ing] the assistance more reliable, flexible and sustainable" (UNESCO, 2005, p. 191). The availability and spread of knowledge in and for the public sphere should also be integrated into policies and laws (UNESCO, 2005, p. 192). This relationship between knowledge and the public sphere would enable colleges and universities to invest more in establishing points of access, purchasing equipment, and instituting comprehensive ICT training for academic staff. It would also enable educational institutions to make long-term investments in local research and development of ICTs and thus to contribute to the successful integration of these technologies into the locally developed curriculum.

Solution 2: Limit the Number of Private Institutions and Establish, Strengthen, and Develop the Public Higher Education System

Local governments should legislate restrictions on the number of private institutions that can be established in a given region and seek ways to establish, strengthen, and develop their public education systems to serve a broad range of community needs. This focus is crucial given the role of educational institutions in facilitating the creation and transmission of knowledge. In cases where local entities forge partnerships with foreign institutions, the terms of agreement must clearly stipulate the benefits involved for the local partners. Such stipulations should include strategies to ensure that those benefits can be fully implemented and should include a clear vision of how the partnership will result in local development. These agreements must prioritize local educators, local knowledge, and the development of digital teaching and research resources in the local language. Above all, access to a university should be a clear priority in order to ensure that universities do not become exclusive institutions for the small percentage of the nation's wealthy residents, thus alienating great numbers of local youth.

Long-term gains should remain a national priority for a nation's education. NGOs need to become more vocal in the effort to maintain the public, universal nature of education. They should also be involved in developing the public sector in order to balance or check the profit-driven tendencies of the private sector. Finally, national governments should ensure that, in negotiating the terms of foreign educational presence in their countries, universities from developed nations commit to assisting local universities in clearly specified ways designed to overcome challenges associated with the globalization of higher education.

Solution 3: Expand Local Capacity by Legislating the Use of Free and Open-Source Software and Providing Academic Staff Access to Connections and Resources

Enabling local control of information production and distribution is among the basic instrumentalities in an information society. Local control ensures that all or most of a society's members have the opportunity to acquire the skills needed to use information as a primary and a positional good. Adopting funding schemes overseen by public rather than private institutions and interests would increase the chances that local universities could spearhead ICT developments that "enable an effective participation by local communities in regional, national and even global decision making processes" (Gurstein, 2003, p. 7). In order for this to happen, initiatives need to be directed toward expanding local capacity for the development, management, and maintenance of ICT facilities. Such initiatives should, moreover, supply the academic staff with stable personal access to high-quality connections and resources.

Because the cost of proprietary software is one of the biggest barriers to participation in the information economy, governments should focus on legislation that supports free and open-source software in order to foster community development and sustainability in the public sphere. This focus should encourage a country or region to use such software in order to gain intellectual independence from the industrialized nations and to establish more local autonomy (Stallman, 2001; Stevenson, 2009, p. 16). This approach would increase the chances that public universities become knowledge creators in ways that are beneficial to the local community. Free software foundations have already emerged throughout the developing world, in India (FSFINdia in 2001), Africa (FOSSFA in 2003), Latin America (FSFLA in 2005), and the Asia Pacific region (FOSSAP in 2005). Legislating the use of free and open-source software would allow for more efficient maintenance and use of ICTs, and it would enable academic staff to develop information in its three functions—as a primary good, a positional good, and as a set of skills.

Solution 4: Adopt Holistic Approaches to the Digital Divide to Develop Teaching and Learning Materials in Local Languages that are Relevant to Local Cultures

The education of those who need to use information in order to turn it into knowledge becomes increasingly important in the global community. As a result, it is crucial to understand how ICT users in a country physically, cognitively, and emotionally go through the process of information retrieval (Gebremichael & Jackson, 2006, p. 275). This "holistic" approach to ICTs in relation to any local population is needed to reduce information poverty and decrease the digital divide. A holistic approach also increases access to and the effectiveness of education.

In this context, information and education professionals from industrialized countries need to assist with the establishment and the expansion of information policies and infrastructure in developing countries. These policies should mandate that digital resources be developed in local languages and that digital literacy be integrated into the local curriculum. This approach would have positive effects on local educational institutions because it would expand the range of resources and strategies at educators' disposal.

At the same time, groups and individuals from developed countries must remain vigilant in order to avoid any unreflective importation of methods and resources that might be irrelevant or detrimental to developing nations and result in forms of neocolonialism (Altbach, 2004). Because ICT is developed within a particular cultural context—generally that of Europe, Asia, and the United States—ICT projects must move beyond the perspectives of those regions and focus on addressing contexts, needs, and expectations specific to the places where the projects will be implemented. Holistic and comprehensive attention can prevent the neocolonialism that might arise from a one-size-fits-all approach (Altbach, 2004; Gebremichael & Jackson, 2006).

Solution 5: Develop Local Systems for the Valuation of Existing Forms of Knowledge

A system for better "valuation of existing forms of knowledge" needs to be established in order to narrow the global knowledge gap (UNESCO, 2005, p. 188). That is, the greatest possible number of people must be equipped with the skills and the educational opportunity to become "knowledge creators." Such a trend is of vital importance to developing countries in which local public systems of higher education need to be strengthened. Local institutions must identify and make use of existing types of local knowledge rather than replace them with imported knowledge from other, economically and culturally more dominant countries. As UNESCO's report (2005) points out, "disregarding the development potential" in existing forms of knowledge can result "in serious mistakes"; this kind of thinking has led to, among other things, "the present higher education crisis in Africa" (UNESCO, 2005, p. 189).

Conclusion

Digital literacy is deeply tied to economic forces, to the contexts of location, politics, and culture, and to the missions of colleges and universities. Some research suggests that "fostering a free and open marketplace" should be "at the forefront of any foreign or international investment" in developing countries (Gebremichael & Jackson, 2006, p. 277; UNESCO, 2005, p. 170). Yet when it comes to higher education and educational institutions' traditional role of promoting knowledge as a public good, the open marketplace approach might be detrimental to long-term national development. It might also contribute to the widening of the global digital divide and the international knowledge gap. The solutions presented in this chapter emphasize the importance of comprehensive and systematic long-term investment in local development. They also consider education as more than a simple commodity; it participates in vital ways in the construction of society and culture. For this reason, education must be treated differently from other commodities. This approach would ensure that future societies and institutions of higher learning exploit the democratizing power of digital media and the media's potential to alleviate existing inequalities.

Endnote

1. The World Bank Group is a collection of five international organizations responsible for providing finance and advice to countries for the purposes of economic development and poverty elimination. They are the International Bank for Reconstruction and Development (IBRD), the International Development Association (IDA), the International Finance Corporation (IFC), the Multilateral Investment Guarantee Agency (MIGA), and the International Centre for Settlement of Investment Disputes (ICSID).

REFERENCES

Aduwa-Ogiegbaen, S. E. (2005). Using information and communication technology in secondary school in Nigeria: Problems and prospects. *Educational Technology and Society, 8*(1), 104–112.

Altbach, P. G. (2001). Higher education and the WTO: Globalization run amok. *International Higher Education.* Retrieved October 10, 2010, from http://www.bc.edu/bc_org/avp/soe/cihe/newsletter/News23/text001.htm.

Altbach, P. G. (2002). Centers and peripheries in the academic profession: The special challenges of developing countries. In P. G. Altbach (Ed.), *The decline of the guru: The academic profession in developing and middle-income countries* (pp. 1–23). Chestnut Hill, MA: Center for International Higher Education, Boston College.

Altbach, P. G. (2004). Globalization and the university: Myths and realities in an unequal world. *Tertiary Education and Management, 1*, 1–20.

Altbach, P. G., & Knight, J. (2006). The internationalization of higher education: Motivations and realities. *The NEA 2006 Almanac of Higher Education, 11*, 290–305.

Atkinson, R. (2001). The globalization of the university. *Nagasaki University of Foreign Studies, Japan.* Retrieved January 5, 2011, from http://www.ucop.edu/pres/speeches/japanspc.htm.

Bagayoko, C. O., Muller, H., & Geissbuhler, A. (2006). Assessment of the Internet-based tele-medicine in Africa: The RAFT project. *Computerized Medical Imaging and Graphics, 30*, 407–416.

Banya, K. (2001). Are private universities the solution to the higher education crisis in sub-Saharan Africa? *Higher Education Policy, 14*, 161–174.

Bollier, D. (2006, October 27–29). The perils of property speak in academia. Presentation at the Canadian Association of University

Teachers conference, Controlling intellectual property: The academic community and the future of knowledge, Ottawa, ON, Canada.

Brown, P. & Lauder, H. (2006). Globalisation, knowledge and the myth of the magnet economy. *Globalisation, Societies and Education, 4*(1), 25–57.

Carnoy, M. (2005). Globalization, educational trends, and the open society. Open Society Institute Education Conference, Education and open society: A critical look at new perspectives and demands. Retrieved January 5, 2011, from http://www.international.ac.uk/resources/Open%20 society%20Institute.pdf.

Crenshaw, E. M., & Robinson, K. K. (2006). Globalization and the digital divide: The roles of structural conduciveness and global connection in Internet diffusion. *Social Science Quarterly, 87*(1), 190–207.

deGannes Scott, B. J. (2006). Can developing countries overcome the digital divide? Information technology in Trinidad and Tobago. *Western Journal of Black Studies, 30*(2), 75–83.

Devlin, M. (2005). Introduction to *The Internet and the university: Forum 2004.* Forum for the Future of Higher Education and EDUCAUSE. Retrieved October 10, 2010, from http://www.educause.edu/ apps/forum/iuf04.asp?bhcp=1.

European Students' Union [ESU]. (2005). *The General Agreement on Trade Services – GATS* (Policy paper). Retrieved January 12, 2011, from http://www.esip.org.

Fisher, Y., & Bendas-Jacob, O. (2006). Measuring Internet use: The Israeli case. *International Journal of Human-Computer Studies, 64*(10), 984–997.

Gebremichael, M. D., & Jackson, J. W. (2006). Bridging the gap in sub-Saharan Africa: A holistic look at information poverty and the region's digital divide. *Government Information Quarterly, 23*, 267–280.

Giroux, H. A. (2004, September 24). An educator's reflections on the crisis in education and democracy in the US: An interview with Henry A. Giroux by Michael Alexander Pozo. *Dissident Voice*. Retrieved January 5, 2011, from http://dissidentvoice.org/Sep04/Pozo0925.html.

Gurstein, M. (2003). Effective use: A community informatics strategy beyond the digital divide. *First Monday, 8*(12). Retrieved October 10, 2010, from http://www.firstmonday.org/issues/issue8_12/index.html.

Huang, L. (2002). Paying for higher education in an international perspective. *Institute of International Education, Stockholm University*. Working Paper Series. Retrieved October 10, 2010, from http://www.interped.su.se/publications/WPS4.pdf.

Jaeger, P. T., Bertot, J. C., McClure, C. R., & Langa, L. A. (2006). The policy implications of Internet connectivity in public libraries. *Government Information Quarterly, 23*, 123–141.

King, R. (2003a). *Globalization and higher education*. Retrieved October 10, 2010, from http://www.acu.ac.uk/yearbook/may2003/kingfull.pdf.

King, R.. (2003b). The contemporary university. In R. King (Ed.), *The university in the global age* (pp. 1–26). New York, NY: Palgrave Macmillan.

Liu, A., Rhoads, R., & Wang, Y. (2007). Chinese university students' views on globalization: Exploring conceptions of citizenship. *Chung Cheng Educational Studies, 6*(1), 95–125.

Longley, P., Ashby, D., Webber, R., & Li, C. (2006). Geodemographic classifications, the digital divide and understanding customer take-up of new technologies. *BT technology journal, 24*(3), 67–74.

Marine, S., & Blanchard, J.-M. (2004). Bridging the digital divide: An opportunity for growth in the 21st century. *Alcatel telecommunications review* (3rd quarter). Retrieved October 10, 2010, from http://www1.alcatel-lucent.com/atr/DATR_quarterly_issues_listing.jhtml.

Mohamedbhai, G. (2002). Globalisation and its implications on universities in developing countries. Retrieved December 15, 2010, from http://ww.w.bi.ulaval.ca/Globalisation-Universities/pages/actes/MohamedbhaiGoolam2.pdf.

Ndroqi, L. (2002). E-learning: Support for high-school networks in Albania. *International symposium on learning management and technology development in the information and Internet age.* Bologna, Italy: University of Bologna.

Nephew Hassani, S. (2006). Locating digital divides at home, work, and everywhere else. *Poetics, 34*, 250–272. Retrieved from http://www.sciencedirect.com.

Newman, F., Couturier, L., & Scurry, J. (2004). *The future of higher education: Rhetoric, reality and the risks of the market.* New York, NY: Jossey-Bass.

Organization for Economic Cooperation and Development [OECD]. (2002). *GATS: The case for open services markets.* Paris, France: OECD.

Oxford Analytica Daily Brief Service. (2003, March 13). Latin America: Digital divide widens. Oxford Analytica Daily Brief Service.

Raikhy, P. S. (2002). Trade in education under the WTO policy regime: Implications for India. In K. B. Power (Ed.), *Internationalization of higher education* (pp. 127–133). New Delhi, India: Association of Indian Universities.

Robinson, D. (2006, October 27–29). An overview of Canada's trade and treaty obligations. Presented at the CAUT Conference, Controlling intellectual property: The academic community and the future of knowledge. Ottawa, ON, Canada.

Slaughter, S. (2001). Reflections on students as consumers and students as captive markets: Complexities and contradictions academic capitalism. Retrieved October 10, 2010, from http://www.aare.edu.au/01pap/sla0242.html.

Smith, M. K. (2002). Globalization and the incorporation of education. *The encyclopedia of informal education.* Retrieved January 5, 2011, from http://www.infed.orgbiblio.globalization.htm.

Stallman, R. (2001). Stallman inaugurates Free Software Foundation India, first affiliate in Asia of the Free Software Foundation. GNU Operating System. Retrieved January 2, 2011, from http://www.gnu.org/press/2001–07–20-FSF-India.html.

Stallman, R. (2003). World Summit on the information society. GNU Operating System. Retrieved January 10, 2011, from http://www.gnu.org/philosophy/wsis.html.

Stevenson, S. (2009). Digital divide: A discursive move away from real inequalities. *The Information Society, 25*, 1–22.

Stromquist, N. P. (2007). Internationalization as a response to globalization: Radical shifts in university environments. *Journal of Higher Education, 53*, 81–105.

Thurow, L. (2005). Why are the fears of globalization so high? *The Internet and the university: Forum 2004.* Forum for the Future of Higher Education and EDUCAUSE. Retrieved October 19, 2010, from http://www.educause.edu/apps/forum/iuf04.asp?bhcp=1.

United Nations Educational, Scientific, and Cultural Organization [UNESCO]. (2005). *UNESCO world report: Toward knowledge societies*. Paris, France: UNESCO.

van Dijk, J. A. G. M. (2006). Digital divide research, achievements and shortcomings. *Poetics, 34*, 221–235.

Washburn, J. (2005). *University, Inc.: The corporate corruption of higher education.* New York, NY: Basic Books.

Woodhall, M. (2001). Financing higher education: The potential contribution of fees and student loans. *International Higher Education.* Retrieved October 10, 2010, from http://www.bc.edu/bc_org/avp/soe/cihe/newsletter/News22/text008.htm.

World Trade Organization [WTO]. (2001). GATS – Fact and fiction. Retrieved October 10, 2010, from http://www.wto.org/english/tratop_e/serv_e/gatsfacts1004_e.pdf.

Young Kim, S. (2008, January 31–February 3). Knowledge intensity of information technology and its implications for the digital divide in the age of globalization. Paper presented at the World Universities Forum, Davos, Switzerland.

Zhao, H. X., Kim, S., Suh, T. W., & Du, J. J. (2007). Social institutional explanations of global Internet diffusion: A cross-country analysis. *Journal of Global Information Management, 15*(2), 28–55.

About the Editors

Kirk St.Amant is an associate professor of Technical and Professional Communication and of International Studies at East Carolina University. He has a background in cultural anthropology, international government, and technical communication. Dr. St.Amant has taught online and onsite courses in technical and professional communication as well as in intercultural communication for different universities in the United States and abroad.

Bolanle A. Olaniran is a professor and interim chair in the Department of Communication Studies at Texas Tech University. An internationally known scholar, Dr. Olaniran's research includes computer-mediated communication and technology use, cross-cultural communication, and crisis communication. His articles have been published in several journals, and he has contributed chapters to many books. He also edited a book on successful cases in e-learning. In addition, Dr. Olaniran serves as consultant to organizations and universities at the local, national, international, and government level. His works have gained recognition such as the American Communication Association's "Outstanding Contribution to the Communication field," among others.

About the Contributors

Francesca da Rimini has been an artist, writer, curator, and editor in the new media field since the 1980s. Her collaborative creative experiments range from VNS Matrix's cyberfeminist computer games and Internet performances to Bumpp's distributed generative artwork. Her master's and doctoral research investigated socialized technologies, cultural activism, and the production of agency using case studies in Jamaica, Hong Kong, and England. She is contributing to a substantial project on informational capitalism at the University of Technology, Sydney.

Arjan de Jager is an information manager at the Vrije Universiteit, Amsterdam. After completing his studies in physics and mathematics, he worked as a lecturer in computing science in Amsterdam and Zimbabwe. In 1998 he became manager of the Country Programme Uganda for the International Institute for Communication and Development (IICD; www.iicd.org) and as such was actively involved in ICT4D projects. His research concentrates on business–IT alignment in the public sector.

Yasmin Ibrahim is a reader in international business and communications at Queen Mary, University of London. Her ongoing research on new media technologies explores the cultural dimensions and social implications of the diffusion of ICTs in different contexts. Beyond new media and digital technologies, Dr. Ibrahim writes on political communication and political mobilization from cultural perspectives. Her other research interests include globalization, visual culture, and memory studies.

Tuğba Kalafatoğlu the founder and president of V♀TE Women in Politics. She is also president of Tuğba Kalafatoğlu & Associates, an international consulting firm. She works as an adviser to governments, international companies, and academics. She was the president of American Communication Association in 2008–2009 and has won numerous awards, including Outstanding Young Person of the World in Politics, Law, and Government Affairs; a GOLD Pollie Award ("Oscars of Political Advertising"); Who's Who in the World; Who's Who in America; and Who's Who in Finance and Business. She holds a bachelor's degree in political science with honors from University of Nebraska at Omaha and master's degree in international affairs, law, and business from Georgetown University.

Kehbuma Langmia is an assistant professor of communications at Bowie State University. He published four books and three articles and coedited two books after earning his PhD from Howard University. Dr. Langmia teaches graduate courses at both Bowie State University and Howard University. He has presented papers at national and international conferences on globalization and the media.

Alireza Noruzi is an independent information consultant, specializing in information services, competitive intelligence, knowledge organization, cataloging, and indexing. He received his PhD from the Department of Information Science at the University of Paul Cezanne in Marseille, France, and his BA and MA degrees in library and information science. His research interests include the Web, information consulting, information marketing, competitive intelligence, and open-access information.

Tatjana Takševa (formerly Chorney) is an associate professor in the English Department at Saint Mary's University, Canada, where she teaches courses on literature, culture, and women and gender studies. Her publications include essays on literature, pedagogy, globalization, cross-cultural communication, as well as a monograph, *Seventeenth-Century Poetic Genres as Social Categories: A New Reading of the Poetry of John Donne.* She is also editing a book titled *Social Software and the Evolution of User Expertise: Future Trends in Knowledge Creation and Dissemination.*

Anas Tawileh is a director for Systematics Consulting and as a consultant for the International Development Research Centre's ICT4D project in the Middle East. Dr. Tawileh has worked on many projects to bring technology to developing countries and has designed, developed, and delivered several training and capacity-building programs and workshops. He holds a PhD and an MSc from the School of Computer Science at Cardiff University and has authored several books and scholarly articles on ICT4D.

Victor van Reijswoud (PhD) is a leading ICT4D researcher and consultant, who works an independent ICT4D and management adviser in Africa. His main activities focus on the areas of free/open-source software and appropriate ICT for development. He has worked as professor and researcher at universities in the Netherlands, the United States, South Africa, Uganda, Burundi, and Papua New Guinea.

Yun Xia is an associate professor in the Department of Communication and Journalism at Rider University, where he teaches print media and digital media design courses. Dr. Xia's research interests include the social impact of computer-mediated communication, educational applications of communication technologies, visual intelligence of graphic communications in new media, and semiotic analysis of communication signs in new media. His articles have been published in journals such as *Human Communication*, *China Media Research*, and *The American Journal of Semiotics*.

Index

Made in the USA
Monee, IL
09 June 2024

59606396R00157